Debt-Free College

79 Secrets for Successful College Financing

MAIN

Debt-Free College

79 Secrets for Successful College Financing

ROBERT A. SPARKS and MAMATHA VADDI

A Perigee Book

A Perigee Book
Published by The Berkley Publishing Group
A division of Penguin Putnam Inc.
375 Hudson Street
New York, New York 10014

First edition: September 2002

Visit our website at www.penguinputnam.com

Library of Congress Cataloging-in-Publication Data

Sparks, Robert A.
    Debt-free college : 79 secrets for sucessful college financing / Robert A. Sparks and Mamatha Vaddi. — 1st ed.
        p.   cm.
    Includes bibliographical references and index.
    ISBN 0-399-52865-2 (trade pbk.)
    1. College costs—United States. 2 Student aid—United States. 3. Finance, Personal—United States. I. Vaddi, Mamatha. II. Title.

LB2342 .S68 2002
378.3'8—dc21
                                                                    2002072511

Printed in the United States of America

10 9 8 7 6 5 4 3 2 1

CONTENTS

Part III: Understanding and Using Financial Aid

Part IV: Staying Ahead

ACKNOWLEDGMENTS

The authors would like to thank their agent, Carole Abel, for making *Debt-Free College* a reality. Thanks also to Jennifer Repo, Christel Winkler, and the rest of the Perigee team for their great work on editing the book.

Robert would like to thank his parents, grandparents, and family for their support, as well as the many professors and teachers who served as mentors, especially Beth Martin and Elva Gladney. Thanks also for the excellent service from the Pflugerville, Texas, post office staff.

Mamatha would like to thank her parents, sister, and brother for their support, as well as her professors and teachers. Thanks also to Ginnie Bivona for her guidance and Beverly Welch for her assistance.

Introduction

Debt-free college is a choice—one that must be made consciously. To do this requires becoming aware of your financial thinking.

More than 50 percent of students graduate with debt. On top of this, the cost of college is continuing to skyrocket. Most colleges seem to assume that students have rich grandparents who will be able to pick up those kinds of costs. This book asks the questions:

- How is it possible to *get through college debt-free?*

- What if you *don't have* rich grandparents?

- What if you are an *adult planning to pursue* another degree or to enhance your current skills?

- What if you are an *independent student* with other financial obligations?

- What if you are an *international student* seeking a quality education?

- What if you are *all of the above?*

This book presents you with a new way to think about finances as a student. This new way of thinking is powerful, because it will reveal how to get an education without debt—something that most people have no idea how to accomplish. Whether you can afford college does not have to be the result of how much money someone in your family hands you. In fact, having things handed to you often leads to bad habits.

Debt-Free College shows you how to graduate debt-free *without* having money handed to you. It will teach you good financial habits that will carry you through college and beyond. It presents a way to think about finance that is advantageous even *after* college.

THE SECRET FORMULA

Debt-Free College is unique. Most college finance books on the market will tell you how to look for scholarships or financial aid. A few of these books will even describe ideas for and philosophies on avoiding debt. This book is different because it:

- Outlines the prerequisites—the lifestyle, the attitude, and the mindset—to avoid college debt.

- Focuses on developing strategies, establishing guidelines, and providing tips for reducing the cost of attendance.

- Provides a comprehensive resource guide with useful websites, telephone numbers, and books to put you on the fast track to debt-free college.

- Includes calendars that outline important deadlines for applying for financial aid, as well as the ideal timeframe to start college planning.

This book teaches you the right attitude to have to avoid debt, while instructing you where to start looking for money. In order to succeed, you need both parts. You need to know what to do, and you need to have the mind-set to do it.

YOUR MONEY'S WORTH

To get your money's worth from *Debt-Free College,* you have to practice. Practicing debt-free finance may be a new skill for you.

You may even feel uncomfortable and be quick to say, "I knew that." Whereas you might already understand the burden of debt, you may not know the steps to avoid it—especially during college.

This book will help you get the hang of debt-free living. At the same time, to add more value, there is a collection of ready-to-use strategies in these pages. In addition to drawing on personal experience, we literally went out and bought college finance books and collected the very best ideas from each. So in case this is the only book you buy, you will *at the very least* have a good chance of getting the very best ideas on the market.

LOOK OUT, MIDDLE CLASS

The need for college education is increasing. Many people in this country are being separated into the category of "have-not" simply because they do not have the income of a college graduate. In fact, we are at a point in time when many people are facing the fact that their lifestyle might not match the lifestyle they grew up with.

America is heading in the direction of tougher times, where unemployment is higher, taxes are higher, and opportunities for higher education are fewer. The fact that college tuition in America increased 234 percent from 1980 to 1995 but the median household income increased only 82 percent makes this evident. Moreover, the American Council on Education reports that more than 50 percent of students who have graduated from four-year colleges are still in debt.

Nonetheless, it is still possible to afford education. People do not have to accumulate massive debt in order to achieve a better job and a classier lifestyle. Now is the time to figure out how you can afford college and avoid debt. It is time to break the destructive cycle of debt that people are incurring in order to afford education. This book can help.

A NEW RESPONSIBILITY

America is the greatest consumer country in the world, with two-thirds of the economy being fueled by consumer spending. This means that America can often pull the rest of the world out of a recession, which is good. Unfortunately, it also encourages values that make it intensely difficult for a college student to succeed financially.

On average, Americans save less than 3 percent of their income. It is the American way of life. You probably have friends whom you classify overall as "responsible" but who still have hefty credit card debt tying them down.

The time has come for a new responsibility. For us to be able to achieve the education we want, get the salary we desire, live the lifestyle we like, and still be able to retire, we must take the responsibility of getting through college without debt.

If you graduate when you are twenty-three and are just paying off your student loans by the time you're thirty-three, you have wasted precious years of earning potential and you have fallen lower in the ranks of the middle class. This is probably *not* what people have in mind when they are working for a college degree.

On the other hand, if you are able to graduate debt-free, or with extra cash, you can take full advantage of your future earning potential and begin to work your way to an enviable position as soon as you graduate.

FINANCIAL INTELLIGENCE

College is a powerful way to accumulate broad and diverse knowledge. You may read enough books in college to make your eyes fall out, but there are other key elements to being successful that are often overlooked. For one thing, learning to build relationships with people is paramount. Additionally, learning to deal with money is crucial.

Financial intelligence is an important skill to learn before and during college. It is a skill that is very different from the knowledge learned in typical college textbooks. With financial intelligence, there is no "right or wrong" answer and no set rules. However, there are principles that are easily overlooked.

There are many brilliant professionals who are financial morons. There are many eminent scholars who have no idea what it means to work within a budget. Such professionals and scholars never learned the basic principles of money, and thus they continue to abuse their finances and slip into an unpleasant cycle of debt.

PREREQUISITES

There is little chance that you will avoid debt if you have no financial plan upon entering college. You may avoid it if your grandparents are going to foot the bill or if your family happens to own oil wells in Africa, but if you are planning on doing the funding yourself, you must be willing to work and to make a plan before you begin.

There is a start-up cost if you plan to graduate debt-free. Part of that start-up cost is your ability to save some money for yourself before you begin. If you are a chronic spender and cannot save, you have no purpose charging into college and believing you can avoid debt anyway. Instead, follow the steps outlined in the next chapters and you will find that your thinking begins to change in a big way. When your thinking begins to change, you will have taken the first steps toward debt-free college.

FINANCIAL KARATE

To recognize debt-avoiding tools takes focus and endurance. It is like learning karate. If you have ever gone to a karate school, you know that expert black belts do not fight full contact with inexperienced white belts. It takes years of learning for the white belt to think intelligently and quickly enough to escape dangerous situations. The same will be true for you as a college student when it comes to money, which is why it is best to begin your training now. The secret to good karate is good practice. The secret to avoiding debt is learning to practice good financial skills. And like a trained martial artist, a debt-avoider must develop self-control and discipline.

In order to be successful, you must be open to new approaches and be willing to think. The authors expect this book to challenge your values and priorities in some way. As you read, you will begin to sense how your priorities will need to change in order to accomplish debt-free college. If you read something in this book and think it would be impossible for you to do it, act upon it, or accomplish it, then you must challenge yourself to consider the possibility. Usually, when you consider a tough new possibility, it helps you see other possibilities that would work just as well but are often a lot easier.

EASILY AND DANGEROUSLY OVERLOOKED

College is going to keep you busy by challenging a bunch of your values at once—friends, popularity, grades, sexuality, alcohol/drugs, and academic dishonesty will all be present. Most people spend their entire four years dealing with these issues while they ignore the fact that they are accumulating debt. The amazing thing is that you will find support groups, counselors, and tutoring for all these issues. But you will probably never find a single group, counselor, or tutor focused on helping you figure out if you are making the right moves financially. People can talk about alcoholism, poor grades, and homosexuality, but they often can't, won't, and don't talk about their spending habits, income, living costs, and savings. That is exactly why so many people never achieve debt-free college.

There may be individual limitations that can make debt-free college more challenging. For instance, if you have a baby or just bought a house, this book might not get you through college debt-free. Even so, you will still learn ways to save thousands of dollars that you will otherwise lose.

This book will give you concrete principles that will help you achieve debt-free college. The authors will use some of their own experiences and strategies as examples, as well as give you profiles of people they had direct experience with.

ROBERT A. SPARKS

I had around $7,000 saved by the time I was beginning college. About $3,500 of that came from saving Christmas money, mowing lawns, and previous summer jobs. The other $3,500 came from working as a waiter. Four years, many jobs, and a scholarship later, I graduated college debt-free.

Like many people, I have been both a spender and a saver. There were times when I would blow my whole paycheck, and there were times when I would save my whole paycheck. I have lived with the benefits and the downfalls of both lifestyles, so I know the temptations and empathize with both sides.

MAMATHA VADDI

As most students do, I fell prey to financial aid myths, and it took me two years to learn the truth. Once I dispelled the rumors, I applied for scholarships and used financial aid. I completed my last two years of college practically free.

With the scholarships and financial aid and a part-time job, I studied in Thailand for six months and completed a second degree.

PART 1 The Basics of Beating College Debt

CHAPTER ONE

Discover Your Financial Attitude

Knowing your habits is key when it comes to developing your financial thinking. You probably think you know your habits, but you are probably partially wrong. Many great philosophers have written that our identities are actually determined by a combination of two factors: who we think we are, and who others think we are.

That is a little oversimplified. You are not simply who you think you are—nor are you the person who everybody else sees. But analyzing your financial habits and understanding how they stack up against others can help put you on the road to debt-free college.

The Journey

Unfortunately, there is no one secret to getting through college debt-free. You cannot expect to open a box of Cracker Jack and find the answer in the surprise. Instead, the answer begins with becoming self-aware.

SECRET #1

You must go through a process of learning how you feel about money, why you feel that way, and what the consequences are.

There are no shortcuts around this if you want to succeed. Learning how to make financial calculations can help you beat debt, but *controlling* money is accomplished by controlling your emotions. This chapter will push you toward a financial epiphany by making you think critically. Discovering your attitudes and beliefs surrounding money is one of the most crucial, yet overlooked, elements of avoiding debt. Take some time now, and the specifics and numbers will come soon enough.

The Pursuit of Your Spending Patterns

Self-knowledge is sometimes shocking. With finance, this concept is all too apparent. Few people know their habits or where they stand in the financial spectrum. Of course, most people know how much money they *make*, they simply do not know what their financial habits are. For instance, if you are responsible with your money 95 percent of the time, but then turn into a crazy spender the other 5 percent of the time, you can really wreak havoc on your goal of debt-free college. Discovering your spending habits, however, will open your eyes to where your money is going and where it *needs* to go to achieve debt-free college.

SECRET **#2**

Knowing your financial habits is a surprise that leads to debt-free college.

Self-knowledge is not something you can accomplish in a day. It is an ongoing pursuit. As you read the rest of this chapter, notice the categories of people presented. Compare their situations to your own. Take the time to begin learning if your financial habits are taking you closer to or further from debt-free college.

Though many things are not worth your time, some things are highly worthy. Recognizing your financial spending patterns is worth your time. Spending patterns are inextricably connected to your attitude about money. Your values are clues to your spending patterns.

If you are the type of person that values spontaneity over dedication, you might have some serious problems holding down a job and earning a steady income. If you value style over economy, you might find it difficult to save for college. If you value risk-taking over safety, you certainly have a chance to strike it big, but you certainly have the chance to bust.

SECRET #3

Going into debt does not have anything to do with whether you are a good or bad person; it has everything to do with your financial habits and your ability to plan and save.

The way to know if your personal characteristics are in danger of leading you into debt is to be self-critical. This is difficult to do while you are blinded by emotions. As humans, we are blinded by emotions from birth to death. That is one reason why it takes such an effort to make penetrating self-discoveries that could eventually lead to financial independence.

When I was sixteen, all my friends were getting cars, and I wanted one, too. In fact, I wanted one so badly that I did not shop around for more than two weeks. I bought a car that seemed like a good deal and was proud of it. Months later, the coolant leaked and the engine blew. I had forgotten to be self-critical by never taking the time to shop, compare, or haggle. Don't be a sucker like the author!

A Deathbed Exercise

There is a good way to test your value system. It is a brief but powerful exercise. Pretend you are at the end of your life, on your deathbed, and you are thinking about the events of your life. The room is quiet, cool, and empty. As you lay there, you begin to think about what your life has meant. Then you ask yourself a question.

Take a minute and imagine it. You are in the silent, sparse room and you are asking yourself this question:

SECRET #4

"What is it I wish I would have spent more time doing?" Your answer will clarify your priorities.

If you are like most people, you will probably wish you had spent more time with your friends and family and less time at work. Surely you didn't wish you had spent more time in the shopping mall. Maybe you wished you had exercised more or worshiped more often. Take a big note—the kinds of things most people wish they had done are not usually things that cost lots of money.

This question has the significant effect of strengthening your priorities and helping you see where your time and money count most. Whereas it is true that some hard work up front is necessary for debt-free college, the benefit of avoiding debt is that you will not have to work so hard and so long in the future. You will not have to spend your time and sweat paying down debt. You can spend more time with friends and family. In other words, you will not "owe" your time and life to anyone, which is what debt does to people.

Types of People and How They Spend

There are many types of people, but let's start by looking at two big categories.

BOOK- AND STREET-SMART

Book-smart people love the classroom. They make good grades easily. They are academically competitive. Street-smart people have outside-the-classroom smarts. They may have decent grades, but they are often not in the top 10 percent of the class.

The significance of these two categories is that they help you understand your talents and priorities—and also the priorities of others who are not like you. You can bet that book-smart friends will have the credentials for college, and they will probably do well academically. They may eventually be doctors, lawyers, and engineers. Street-smart people, on the other hand, might end up owning their own businesses.

Being book-smart is good, and being street-smart is also good. But being book-smart *and* street-smart is the best.

SECRET #5

Learn balance, so you will be able to recognize great financial opportunities and have the know-how to seize them.

You may have the natural tendency to be one way or the other, but you should make an effort to embrace the other half of the picture, too. If you are always reading books, you should try to increase your life experience. If you are never reading books, you should try to read some books. This balance is critical for the type of person who wants debt-free college.

 TRIVIA: Approximately 70 percent of students who go to college do so *just* to make more money—*www.funtrivia.com*

OTHER CATEGORIES

There are many other types of categories besides street-smart and book-smart that you need to think about before you understand your tendencies with money.

What you value, what you believe, and what you feel ultimately shape you and your financial habits. If someone practices a religion that teaches them "money is the root of all evil," that person will probably spend very little time thinking about money or learning to manage it. Thus, that person will likely have poor money-management skills. That is not to say that he would lead an unhappy life. He might even think that someone is quite dumb to spend his time writing a book on avoiding college debt.

The following are sketches of fictional people that will help you flesh out additional financial categories. You will probably see some patterns that match your patterns and also some that represent the opposite of yours.

SECRET #6

Understanding other people's financial habits will extend your own critical thinking.

There are no right or wrong personal characteristics, but there are cause-effect relationships that make debt-free college easier to handle. Some of the following characters may be at different points in their lives than you are, but that doesn't matter—just think about whether you agree or disagree with their lifestyle.

Bob

Bob has spent a nice life earning money and is now considerably wealthy. But he also has an extreme fear of losing his money. Thus, he keeps his money in government bonds and pretty much nothing else. His money is very safe, but his money does not grow. He is satisfied with working for every dollar he spends.

Bob values security so much that he ends up overlooking opportunities to make more money.

Maria

Maria is twelve and likes to work at her father's store. Her father pays her for the help, and Maria saves the salary and buys nice things for herself when she feels like it. She has many more nice things than either one of her sisters, who are ten and fourteen. Her sisters do not help in the store and do not have an interest in earning money.

Maria values working, saving, and living within her budget.

Cindy

Cindy is twenty-one and very unselfish. She is always devoting her free time to community service projects. Everybody loves Cindy, and everybody goes to her for advice and nurturing. If she has any extra cash from her paycheck, it goes to helping charities. Cindy is trying to make it back to college, but she always seems to be too broke to make it happen.

Cindy is such an unselfish person that she overlooks the concept of saving money altogether.

Max

Max is thirty and just got a loan to help consolidate his credit card debt. He makes a lot, but he spends a lot. With the lower monthly interest on the consolidated loan, he feels that his high salary will allow him to pay off his debt. Because of his high salary, he recently qualified for a mortgage loan, so he bought a house and some nice furniture.

Max likes to spend money he does not have; he's relatively comfortable with debt.

Rashad

Rashad is committed to his dream of traveling throughout the world. His family is upper middle class. Though he is twenty-three, Rashad does not work. He is convinced if he does not see the world while he is young, he never will. He has not completed any college, but he has fantastic knowledge of different countries. He is not really sure if his parents expect him to pay back the money he is borrowing from them to fund his expeditions. He does not know if his cultural knowledge will help him to get a high-paying job.

Rashad knows a lot about cultures and is comfortable with the idea of not being able to support himself financially.

Five Truths of the Financial Mindset

Once you truly commit to the idea of debt-free college, you will begin to find ways of making it happen. The first step is being willing to take the risk of debt in order to go to college. The next step is to manage that risk and continue to want debt-free college. There are important truths about success that hold for debt-free college, too.

1. You must want to do the thing you are doing in order to do it well.
As humans, our potential and our energy are closely related to our motivation. In other words, our success depends on our desire. Someone who has less talent or less money can still beat someone who has oodles of talent and lots of money—if they *want* to. If you only "kind of" want to graduate, then you may only "kind of" finish college. If you only "kind of" want to avoid college debt, then chances are you will only "kind of" avoid it.

2. To succeed, you must stay hungry.
You have to find ways to motivate yourself. The path to debt-free college can be monotonous and discouraging, but you have to find ways around those times. Do whatever it takes. If hanging upside down motivates you to learn and spend better, then hang upside down every day. Find a way to stay hungry so that you will stay committed.

3. Your aptitude is your advantage.
When you begin to realize what type of person you are, you will begin to realize secrets about yourself. You will begin to discover why you have inherent advantages in certain areas. If you tend to be a hard worker, you will probably work your way into a higher income quickly. If you are an entrepreneur, then you may have the tendency to form businesses. If you have a talent for working with people, then you may become a negotiator or a counselor. *When you find your aptitude, you can use it to your financial advantage.*

4. What is strength in one situation is *not* strength in other situations.
There is one aspect of aptitude that people do not often think about. What counts as strength in one situation translates to weakness in another situation. Thus a hard worker, despite a high salary, might not be a fun person to be around because his approach is so

serious and resolute. The entrepreneur, with his dreams of a successful business, might overlook religion because his approach is so worldly and materialistic. The negotiator, always focusing on other people's disputes, might not take the time to keep his personal life in order.

It is important that you begin to see where your "strengths" are leading you financially. If you value saving your money, which keeps you from spending on college, your personal growth and potential income level is suffering. Everyone has financial strengths *and* weaknesses. The homeless person down the street has them, and Donald Trump has them. Unfortunately, weaknesses are something that we are born with. Fortunately, we do not have to accept them. We can choose to recognize them and do something about them.

Learning to use your strengths and defend your weaknesses is a lot like being a referee. Imagine there are two boxers inside your head, and one is always beating up on the other. In fact, the stronger one is dealing low blows to the weaker one, yet the referee does nothing. The referee is unfair because he is naturally lazy. It is only when the referee has some pressure put on him (you learn to guard against your financial weaknesses) that he begins to call a fair fight and the weaker opponent has a chance.

People tend to dominate with their strengths and ignore their weaknesses. This is not a good way to avoid debt during any time of life, and especially not in college, when you are forming life habits. In order to avoid debt, you must find a *total* solution, which means that you must call a fair fight and develop your areas of natural weakness.

5. Priorities sharpen the goal.

Whether you just graduated high school or are thirty and have two kids, you must set your priorities before jumping into college. If you are not sure you really want to study and budget for four years, then debt-free college may not be for you. If, on the other hand, you decide that education and avoiding debt is worth four years of effort and economy, then debt-free college is a strong possibility. Debt-free college is a mindset.

Instead of spending $30 at an arcade, you might decide to spend

$7 at a movie and put the extra cash toward paying for college. That is a small example—just think of the power you will have to change your life when you consciously apply techniques to align your long-term goal of debt-free college with your day-to-day life of earning money and studying.

Controlling financial habits is like losing or gaining weight. Everyone wants to lose or gain weight. How hard it will be to achieve the "correct weight" depends on how far you have gone in the wrong direction. People will diet, exercise, or load up on food. They will then weigh themselves to see if they have made progress. It is the same way with money. You must diet or possibly "load up" to get yourself to the right balance of spending, earning, and saving. Just like changing your weight, managing money is a process of ongoing correction.

 TRIVIA: At a rate of 31 percent, Austin, Texas, has the most college graduates. At a rate of 6 percent, Newark, New Jersey, has the least college graduates—*www.funtrivia.com*

Get Your Priorities Straight

If you focus on a few basic principles, you will uncover your financial strengths and weaknesses.

Understand Past, Present, and Future—Decide what it is you really want. Take a weekend, take a year—whatever it takes. You need to find out three things:

- Where have you been? Have you had a steady job?

- Where are you? Are you in debt?

- Where do you need to go? How much money do you need for college?

Integrating your past, present, and future helps you find your path. Maybe you have always worked, are never in debt, and are saving for college. If so, you're in good standing. Maybe you have always worked, but you are in debt and unable to save any money for college. If so, you need to adjust your financial habits.

Think Before You Leap—Attitude gives you the energy to control your money. Tools harness your energy. In order to make a successful leap, you have to know where you are jumping. This book will sharpen your knowledge and reveal practical approaches for making a successful leap.

Plant Your Seed—An acorn buried by a squirrel produces an oak tree, not an apple tree. Likewise, you will not be able to go to a costly school without getting into debt unless you have a way to pay.

As people, we live our lives based on relative truth. Two people can feel exactly opposite about money and *both* be right. They would both be right because they have different backgrounds and different financial situations. They have been taught to respond to money differently. This affects the financial decisions they make. Examining your financial history will provide insight into who you are today.

SECRET #7

Your financial standing today is a result of your choices with money yesterday; your choices with money today determine your tomorrow.

The Past

A big part of who you are is where you came from. If you grew up in the harsh clutches of the inner city, you are going to feel differently about money than someone who grew up on Fifth Avenue in Manhattan. If you had parents who managed their money well, you will have different ideas about money than if you had parents who could never hold onto their money.

For example, take two people who grew up in lower-income housing. One might grow up accepting this lifestyle and accumulating debt. The other might grow up hating lower-income housing and work his way to financial prosperity. Both have the same physical background, yet both feel differently about success, about the future, and about money. *Different mindsets* cause them to end up in opposite places even though they share the same background.

The Future

What you want to do with your life affects who you are today. If you plan to be a business tycoon someday, your values are different than someone who merely wants to support a family and take a vacation every three years. Either way, whatever you want to become is strongly tied to the values you currently have and the way you feel about financial success. Either way you go, it is still good to avoid debt. Although the specifics of avoiding debt are different for different pursuits, the basics are the same.

The Present

"What you are doing" is otherwise known as the present. After you have considered your financial past and your future goals, you will have an idea of how you feel about money at the present. Once you know this, you will be more conscious of your *emotional intelligence* when it comes to money. When you reach that point, it is time to start questioning whether you are making the right day-to-day moves to get to where you want to go.

Some people have difficulty pinpointing their feelings, but surely you have done it at some point in your life. It begins with education and thought, followed by action. If you are learning a radical new idea, you will probably not accept it right away. As you learn more about the idea, you may come to accept it, then take action. When you take action, you are not sure of what the outcome will be, yet you hope for a good result. Through motivation and hope, you create the desire and feelings that end up changing your situation.

THINK BEFORE YOU LEAP

There are honest limitations to what you can accomplish, even when you know what you want out of life.

You might want to attend a private college that has a total cost of about $26,000 a year. At that rate, it will be very difficult to avoid debt. The private college may offer an excellent education, but the same time, it may be overpriced.

SECRET #8

It is important to weigh the cost of the education you want with the benefit it will provide.

A good education is valuable, but so is staying out of debt. Often, many "good" colleges are overrated; they get more points from their name than from their professors or their programs. Choosing a college based on value instead of name is an important part of debt-free college. Furthermore, if an *expensive* education is the only thing that is important to you, you could easily overlook the goal of getting a *quality* education.

Quality and expense are not the same things. Sometimes things are expensive because they have high quality, but often they are expensive only because they have been marketed well. It is a lot like buying shoes. You can spend between $100 and $140 to buy a new pair of Nikes. The Nikes will usually look good, feel good, and last about two years. You can also get the same style of shoes—but a different brand—and pay around $40 to $50. Guess what—the shoes will still look good, feel good, and last about two years, even though they are not Nikes. Finding a college is very similar; you can find one with high value that will be affordable, or you can find one with a name brand that has a high cost. There are many colleges that are affordable and still provide excellent educations.

DEBT-FREE COLLEGE PYRAMID

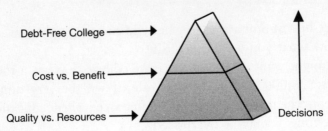

Debt-Free College ————▶

Cost vs. Benefit ————▶

Quality vs. Resources ————▶   Decisions

SECRET #9

Choose which resources you are willing to pay for.

Even though you can buy generic shoes and save money, there is an economic principle called scarcity that prevents everything from being a bargain. The principle says that due to so many people in the world and so few resources, resources end up costing a lot of money. If you want the convenience of living in the center of the city, be willing to live in an older, smaller place. Places to live in the central parts of big cities are scarce. If you want a big, modern place, be willing to move to an inconvenient location where those types of houses abound. Either way, you will have your problems, but you will save money by prioritizing your wants. Just like a nice apartment in central London, spots in a prestigious school are scarce, so you must be willing to pay a premium to attend.

SECRET #10

Align your decisions with your debt-free goal.

By learning what motivates you, your priorities become easier to see. By doing something boring and menial—perhaps working a fast-food job—you learn what does *not* motivate you. Once you learn to be motivated by debt-free college and make it a priority, you will see how to use your time effectively to accomplish your goal.

You must be brutally honest with yourself if you want to avoid debt. You must look at how much money you have, how much income you will be able to make, and the average cost of the college you wish to attend. In other words, you have to learn **The Basic Debt-Free Equation:**

THE BASIC DEBT-FREE EQUATION

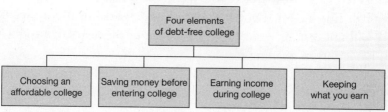

Take a minute to look at this equation. Study it until you have at least a ballpark guess what each variable is like for you. These variables are covered in the next chapters, so you will be able to recognize them at a conceptual level as well as in day-to-day life. Once you recognize them, you will have an advantage—and you will be empowered to beat debt.

This equation may look simple on paper, yet when it comes to day-to-day life, the equation is difficult to see. This is partially because we often think in terms of what we need instead of what we can reasonably afford. At first, you may feel that you need to go to a prestigious private college. After you evaluate the cost benefit, you may realize that you are going to incur some heavy debt to attend a "name-brand" college.

Until you have an idea where you are *numerically* for each part of the debt-free equation, you will really not know where you are heading. Merely thinking about something does little good. Putting it down in a plan, using words and numbers and goals, and forecasting does a lot of good. You will understand after you have sat down and done it.

One lucky thing is that you are likely to have a much simpler situation than a fifty-year-old (apologies to those reading of that age). When you are younger, and not as worried about retirement, and have fewer people depending on you, the planning process is simpler. There are fewer variables when you have only yourself to consider and a lifetime ahead of you.

Now is the time to make the habit of sitting down and planning. Then, when you are forty or fifty years old and someone asks you how much money you will have in ten or twenty years, you will be able to tell them how much you will have and why you know that. You will not have to worry and fret and work until you are old. You will understand your money because of the years of experience you have with managing it.

TIP: One key aspect of debt-free college is choosing an affordable college. While choosing a college, you should examine how each college measures up to your criteria, both financially and intellectually. One way to do this is to use a grading system. With the grading system, you distribute 100 points evenly across selected criteria. In each category of your criteria, determine the highest and lowest points. When you add them up, you will know which college best meets your needs. By grading colleges, you make certain that the college is worth the cost. The following table shows how the grading system worked for one of the authors.

University	Prestige (30)	Cost (20)	Campus (20)	Faculty (15)	Major (15)	Total Points
University of Texas	15	20	15	15	15	80
Cornell	30	10	10	15	10	75
Princeton	30	10	10	10	5	65

With cemented priorities, you will find it easy to tap into the huge supplies of energy and potential that are locked away inside you. The longer you wait to use that energy to your financial advantage, the harder it will eventually be for you to get debt-free college. If you have not made this a priority, your efforts will lack direction.

PLANT YOUR SEED

There was a wise humanities teacher at my high school. As a class, we were struggling with the idea of free will. Most of us felt that we could become anything and do anything we wanted with our lives. We felt that the idea of fate was rotten. The teacher pointed out that:

SECRET #11

An acorn grows into an oak tree.

At first, we did not think about the significance of what she said. After we thought about it, we realized what she meant. An oak seed *does* produce an oak tree. An apple seed *does* produce an apple tree. The oak tree will never bear fruit like the apple tree. The apple tree will never be as tall or as stately as the oak. The mesquite tree may be overlooked by everyone, but it will lead a safe life because it is hardy and has thorns that protect it from hungry animals.

Some people will be presidents, and some will be mailmen. Some will be astronauts, and some will be teachers. The point my humanities teacher was making is that we are all born a certain way, with certain potentials. However, we must use our free will to reach our individual potential.

The tree analogy uncovers a basic financial truth. If you feel the pain of realizing you may not ever go to a "name-brand" school, just remember what kind of tree you are (also remember that "name-brand" is not the same thing as high quality). In fact, that is the fun part of the analogy. If you are an apple tree, it is still up to you to decide how many apples you will produce. If you produce many apples, you will have more friends and more success than the stately oak that went to Harvard but was too lazy to produce any leaves.

In my opinion, you do not have to limit yourself to being just one tree. If you have ambition, intelligence, or determination, you can shift yourself into a new type of tree over time. If you start off in life as a scrawny mesquite, but are determined to become a stately oak, you can do that. Despite my teacher's point about fate, you can beat the odds *if* you believe you can—as long as you believe for long enough and hard enough. Just look at former President Bill Clinton. He grew up in a rather . . . well . . . backwater part of the country and went on to lead the free world. He not only beat the odds, he walloped them.

Write Your Own Chapter

Hopefully, you have had a few insights about yourself from reading the last few pages. If you want to really make some progress, you should try to write your own chapter. Find a quiet room and organize your thoughts. A quiet room is a powerful tool for reflection. If you point that tool upon yourself, you can make financial self-discoveries.

Don't just "think it out." Thoughts are loose things that fade like the wind. Sit down, brainstorm, list, categorize, and write down your reflections. You may come face-to-face with some realities you did not expect to find. In the end, the exercise will help you to understand your beliefs and also where you stand in the spectrum of college finance.

Now, find a quiet room, sit down, and write your personal chapter that covers these points:

- **Your background**—Just the facts. What kind of neighborhood you lived in, and what kind of shoes you wore.

- **Your emotional base**—The feelings of your family and friends toward money. Whether you took vacations frequently or hardly ever. Whether you had the tendency to spend or save.

- **Your categories**—Are you book-smart or street-smart or both? Are you similar to Rashad, Max, or Cindy in any ways?

- **Your priorities**—Why do you want to go to college? How do you feel about taking on debt to go to college?

- **Your reflection**—Have you ever been motivated by a boring job? What do you do to make discoveries about yourself? Have you always thought that personal reflection was hogwash and therefore never tried it?

- **Your dreams**—What kind of tree are you? What kind do you want to be?

- **Your direction**—Where do you stand on each section of the debt-free equation? Where do you want to stand?

If you think and write on these questions, you might fill half a page, or you might write twenty pages. Either way is fine. The point is that you will begin to know yourself better after you write down the words. Because knowing yourself is crucial to understanding your financial habits, taking a few minutes to write is worth the time. In fact, the cost/benefit of writing a chapter about your habits is excellent—it is a sheet of paper, some ink, and ten minutes in exchange for better self-knowledge that you can use to help you in your goal of debt-free college.

The Next Step

In the next chapters, you will learn to crystallize the debt-free equation, break it apart, and put it back together. Then, once you adapt your thinking and your feelings to the equation, you will be able to get on track to beating debt. Before you move to the next chapter, however, take one last look at the equation and try to imagine what each of the blocks *feels* like in real life. Ask yourself why you feel the way you do about each block and try to pinpoint which blocks are the most uncomfortable or the most confusing. Also think about which blocks make you feel the most positive.

Remember that it is just as important to establish how you feel about money and savings as it is to develop your ability to add numbers and make budgets. People who avoid debt tend to have a different mind-set about money than those who accumulate debt. Yet most people do not really know their mind-set about money if you ask them. This is primarily because they have not thought about it, talked about it, or discussed it. Spend a few moments looking at the equation and examining your feelings.

THE BASIC DEBT-FREE EQUATION

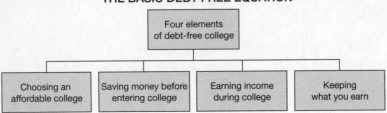

CHAPTER TWO

Charting a Financial Plan:
Your Future Starts Here

You may have heard the Biblical story of David and Goliath. Two warriors, David and Goliath, were on opposite sides of a great war. Little David challenged giant Goliath to a one-on-one battle. Everyone laughed; David would be killed. But when David strolled onto the field, took aim at Goliath, and slung a rock that struck the giant in the head and killed him, people stopped laughing—and David became king. Such is the power of a plan and learning to take aim—two things you must do for debt-free college.

The Cause/Effect Relationship

If you ever stop to think about what you actually know about something before you get involved, it might amaze you. We use computers without knowing how they work, we take prescriptions without knowing how they cure us, and we form relationships without knowing people's backgrounds. There is simply not enough time to research, plan, or know about everything we do. Even many of the smartest professionals in the world know little about "why." Instead, those professionals settle for knowing a few simple cause/effect relationships—and from those relationships they make broad decisions.

Your mission is to learn a few financial cause/effect relationships before you charge into college. Once you understand the relationships, you will be armed against college debt. There are two primary tools you can use to understand financial cause/effect relationships:

- **The balance sheet**—provides a snapshot of your financial status
- **The income statement**—helps manage income flow

These two items are rich with financial information. The balance sheet and the income statement determine whether businesses survive or become history. The same goes for your bank account. Here is what the balance sheet and income statement look like:

BALANCE SHEET

ASSETS		LIABILITIES	
Stocks, Mutual Funds, CDs $		School Loans	$
Real Estate	$	Car Loans	$
Businesses	$	Credit Card Debt	$
	$	Retail Debt	$
		Bank Loans	$
		Mortgage Balance	$
Total Assets:	$	**Total Liabilities:**	$
Net Worth:	$		

Net worth is the difference between total assets and total liabilities. You would like to have more assets than liabilities!

INCOME STATEMENT

INCOME		EXPENSES	
Active Income			
Salary Income	$	Tuition	$
Real Estate Income	$	Rent/Mortgage Payment	$
Business Income	$	Credit Card Payment	$
	$	Car Payment	$
	$	Retail Payment	$
Subtotal	$	Taxes	$
		Other	$
Passive Income			
Interest (CDs, bank account)	$		
Other	$		
Subtotal	$		
Total Income	$	*Total Expenses*	$
Monthly Income:	$		

Monthly income is the difference between total income and total expenses.

The balance sheet and income statement are elusive for most people. They are even elusive for the federal government—there are entire departments for monitoring finances and spending, yet the national debt still soars. We all know that if you spend more than you make, you go into debt. Yet so many people waste away in debt and are never able to get ahead in life. The time to get ahead in life is during college; this is done by staying out of debt. Staying out of debt is accomplished by understanding the impact of these two financial statements.

Income Statement

Let's break down the income statement piece by piece. If we start with the last line on the income statement, we see the words

"Monthly Income." This reveals the purpose of the income statement.

SECRET #12

The income statement tallies your cash inflow and cash outflow.

An income statement tells you whether you have positive or negative income. Negative income is what puts people into debt.

As a student, one big problem is that you are likely to have expenses in each category of "Expenses," yet only one or two marks in the category of "Income." Expenses include taxes, rent, car payments (if you have a car), credit card payments, plus the loose cash you might plunk down for new clothes or a bigger TV.

You have to have a big gravy train to handle so many expenses, but as a student, you are likely to have income from only two categories—salary and passive income. Moreover, your salary is likely to be low. *Passive income*—money you're not working for—is more than likely your bank account interest or the dollars that Mom and Dad send your way.

Once you see the facts on paper, it is easy to see why debt is so difficult to avoid as a student. Money is flowing *out* of your pocket in excess, but money is flowing *in* to your pocket in only a few categories.

MAKING AN INCOME STATEMENT

Composing a rough income statement should only take a few minutes. Use the income statement from the previous section to input your financial information. Leave any categories blank that do not apply to you. Add all your income streams, then deduct your outflow streams. Then you will find out if you have a positive or negative flow.

Most people have a good idea of how much their *nominal* income is. It is likely, however, that you do not have a solid idea of how much you are spending each month, or in other words, what your *outflow* is. As a consumer-oriented society, we generally don't focus on how much we are spending—we just spend, then wonder how we got into debt later. If a debt-ridden person had been making income statements all along, he would not have to wonder why debt was smacking him around. It would be very easy to see how debt took over if we looked at the history of a debtor's monthly income statements.

At some point, you need to assemble a detailed income statement. Include every expense—gas, paper plates, cigarettes, and newspapers. Even include bubble gum. Only if you account for every little thing will you be able to get an accurate idea of the big picture. Additionally, there is an expense that is almost always overlooked. That expense is taxes.

AFTER TAXES

You need to figure out how much you are paying in taxes. No one enjoys thinking that they may have to work from the month of January through the month of May just to pay taxes. But learning to think in terms of after-tax dollars is exactly what you need to do—and the income statement will help with this.

If you are discouraged from filling out your income statement because you do not know how to calculate the amount of taxes you are paying, don't despair. It is actually quite easy. You merely need to find the stubs of a few old paychecks (assuming you are working), then scan the categories until you find the tax deductions made by your employer. This will give you a ballpark estimate of your tax expense—assuming that you are not having the government take out more money than necessary.

Once you have figured out how much money you have *after* taxes, you will probably have an awakening experience. You will realize that for every eight hours of time you spend working, you are actually only receiving salary for five, maybe six of those hours.

It is a nuisance to calculate after-tax income, and it is infuriating to discover how much of your budget income tax consumes, but it is a crucial thing to know if you plan to avoid debt. If you do not know, you will never master the income statement. Not knowing means you will never avoid debt unless you do it by luck. Begin your journey by taking a break in your reading and figuring out just how much you are making after taxes. Take the time—now—and begin making yourself an expert.

Balance Sheet

The balance sheet is also important, especially over the long run. The first thing to know about the balance sheet is that:

SECRET **#13**

It is better to have assets than liabilities.

But what in heck are assets and liabilities, you ask?

ASSETS

Assets are things that put money into your hands. They are bank accounts, CDs, stocks, bonds, real estate holdings, or businesses. Bank accounts, CDs, stocks, and bonds put more money into your pockets by yielding interest or dividends. They basically pay you just for having them around—something most of your friends probably don't do.

SECRET **#14**

Assets pay you money for keeping them around.

By creating money for you, assets help you achieve debt-free college. But assets are downright hard to come by.

LIABILITIES

Liabilities are easy to come by. They are purchases such as a new pair of shoes, a car, or a nice apartment. Liabilities lead to debt because they cost you money rather than making you money.

SECRET #15

Consider anything that causes you to spend money a liability.

Because assets are so difficult to obtain, it is imperative to learn how to manage liabilities. In other words, if you do not have a big bank account or stock portfolio, do not assume retail debt or take out bank loans. You are going to have a hard enough time avoiding college loans, so it is crazy to indulge in any other type of debt.

MANAGING LIABILITIES

You can manage liabilities on the balance sheet through your monthly income statement. If you keep your income positive, you will not go into debt. If you spend money you do not have, you *will* go into debt. By keeping your monthly income positive (or as positive as you can), you will naturally begin to avoid liabilities.

SECRET #16

The way to avoid liabilities is to manage them through financial planning and self-discipline.

In other words, if you can manage to take out no loans and still keep your monthly income positive, you can get by without making a balance sheet. Yet the irony is that you will not know this unless you have done the calculations. After you have done them, you will begin to see just how important keeping a positive income is. Keeping a positive income is the name of the game in achieving debt-free college.

First Two Years

The first two years of college will probably be the most expensive. Much of the reason for this is that when you are learning a new system, you do not have experience with it, so you are not as efficient.

It is very difficult to avoid a negative income during the first two years. This is why it is important to have a sum of money saved as you begin your college years. This way you can "loan" money to yourself from the asset column of your balance sheet. Remember— assets are bank accounts, CDs, stocks, or bonds.

TRIVIA: Education leads to longer life. Research shows that college graduates outlive those who never completed high school—*www.useless knowledge.com*

THE ASSET BASE

The amount you have saved before beginning college is your **asset base.** Having a few thousand dollars saved as you enter college is similar to having a down payment when you buy a house. It is merely the startup cost of getting what you want. Asset bases can be difficult to save, but you do not need a humongous one *if you choose a college that fits your budget.* In fact, if you work hard and save well, it may take less than six months to save a substantial amount.

It is essential to have at least a small asset base as you enter college. You will probably only need between five and ten thousand. That is not very much money considering that an education will change the entire course of your future earning potential. Additionally, if you find yourself unable to accumulate an asset base before you begin college, you have yet to learn the skills of saving and budgeting. In such a case, you should continue to learn and practice those skills until you can accumulate an asset base. By building an asset base, you prove that you know how to manage money and are ready for the greater challenge of debt-free college.

BUILDING AN ASSET BASE

Because the first two years of college will generally be more expensive than the final two, you need to build an asset base *before* you begin college. (Remember an asset base is on the left side of your balance sheet.) A typical asset base consists of a short-term CD or a bank account. These two types of assets yield relatively low interest but are extremely liquid. *Liquid* means they are assets that can be called on quickly to provide cold, hard cash—which is exactly what you will need to pay tuition every semester.

You will need to build an asset base so you do not go into debt during your first two years. If your income statement is negative the first two years (you spend more than you make), then you will borrow from your asset base and avoid debt as opposed to taking out a bank loan.

Unless you are going to an extremely inexpensive college, building an asset base is nonnegotiable. You simply have to save up some money before you begin college. I saved around $7,000 before I began college—about half of that was made by working as a waiter the summer before I began college. If the idea of saving $7,000 terrifies you, you need to ask yourself why it is so scary. If you have a jobless husband and two kids, that is more understandable. However, if you are single or still living with your parents, saving a few thousand dollars should be a snap. If saving some money seems like an impossible task, however, you need to ask yourself *why* it seems so impossible. The answer might lead you directly to your primary financial weakness.

It is important to learn the skill of saving money before you plunge into a hyperexpensive environment like college. To save money, you might have to work more and spend less. You might have to give up certain things that you are used to. If you are only half committed to debt-free college, then doing extra work or giving up a few luxuries—Starbucks Coffee or a pair of Nikes—will seem like a big deal. But if you make debt-free college a priority, the luxuries you forfeit in order to reach your goal won't seem so critical.

The Debt-Free Equation

The size of the asset base you will need depends upon the following:

- The expense of your selected college

- The amount you can save

- The amount you can earn

- The amount you have already saved

In other words, the size of your asset base depends on The Basic Debt-Free Equation. As you can see, the basic equation to avoiding debt is not complicated *on paper*.

THE BASIC DEBT-FREE EQUATION

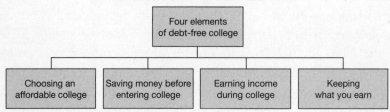

During day-to-day life, it is easy to get off track in any of the four areas. Let's do a random projected example for the first two years.

INCOME STATEMENT (YEARLY)

INCOME		EXPENSES	
Active Income			
Salary Income	$ 14,000	Tuition, Room, and Board	$ 14,000
		Credit Card Payment	$3,000
		Taxes and Other	$800
Subtotal	$ 14,000		
Passive Income			
Parents	$ 1,200		
Subtotal	$ 1,200		
Total Income	$ 15,200	*Total Expenses*	$ 17,800
Monthly Income:	$ (2,600)		

In this example, we are spending $2,600 we do not have. That's being $2,600 in the hole! While you are still establishing yourself during your sophomore year, you might spend a similar amount. Thus, in order to cover the first two years of this type of spending, you have to come up with about $5,200. If you have already built an asset base, you can "borrow" from yourself.

Before the school year, your balance sheet would hypothetically look like this (assuming a $5,200 asset base):

BALANCE SHEET

ASSETS		LIABILITIES	
Stocks, Mutual Funds, CDs	$ 5,200	Tuition	$
Real Estate	$	Car Loans	$
Business	$	Credit Card Debt	$
	$	Retail Debt	$
		Bank Loan	$
		Rent/Mortgage Payment	$
Total Assets	$ 5,200	**Total Liabilities**	$ 0
Net Worth:	$ 5,200		

Let's say the first year puts you in the hole by $2,600. This would make your balance sheet heavier on the right side:

BALANCE SHEET

ASSETS		LIABILITIES	
Stocks, Mutual Funds, CDs	$ 5,200	Tuition	$ 2,600
Real Estate	$	Car Loans	$
Business	$	Credit Card Debt	$
	$	Retail Debt	$
		Bank Loan	$
		Rent/Mortgage Payment	$
Total Assets	$ 5,200	Total Liabilities	$ 2,600
Net Worth:	**$ 2,600**		

But since you will not actually "owe" yourself, your balance sheet will actually look like this:

BALANCE SHEET

ASSETS		LIABILITIES	
Stocks, Mutual Funds, CDs	$ 2,600	Tuition	$
Real Estate	$	Car Loans	$
Business	$	Credit Card Debt	$
	$	Retail Debt	$
		Bank Loan	$
		Rent/Mortgage Payment	$
Total Assets	$ 2,600	Total Liabilities	$ 0
Net Worth:	**$ 2,600**		

You will *still* have no liabilities. The significance is that you were able to build a $5,200 asset base before you began, so you avoided debt. In addition to being a training ground for good financial habits, building an asset base is important because it allows you to avoid debt down the road. The asset base is not meant to cover the entire cost of the year; it only covers the portion of the money you fail to come up with.

In our example, we spend $2,600 more than we make the first two years, so we would want to have an asset base between $5,200 and $8,000 before entering college. That will cover the expense for the first two years, plus a portion of the final two years. Eight thousand dollars is a chunk of money, but if you learn how to earn and save, you could probably come close to saving that amount in a year.

 TRIVIA: The average college student attending a U.S. college reads around 60,000 pages in four years—*www.uselessknowledge.com*

COVERING INSURANCE

When you are a student, it is easy to think that insurance companies really have it out for you. There are a lot of insurances you can purchase, and many of them are downright necessary—health, car, dental, and optical. If you are under twenty-four and have generous parents, you might get a break on insurance, but do not worry if your parents are unable to help you with this expense. Once again, turn to your college for help. Colleges almost always have insurance plans for students; they get reduced prices by having many students join one giant plan. Additionally, if you attend a state college, this makes sense for the same reason that college housing is relatively inexpensive. Thousands of taxpayers are indirectly coming to your assistance. You should let them.

Last Two Years

You might be wondering how the last two years are going to be covered when the asset base does not fully pay for them. For now, just assume that if you play your cards right during the first two years and develop good financial habits, the last two years will be easy. Nothing is easy *while* you are learning to do it. Then, once you have perfected the system, you can do well without even thinking about it—plus you begin to recognize powerful new opportunities. In fact, those opportunities are there from the beginning; however, they take time to recognize and seize. There is more detail on the last two years in chapter 7.

Simple as Pie

You may not be a numbers kind of person. If you are not, there is also a graphical way to analyze the numbers. Graphs make numbers easier to interpret. What you see below is an **Expense PIE** (*EP*).

To obtain debt-free college, you need to at least achieve the **Break-Even Level of Expense** (*BELE*) in order to avoid cutting into your asset base.

BREAK-EVEN LEVEL OF EXPENSE

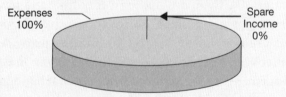

Expenses 100%　　Spare Income 0%

At the BELE point, expenses exactly match income. You are basically one dollar away from debt. At this point, you are dangerously close to debt but technically still okay. This would be better:

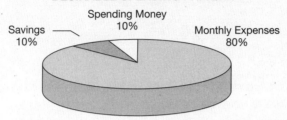

DESIRABLE SPENDING PATTERN

Spending Money 10%

Savings 10%

Monthly Expenses 80%

If you manage your money well, it is possible to achieve this desired spending pattern while still in college. Even if you could never actually have 10 percent saving money and 10 percent spending money, it helps to keep the goal in mind.

Someday after graduation, when your income level is higher, this would be even better:

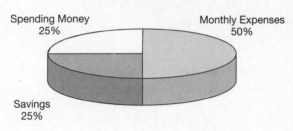

DESIRABLE SPENDING PATTERN
(Post Graduation)

Spending Money 25%

Monthly Expenses 50%

Savings 25%

Unfortunately, the harsh reality is that most students have a far uglier PIE. They have a deficit, which means that they not only spend the whole PIE, but they also spend PIE that they do *not* have. When you run a deficit for the year, the PIE actually looks like this:

DESTRUCTIVE SPENDING PATTERN

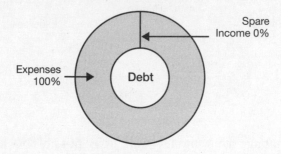

With a destructive spending pattern, you have no extra income because your expenses are already 100 percent of your income, plus some. In the middle, a giant hole represents the debt you have accumulated. Each hole you make is money you will have to pay back later—*with* interest. Holes represent many future hours of your time and a lot of your sweat. Holes keep you down and hold you there. Most students have such a substantial "debt hole" by the time they graduate that it keeps them strapped for years.

The huge problem with this . . .

DESTRUCTIVE SPENDING PATTERN

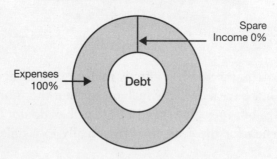

. . . is that someday you have to come up with this . . .

However, while you are trying to come up with the money, your debt suddenly turns into the following because of the negative cycle you have established . . .

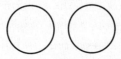

. . . and then, due to interest, before you know it, you have a lot more to pay back than you even want to think about.

This pattern of increasing circles represents the destructive cycle of debt that so many students succumb to, but which you must avoid. You should be aiming to have not even a single dollar of debt to repay.

If you have the benefit of an asset base, a destructive spending pattern can be turned into a break-even situation:

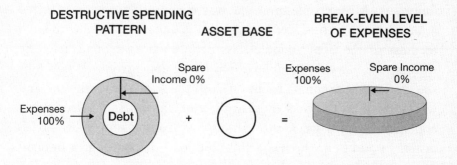

Because it is amazingly difficult to avoid debt during the first two years of college, it is important to build an asset base (the amount you save before you begin college). Building that asset base is a financial training ground for developing your skills before you face the real thing. Now let's look at an example:

KATIE

Katie attends a prestigious university in the Northeast. The university has a technical focus, and though Katie is not a highly technical person, she has another talent. She fashions herself to make money.

Katie comes from a poor family. Her father left when she was young, and her mother has a partial disability that prevents her from working full-time. Along with Katie's financially humble childhood came a fierce determination to lift herself above her circumstances. She applied this to the classroom throughout her younger years.

Katie knows how to market herself—undoubtedly she put together some fantastic applications for college. The result was her acceptance at a top-tier university. The icing on the cake was a formidable scholarship that would cover nearly all of her tuition and living expenses. Katie did not stop there. She applied for many more scholarships and received a good amount of those. In fact, she should be able to finish a double major without personally paying anything for tuition or living. Katie is also a master at securing high-paying internships.

Despite her scholarships and internships, Katie is in debt. You would never know it by looking at her. She dresses lavishly, has a nice car, travels and gambles frequently, and attends a high-cost university. Most people think she was born into money or inherited a nice sum. Not true. Her background is underprivileged compared to most of the upper-middle-class people who surround her. The clothes, car, jewelry, gambling, and travel come from the two jobs she works. She commits to an internship during the workweek and works retail on the weekends. In the end, she works between thirty and fifty hours a week throughout the year to supply her lavish tastes. In addition, she has a full-time load of classes at a difficult university!

Katie's Lesson

Katie is an ultraproductive, ambitious, and intelligent person. But there is one area where she lags—and lags badly. You guessed it—money management. Katie may have been able to cover all her college expenses with her scholarships, but that is not the way she is heading. She also may have been able to accumulate a modest car and some nice clothes by working part-time. Instead, she works full-time, or overtime, has many nice things—and is building debt as she goes.

SECRET **#17**

Immediate gratifications are quick to fade and quick to destroy.

WHAT KATIE COULD HAVE HAD

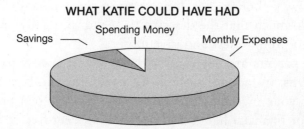

Savings — Spending Money — Monthly Expenses

Katie could easily have achieved this pattern even though she attended a high-cost, private university and had low net wealth and a relatively low income. Her scholarships could have covered her tuition and living expenses. Instead, she showers herself with luxury goods and ends up with a PIE that leads to a destructive cycle of debt.

DESTRUCTIVE SPENDING PATTERN

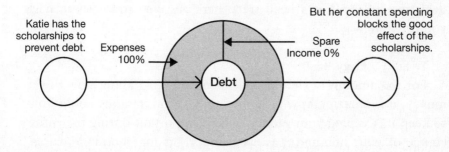

Katie has the scholarships to prevent debt.

Expenses 100%

Debt

Spare Income 0%

But her constant spending blocks the good effect of the scholarships.

Instead of focusing on her long-term financial health, Katie thinks only of immediate gratification. Though capable of freeing herself, she will remain locked in a cycle of debt until she learns to see the truth. Katie's work ethic and productivity are exemplary, but her "I must have it *now*" attitude leads to credit-card debt.

SECRET #18

Slow down when it comes to credit cards.

Just because Katie does an above-average job at earning money does not mean she can ignore saving her money. Katie does not think this way though. She feels because she works so hard and produces so much that she deserves to spend. In reality, she would do better to produce less and save more.

If your parents are not good with money, it is easy to fall into their patterns. In fact, falling into their patterns can be a tempting excuse for your own financial sloppiness. But the real problem is always poor financial habits and not making debt-free education a priority. Many self-made men and women overcome difficult circumstances and deplorable environments all the time. Refusing to give up old habits is no excuse for financial laziness.

Avoiding Liabilities—Nine Strategies

Liabilities come in many forms that are easy to overlook. Unfortunately, they are generally luxuries that are tempting to buy. But liabilities sink you into debt. Thus, avoiding liabilities is crucial to debt-free college. For a head start, here are nine strategies to help you on your way.

1. Start a Piggy Bank

For the amount of time people spend thinking about how to get money, it is amazing how little time they spend thinking about how to keep it. Keeping your money will be important during the entire course of your life, and it is even important for multimillionaires.

Keeping your money is especially important during the college years because it sets the tone and pace of your life after graduation, which is the most crucial period to accumulate equity instead of debt. Equity created during your teens, twenties, and thirties has a lot of time value.

It is a lot like a piggy bank. You make small contributions over time, and the contributions build up. By training yourself to give up small amounts, you ultimately accumulate a large amount. Then, you get to break the piggy bank open and reap the rewards. If you can simply stash away small chunks of your income—even $10 or $15—on a regular basis, you will be amazed at how much you have accumulated when it comes time to pay tuition.

Fresh Fish

The first year of college will be amazingly expensive for you unless your parents or a rich relative decides to funnel money your way. Even if you do get "free money," you might still feel broke, as I learned from a freshman named Joe.

Joe came from an upper-middle-class family. He had nice shoes, lots of CDs, good stereo equipment, and fine cologne. He spent a great deal of his time shopping. The problem was that by the end of the month he couldn't even afford to chip in for a pizza. That was when he told me that his parents were giving him $700 a month, but he was often still broke. The $700 allowance did not even include tuition and rent, which his parents paid for entirely. Suddenly, it was obvious that many freshmen have no concept of the income statement or balance sheet, or the economic danger they face in setting such destructive spending habits.

Joe is typical of many freshmen. Most freshmen are not handed $700 a month by their parents, but many blow their money on junk that accumulates in their closets. They are often strapped for cash, yet they buy things left and right. They fall into a vicious cycle of spending. This cycle is especially destructive to a college student trying to earn high grades. The true "currency" of college is grades, not $100 spent on a ticket for a hot concert. Your grades are currency, because if they are good, you build a better future for yourself.

Many freshmen struggle with low grades and poor study habits. Those low grades and poor study habits are frequently linked to money in some way. Oftentimes, it is because they work excessively. And some people have a genuine reason to struggle—their families are of a lower socioeconomic class, and they have to earn a lot of money themselves to pay for college. But others work excessively and then use the money recklessly. The key is to use the money you earn for rent or tuition—not junk food, name-brand clothes, or a new car. How can one spend time learning and earning good grades if they are always working to buy more junk?

2. Establish Good Financial Habits

The most important thing to realize is that *you* determine your spending habits. You are more likely to spend lots of money if you grew up in a rich family and were indulged, but ultimately it is your comfort level with debt that will determine if you tend to fall into debt. The most important thing is to be aware of your attitude toward debt, money, and saving. Most people do not really know where they stand. Once you know your attitude, it will be possible to form a specific plan—to determine how much money you can earn, how much you can let yourself spend, and where you will be in four years.

TIP: There are several tools to help manage the cost of living expenses. The following websites have financial calculators to help with expense management:

- *www.salliemae.com*   • *www.collegeboard.com*
- *www.collegesavings.org* • *www.finaid.org*
- *www.wiredscholar.com*

3. Perform Cost/Benefit Analysis

Should you be accepted into an elite private college, you need to evaluate your financial situation and determine if you can afford four years there. Next, you must decide if the college has a strong enough cost/benefit value. Weighing the cost/benefit of the college is vital. If you go to an inexpensive college with high value, you could easily come out ahead of where you would be if you went to a "name-brand" college and accumulated $30,000 in debt.

But you must consider the prospects of what you can do with a fantastic education, too. If you graduate from Harvard with $80,000 of debt and plan to teach high school English, you are in for a hard life of debt-repayment. If, however, you graduate from a community college debt-free, but you could have graduated from Harvard with merely $5,000 of debt, then you might have made the wrong decision. It is good to be against debt; it is not good to be unreasonable.

4. Live Within Your Means

After you have picked out a college and received an acceptance letter, you have to make the next biggest decision—where to live. Where you live, should you choose a reasonably priced college, is the most vital question in determining whether you will be able to beat debt as a student. This question, this problem, this challenge, will be referred to throughout this book. Where you live is inextricable from how much you spend. How much you spend determines your debt. The cost of where you choose to live can be a big financial problem, but it is amplified during college for two reasons:

- You are already paying a lot of money to go to college.

- You are (probably) earning very little while you are in college.

Family and Friends

If you go to college in a city where you have family or friends, it is wise to consider the possibility of living with or renting from them. Cheap housing is not easy to find! The benefit of living cheaply with family or friends is worth pursuing.

Though your friends may decide to go for apartments and encourage you to do the same, you should consider an alternative form of housing that could mean the difference between achieving debt-free college or not. If offered, you should consider college housing.

The cost of college housing at state schools is low for a good reason. State schools do not exist to make money. In fact, everyone paying state taxes is helping to subsidize the cost of the college housing. If you are not going to a state college, but college housing is still offered, it is probably *still* reasonably priced because the college itself subsidizes the housing to a point.

There are advantages other than cheap rent if you live in college housing. There are no separate utility bills, and food is generally part of the package. Nearly all college housing is on or near campus, so you can choose not to have a car—or at the least will not have to spend as much on gas and maintenance as you would if you commuted. Having one bulk "living cost" also makes it easy to predict how much each month will cost you. You will not have to guess about how much your water bill will be, how much you will have to spend on food, or whether your rent will increase in a few months. Avoiding small expenses adds up tremendously over a period of months.

On average, about two-thirds of students' annual college expenses are housing and food. (Schools with very high tuition are an exception.) That leaves only one-third of the PIE for tuition, books, entertainment, and everything else. In other words, this is what the average student spends on housing and food:

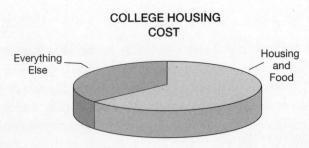

College housing keeps the cost of living to a reasonable percentage of your PIE.

The above figure shows what your expenses will probably look like while living in college housing. However, if you decide to live somewhere plush, your expenses will probably look more like this:

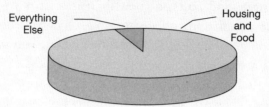

LUXURIOUS COST OF LIVING

A luxurious cost of living consumes an unacceptable percentage of your PIE.

The type of PIE above leaves little money for other, more important, expenses such as tuition, and thus quickly leads to this:

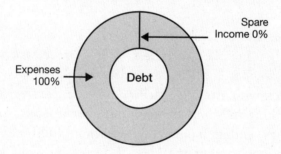

DESTRUCTIVE SPENDING PATTERN

Granted, there are disadvantages to living in college housing. If you like to eat, the food is sometimes bland. If you like to party, there are often rules against alcohol. If you are Romeo or Juliet, the housing may not be co-ed. Yet on the reverse side, college housing is relatively cheap, which is what you need to achieve debt-free college.

The idea of living in a college dorm, for many people, is difficult to accept. In fact, many students choose not to live in college housing or leave it as soon as they can. The problem is that they replace low-cost dorms with relatively expensive living conditions. People often say that they "split the cost of living with roommates," which "makes it cheap." Such an approach helps, but if you live in a dorm, you also split the cost of living with roommates, and there are no surprise utilities, food costs, or rent increases. It is easy to budget forecast while you live in college housing. Once you become aware of your spending habits and the need to budget, you will welcome expenses that are relatively low and easy to forecast.

There are alternatives to college housing. Private co-ops are often excellent deals. They are seldom glamorous but usually affordable. Perhaps you can strike a deal with the landlord for reduced rent by providing some basic facilities maintenance. Or possibly you can find a clean efficiency in a run-down area. Maybe an older lady will let you board for free if you agree to walk her dog and do lawn maintenance.

There are many ways to find affordable housing—all it takes is a little research or creativity to find them. The authors advocate college housing because it is the most straightforward, widely available, easiest way to predict and manage your expenses.

5. Set Standards of Living

Finding housing that *costs less than average* is key. In other words, your standard of living must decrease. Living in a new apartment complex with attractive facilities in an expensive city is fine if you are working full-time for good pay, but it is disastrous if you are a student spending money to go to school full-time.

You may not support the idea of decreasing your standard of living, but you must agree that if someone suddenly severs her income and drastically increases her spending, only two things can happen. She will go into debt, or she will spend her savings. The balance sheet and income statement illustrate this. Living as a student is no different than running a business—you can choose to stay out of debt, or you can be lazy and let it swallow you whole.

You must find ways to decrease your living costs. This is the important thing to know. No matter how much you agree to that principle in theory, you may find it hard to do when the time comes. It is quite easy to *say* you are committed to debt-free college, yet actually only be a pretender. If you are totally unwilling to sacrifice your standard of living, you are not committed.

Mary's Standard

Mary knows exactly how much she can afford to spend before she goes to look at a new apartment. She shops around among complexes. She is not really happy with the poor paint job of the apartment she can afford, but a complex across the street certainly catches her eye. She goes to see it. It has fresh paint, a nice pool, and there is green grass and a gazebo on the north end. Once she sees the new complex, she relentlessly compares it with the older complex. She does this as she drives home, as she fixes dinner, and even as she sleeps.

"You only go to college once," she tells herself. "A part-time job would make up the difference in the cost between the complexes," she reasons. "And think of how much your friends will like it, and Mom and Dad will certainly like it when they visit, too."

She envisions and envisions and envisions herself in the new complex. Over the next month she does so much envisioning that she is willing to pay an extra $250 a month to live in the nicer complex than she would pay to live across the street, where the paint is older and there is no gazebo. Thus, the liabilities enter, and thus debt begins.

6. Know the Point of Overextension

People like nice things. The problem is that until you can afford nice things as a relatively small percentage of your income instead of by earning $9 an hour at a grocery store, you will overextend yourself if you buy them. Mary is not going to care much about the nice gym at her new complex when she returns tired from sacking groceries and needs to finish her homework before her 8 A.M. class the next day.

You must not let yourself fall into the trap of overextending yourself. You can avoid this trap by making commitments early and sticking to them. For example, the reason some people are able to enjoy a dorm is because they never choose to tour expensive apartment complexes. They know they might not be able to resist the temptation if they started sampling luxury. There is an old saying that explains it: "If you do not wish to fall into the water, then do not go near the edge."

The way to stay away from the trap that Mary fell into is to make a budget. For example, determine that you can spend $425 a month for rent *at the most,* then only look at complexes you know cost $425 or less.

7. Six to Eight

Most students have classes between the hours of eight to five— just like business world hours. (Most professors will tell you that students should study for two hours for every one hour they spend in class. This would mean that students should actually have a schedule similar to a forty-hour workweek. From the authors' experience, about one percent of students actually do this.) This means that you should have the rest of your hours—six in the evening to eight in the morning—to work.

Working is one aspect of financial strategy you cannot afford to be wrong on. There are few other ways to accumulate the asset base you will need other than working and saving. Hopefully, you will begin working before classes even begin. If you already have a job when classes start, you can simply continue working the same job and reduce the number of hours you work. This is a huge bonus for several reasons:

- The beginning month of classes is expensive. By already having a job, you won't waste any time looking for ways to make money.

- It will be easier to already have a job lined up because classes are always a shock at the start—from the first-time freshman to the slacker senior who lounged for the entire summer.

- Tests are stressful. By already having a job, you will not have to add to your stress with a job hunt or by having to learn a new skill. All you will have to do is maintain what you already have going, which may be sometimes boring, but not very difficult.

If you cannot already be working by the time you start college, find work quickly. The worst thing you can do for your financial situation is live off your savings. You will have to live off your savings anyway, but your goal is to minimize the amount you drain them.

Think of it like sleep. You can get more done today, whether it is work or partying, if you deny yourself some sleep. The next day, however, you will be tired, and you will lose productivity. By not sleeping one day, you borrow energy from the next day. With money, this concept is even more harmful. If you borrow money today, you have less money for tomorrow. And not only do you have less money, but you also have a smaller sum to accumulate interest with, thus your income decreases even farther.

8. Streamline Your Schedule

You should think about what type of job will benefit you the most. Many students prefer to work a job for a few hours a day, each day of the week—usually desk or office jobs. This means that they earn small amounts of money many times a week. This is not the most efficient method. It is better to work two or three days a week and for a greater number of hours during those days. This is better because it will reduce your "overhead."

Overhead is transition or start-up time. In this case, overhead is time wasted coming and going to work, getting set up at work, clocking in, clocking out, taking breaks, etc. If you work for a few hours each day almost every day of the week, overhead is a huge percentage of the actual time you are working and earning. If you instead work only a few days, but for longer hours, you will reduce your start-up, transition, and shutdown overhead. The significance is that you will get a greater financial return on your time and energy.

If you can, keep your college skill set in mind when choosing a job. By aligning your skill set and your job, you can improve your résumé as well as use your college skills to earn a higher salary.

9. Balance Work and Study

You should seek a work/study balance that will benefit you academically. If you work too much, you will have the tendency to wreck your grades, which will only damage you financially in the long run. If you work too little, you will end up with greater amounts of debt, and you may never develop a strong work ethic either. If you find the right balance, you will actually improve your grades.

Mark was a slacker during college who discovered something interesting about the work/study balance. His parents did not want him to work because they thought it would harm his grades. So he did not work, and he made poor grades anyway. When Mark chose to work against his parents' will, an interesting thing happened. His grades, though never stellar, improved. He later told me that work made him organize his time and start using the many hours of the day he had usually wasted.

Work teaches you to channel your energy, be reliable, and have an end in mind—a paycheck. Grades must be earned just like pay, and you will find that work is a valuable paradigm for good academic habits.

CHAPTER THREE

The College Money Game:
Playing Defense and Offense

Despite your best efforts, you may find yourself in the hole during your first and second years of college. If you have forecasted for such a loss, you should have the asset base to cover that cost. At the same time, it should motivate you to perfect your system for earning and spending money in a debt-free way.

As a student, it is easy to feel that you are doing your part by not buying new video games, magazines, or clothes all the time— especially if you are from a middle-class family who takes those items for granted. There will certainly be enough people around you buying things and joining expensive clubs. But if you are comparing yourself only to big spenders, you are not being critical of yourself. If you want debt-free college, you have to do more than just minimize a few wild expenses.

For debt-free college, you have to be crafty. You must watch closely for early warning signs of debt. Yet you must also be aggressive in pursuing a better financial position for yourself so you can safely reach your goal.

 TRIVIA: On a personal finance skills test given to high school seniors, the average score was 57 percent, a flunking score. Only 5 percent of the seniors scored a C or better—*www.jumpstart.org (School Zone: College Students and Credit Cards)*

Wants Versus Needs

Learning what is and what is not essential is a gradual process. For most people, it is a lifelong process. The problem is that we are raised in a society with such a luxurious standard of living that we forget what is necessity and what is luxury. Generally speaking,

- Shopping for an extra blue shirt at Bloomingdale's is a luxury; shopping for underwear at Wal-Mart is a necessity.

- Eating shrimp at Pappadeaux is a luxury; making a trip to the cafeteria and eating fried fish sticks is (unfortunately) a necessity.

Luxuries and necessities are relative. When an average student thinks of the word *cheap,* they might think of Wal-Mart. The bum down the street may think of Goodwill. Tiger Woods might think of Saks Fifth Avenue. There is no absolute truth when it comes to finance, and this is why it is so seductive to be trapped into competition with someone that has far greater wealth or income than you.

SECRET #19

Luxuries and necessities are relative.

The fact that luxuries and necessities are relative is the ruination of many people. We live in a society where public displays of wealth determine social status. We continually strive to move up the social ladder. This basically means spending money, or "keeping up with the Joneses." Many people gradually accept the standards of living of *other* people who are actually much wealthier than they are.

In other words, we spend, spend, spend because we are told that is the way to get ahead in life. That philosophy destroys the goal of debt-free college. For instance, if you join a fraternity your freshman year that will cost $4,000 a semester, that's $32,000 over four years! But many people cannot turn down the chance to join a fraternity—it becomes a matter of pride for them.

If you begin to feel that way, remember that there are different playing fields of equality. Socially, you are probably the equal of the fraternity members. Financially, you may not be. Their fathers may be lawyers and doctors; yours may be a hard-working janitor.

HOUSING AND FOOD—CHRONIC EXPENSES

People can usually go without new clothes or a new car, but they cannot go without housing or food. Housing and food is a problem area. Students want to live in a luxurious apartment with spas, rose gardens, and personal washers and dryers. Most students, however, can barely afford the bland lifestyle of dormitories without going into debt.

The financial reality is that housing and food will probably take up the biggest part of your PIE. The average PIE for housing and food looks about like this:

HOUSING AND FOOD COST

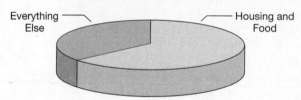

If you succumb to wants instead of sticking to needs, your new luxurious housing and food PIE would look something more like this:

HOUSING AND FOOD COST

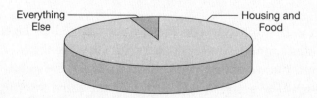

If you have such a big percentage of your PIE being taken by housing and food, then you have very little money to put toward tuition, clothes, a car, or savings—*the basic needs*. You have to take the small things seriously, too—they add up!

- A $30 subscription to the city newspaper

- Pizza boxes in your trashcan when the cafeteria would have meant free/cheap food

- New $100 athletic shoes

These small expenses do not seem like much individually, but if you add them up, they probably equal money you do not have. It is money that is being sucked from your asset base, a.k.a. your bank account. And since you probably do not have an expansive bank account, it is a dangerous idea to get in the habit of borrowing too much from yourself. Borrowing too much leads to the ugly donut circle.

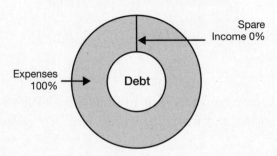

DESTRUCTIVE SPENDING PATTERN

Spare Income 0%

Expenses 100%

Debt

The More Game

Have you ever stopped to consider why someone like Tiger Woods or Bill Gates continues to work so hard? They are the best at what they do and the wealthiest people in their respective fields, yet they never let up. The secret is that they face the same insecurities and the same greed that the rest of us face. We want more than we have—more money, more power, more adventure, more spirituality, more intelligence, more status, and more reputation. Reaching for more is the progressive nature of life, and it helps us get what we want. Yet you cannot do better by getting into water that is over your head.

SECRET **#20**

To get more, it is necessary to live lower.

Reaching for more is a good thing. It is otherwise known as ambition, and it is what drives accomplishment. If you do not think that reaching for more is a good thing, then think of the opposite, which is reaching for less. A life in which someone continually struggled to have less, do less, and accomplish less would be dull and pointless. If you lived that way, you would be in a continual state of decline and would have nothing to look forward to.

Reaching for more too fast and too soon *can* be a bad thing. For example, a software tycoon releases a successful piece of software that is well received in the marketplace. But in the rush for even more success, the tycoon orders his company to hurriedly develop a new piece of software and immediately releases it to the public. People rush to buy the new software and find out that the software has been prematurely released and has many bugs and glitches. The company loses market share and spends time fixing problems instead of developing more solutions. The company would have been better off to wait until their product had matured and been rigorously tested before they actually started selling it. The company went for too much, too fast. The same bust can happen to you if you reach for expensive social jumps without the income to support it.

On the Defense

There are defensive and offensive ways to think of money. As a college student, defense is usually easier. This is because when you are young your experience is small, and thus your wages are likely to be small also.

College debt is a paradox. You go to college for education and to increase your earning power, but in order to avoid college debt, you need the higher earning power. It would definitely be easier to avoid debt with a higher salary, but the chances for a high income as a student are low. It is often best to work with what you have instead of waiting for something to be handed to you. This is where financial defense comes to play.

SECRET #21

The philosophy of working with what you already have is a defensive philosophy. Defense is about saving your money and reducing your spending.

Your goal should be to develop a superior defense by the time your junior year begins. Once you master a defensive philosophy, you can live on little while you begin to focus on an offensive philosophy. A good offensive philosophy can be lucrative, but offense is also more risky and more challenging. With an offensive philosophy, the stakes are higher. That is why it is wise to master a defensive philosophy first—then you will have something to fall back on if your first attempts at offense flounder.

BECOME LIKE THE BUDDHA

Siddhartha Guatama, the Buddha, lived around 500 B.C.E. He gave up a life of aristocracy to find nirvana, a serene state in which he purified himself of the greed and selfishness that torture men. As a student, you need to find four years of financial nirvana. You will be spending quite a sum on tuition, books, room, and board, so you should try to reduce your material desires for a few years and save. There will be a time to shed the ascetic shackles of financial Buddhism—that time will be your debt-free graduation.

College is an adventure in financial realization. If you want debt-free college, you must give up some luxuries that you are accustomed to. If you grew up taking a vacation every year, don't expect to do so during college unless someone else is footing the bill. This may seem basic, yet you will find that for some people, it is elusive.

SECRET #22

Financial nirvana requires a change of financial lifestyle.

Few people pause to think about exactly how much they spend, what they spend on, and what they might be better off *without*. Instead, people usually take the beliefs and lifestyle they are born into.

Here is an analogy. You are probably the same religion now as you were when you were a kid. You may have switched from Catholic to Baptist, but it is unlikely that you have switched from Southern Baptist to Buddhist, or from Hindu to Muslim. Few people genuinely consider a radically different lifestyle than the one they have inherited. It is no different with money, yet with money you can end up doing yourself a world of harm.

Take a look at a letter from a poor soul who did not play any financial defense while sailing through college:

Dear Susan & Co.,

I have a total student loan debt of around 45,000 dollars. Also, I have about 4,000 dollars of credit debt from school . . . would I be able to put that debt into the student loan consolidation as well?

My repayment is going to take effect next month, and I need to take action right this second, if I am to pay rent and other living costs AND pay my loan and credit bills! What are my options? I AM SHAKING IN MY BOOTS!!!! Help me ASAP PLEASE!

Jon

—http://www.cccsintl.org/susan/cd.htm

LIMBO

Limbo is a game where two people hold a stick and everyone else must arch their backs and walk under the stick without touching the stick and without falling down. To do well, you must be flexible, crafty, and persistent. You have to fight for every inch to make it under the stick. Making yourself a budget in college is a lot like that. You have to squirm, wiggle, and finagle your way through difficult positions to reach the goal of debt-free college.

SECRET #23

Careful budgeting means knowing how low you can go.

The first step in solving your financial problems during college is to find out how much you *could* spend, then spend *less* than that amount. If you always spend as much as you could, then you will end up as many indebted Americans do—with a nice car, with good vacation stories, and with plenty of debt.

While you are in college, it is more important to limit your financial bleeding—and everyone must bleed since expenses are high and income is low—by rejecting certain luxuries you are accustomed to. Think of it as changing your financial religion.

TIP: One way to limit financial bleeding is to avoid overpaying tuition in the long run. To do this:

1. Enroll only for the amount of hours you can manage.
2. Never drop courses mid-semester.
3. Take summer courses at community colleges.

RULE YOUR PLASTIC

You must get your credit card situation under control. For undergraduate students, the average credit card debt rose from $1,879 in 1998 to $2,748 in 2000. During the same period, the percentage of students with four or more credit cards rose from 27 percent to 32 percent, according to Braintree, Massachusetts–based Nellie Mae.

As you are reading this, the figures for average credit card debt will have already increased. The figures reflect the destructive spending patterns of many young students. Credit card companies have increased advertising on college campuses in order to extend their market. Credit card debt is a financial cancer that sucks you into the negative cycle of debt. If you have difficulty handling credit cards, do not tempt yourself by having any.

There is a word that summarizes the concept of spending less than you normally do. This word is painful. In a consumerist society, you must be careful when you use it or people will deem you a leper. The word is *frugal*.

SECRET #24

If you make less, then spend less.

You must be frugal if you wish to avoid debt. This means spending less than you can afford to. If you can afford a new car, buy one that is two years old instead. If you can afford to buy brand-new textbooks, buy them used instead. For you seniors, if you can afford Guinness, buy Budweiser instead.

If you suddenly find yourself with credit card debt, you need to get control of the situation right away. Stop overspending, and use the following tips to make sure your credit card doesn't eat you alive:

- Set up a budget

- Pay off your credit card balance every month

- Pay more than the minimum if you can't pay the whole balance

- Ask your credit card company for a lower interest rate (They'd rather lose interest than have you go bankrupt.)

- Transfer your balance to another credit company with a low introductory rate and pay it off quickly

- Take out a low interest loan from the bank and pay off your credit cards

- Use a debt-reduction calculator to find out how long it will take you to pay off your credit cards (www.lssmn.org/debt/calculator.htm)

- Learn to pay in cash

- Read the fine print when signing up for any new credit cards

- Seek help from local, nonprofit credit counseling organizations

- Limit yourself to only *one* credit card

- Freeze your credit cards in water and keep in the freezer

- Cut up your credit cards if you cannot control them

CHOOSE YOUR PEERS

Your ability to live frugally is going to depend largely on the social groups you select. Even if you have the independence of a cat and the stubbornness of a mule, you will be affected by your peers. You may never fully accept their customs and dogmas, but their philosophy will surround you at all times and silently affect you.

How many lawyers do you know of who drive a 1990 mint green Ford Fiesta? How many janitors do you know of who drive a late model BMW? Probably none, on both accounts. But there really are frugal lawyers and high-life janitors. The point is that some lawyers are frugal when compared to other lawyers, and some janitors are high-life when compared to other janitors. You cannot compare apples to oranges, and you cannot compare janitors to lawyers—not financially anyway.

SECRET #25

Friends affect you financially.

Think about this again. You cannot compare apples to oranges. If you are an apple, you better make sure you put yourself in a group with other apples. Do not join a fraternity that will charge you $10,000 a year and force you to have a high level of social spending when you come from a family of elementary school teachers and are barely making the minimum monthly credit card payment.

If you think this is an obvious point, you are right. It *is* an obvious point as a line in this book, but in the real world, where there is pride and competitive jealousy and greed, the ego will ignore the obvious and accept the destructive. That is why you must make debt-free college your priority now and begin your good financial habits now. Then, when you begin to face high levels of social pressure and become confused, you will be able to return to your foundation, which you are laying as you read this book.

To give you an example of the types of poor financial decisions that pride may lead to, I point to my sophomore year. During my sophomore year, I accepted a promotion from waiter to manager. I went from making $12 an hour to making $7 an hour. Most waiters would not have taken such a promotion, yet I jumped at the chance. I wanted to wear a white shirt and tie, and I was willing to take a $5 an hour pay cut to do it. Financially, it was a mistake, no matter how much I enjoyed wearing a tie.

MAKE PRACTICAL DECISIONS

Because I felt the need to be a manager, I suffered in other areas. My pride was puffed from wearing a tie to work, but my pocketbook was weakened from the pay cut. In fact, I earned so much less as a manager that I ended up with $4,500 of debt my sophomore year. I used almost my entire asset base! I was going to have to find a way to achieve this for the next year . . .

BREAK-EVEN LEVEL OF EXPENSE

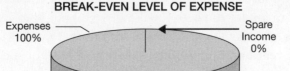

Expenses 100% — Spare Income 0%

People who live at the break-even level of expenses quickly fall into a destructive spending pattern. The break-even level of expenses is nearly impossible to maintain. Either you have a little left over, or you go into debt. People who teeter-totter at the break-even level for very long end up sinking under the sudden, unexpected expenses that inevitably turn up.

SECRET #26

Financial decisions should mirror financial goals.

Had I chosen to be a waiter instead of a manager, I would have had about $3,000 left as an asset base for the next year. That alone should have been enough to get through another year as long as I continued to work full-time during the summer and part-time during the school year. In other words, it would have been possible to "fill in" the debt.

DESTRUCTIVE SPENDING PATTERN   ASSET BASE

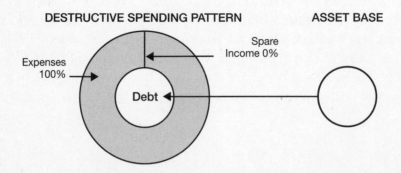

Expenses 100% — Spare Income 0% — Debt

STRIKE A BALANCE

The best way to handle the "more money versus better job" situation is to compromise. If you have high-level work that pays poorly, and low-level work that pays well, then strike a combination between them. When you begin to earn more money, whether this is during college or after college, there is going to be temptation to spend more. Unfortunately, many people who run into windfalls do an excellent job of proving that "a fool and his money are soon parted."

A fine example of a group of people who have fantastic amounts of money and oftentimes no money management skills is athletes. There are many athletes who have made millions in their careers and are now broke due to despicable money management and poor self-control. Two poster children of that lifestyle are Dennis Rodman and Darryl Strawberry. People love them both, but both hover at the point of financial meltdown at all times.

If you wish to know where doing well *and* spending well leads, you should read a book called *The Millionaire Next Door* by Thomas Stanley and William Danko. This book is filled with powerful facts and subtle opinions about financial philosophy. You will be very surprised that the vast majority of American millionaires have their fortunes linked to a philosophy of spending wisely. If it has worked for them over a lifetime, surely it can work for you while you are in college.

If you are forced to reduce your hours or take a pay cut along the line, you need to compensate within your budget. You need to find ways to reduce your spending so that your asset base does not deteriorate rapidly. As your understanding of money grows, you will learn an important financial truth. You may not believe it when you first read it. Most people have been trained to believe the opposite, so the reality sounds crazy. The truth is:

SECRET #27

It is not how much you make, but how much you keep that is important.

If you do not believe this, think about why so many doctors and lawyers in this country are not wealthy. They make plenty of money and thus most people think they have big bank accounts and lots of stocks. But much of the time this simply is not true.

Doctors and lawyers are oftentimes as debt-ridden as the average middle-class Joe. Despite their professional sophistication and high incomes, many have not learned an important financial lesson. They have not learned that it is how much you *keep,* not how much you make, that is important in conquering debt. If you can learn not to make the same mistake, you will be able to graduate from college debt-free, and you will have an excellent chance of accumulating more wealth than the average doctor or lawyer.

TRIVIA: Ramen noodles, a popular meal for college students, were invented by Momfuku Ando in 1948. Now, these noodles are consumed in more than eighty countries—*www.uselessknowledge.com*

SHELF BONUSES

You probably will not have to worry too much about promotions while you are in college. They are few and far between when you work mundane, part-time jobs. But the financial temptations that promotions introduce are important to consider. There are many types of promotions in a lesser sense—an increase in allowance, a cash gift, a new scholarship, or a higher-paying job.

Any of these would tempt the average Jack or Jill to go out and buy something new and nice. Just remember—as a student, you are probably spending thousands of dollars a year that you are not actually earning. Thus, you must shelve your temptation to spend more if you get a promotion. Save the windfall and take yourself closer to debt-free college. New Nikes may make you happy for a week, but a bigger asset base will make you happy for months and years.

SECRET #28

Small gains in assets, if not managed, can lead to big liabilities.

Promotions are one of the best opportunities to "do well, but still spend well." In general, they give you a chance to make more, have more prestige, and also lift yourself away from the cycle of debt and into the cycle of wealth. Envision the cycle of wealth as the exact opposite of the cycle of debt. At the very least, should you get a (financial) promotion while you are in college, you will have an excellent new tool for a debt-free education.

LEARN FROM THE AMISH

In Amish country, whenever a family's barn or house burns down, the surrounding Amish neighbors leave their own farms and work with the afflicted family to rebuild the barn or house. The destruction of a house is considered such a problem, such an evil for the community at large, that everyone temporarily abandons the problems on their own farms and goes to work rebuilding the house of the afflicted family. That is a powerful statement on Amish values.

Think of your personal debt as the destruction of your house. You should learn to hate debt as much as you would hate to have your house and belongings charred to rubble.

SECRET #29

Think of consumer debt as of your house burning down.

Now, remember you are Amish—so you *must* redirect all your efforts toward putting out the fire (debt) and rebuilding. There should be no energy wasted on anything else until the effort is accomplished. If it is time to harvest, then forget the harvest and dedicate your energy to rebuilding the house.

Many people work from paycheck to paycheck just to pay the interest on their debts. Some are never even able to reduce the balance of their debt because the interest payments alone eat them alive. In effect, debt burns down those people's lives, forcing them to work hard and never letting them break free. Such people learn to work very hard but stay quite stationary—smack in the middle of the poor farm. Do not think that you are immune from the danger. The average U.S. family reserves a little more than 14 percent of take-home pay just to pay down debt (Newshouse News Service).

You should approach the situation like the Amish do, which is to devote every resource necessary to rebuild your house. Suggesting that your friends come to your aid and give you their paychecks until you are out of debt will only get you laughed at. Instead, find a way to rearrange your finances so you will not catch fire and burn yourself down.

USE SUMMERS PROFITABLY

An excellent way to rebuild your asset base is to use your summers profitably. During the school year, your asset base is slowly burning down. The summer is your time to rebuild. The hard work will likely clarify your priorities—while you save money. If you have the opportunity to move back home, or live with a relative for free, then you will do even better.

SECRET #30

Summer breaks are chances to repair your asset base.

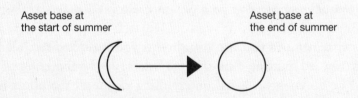

Asset base at
the start of summer

Asset base at
the end of summer

It may or may not be practical for you to use the move-home-for-the-summer approach to gain money. You might have a lease on your apartment that prevents it. You might have a family or a girlfriend that prevents it. Basically, there are many ways for a fire to start, but there are also many ways to put it out.

Let's say you must keep your apartment lease over the summer but are rapidly nose-diving toward debt. This would be a good time to forsake summer school, work overtime, and decrease spending on luxuries. You will probably not be able to save nearly as much this way as you would if you could move in with a family member for the summer, but you should still be able to save quite a bit. This is actually another argument for living in college housing—you will have exactly the lease duration you wish, because most spring/fall college housing closes for the three months of summer.

MANAGE RESOURCES

Managing resources is an important defensive approach, but it borders on offensive. It requires creative thought in order to produce better results that will benefit you more. Resource management requires rearranging your current resources in a new way—a way that will produce more money or more time for you. This can be as simple as piggybacking your tasks, or as difficult as revamping your entire daily schedule to use your time more efficiently.

SECRET #31

> *Resource management is learning to think of your resources holistically.*

In other words, you have far more than just one resource. How much money you earn is only one resource. Your other resources are things such as physical and mental health, your grades, your clothes and transportation, your time, and your contacts. Your resources are all valuable, whether or not they are directly making/ costing you money. If you can think up ways to rearrange those resources so you are getting more without exerting more then you add value to your life.

One way to practice better resource management is to focus on your work schedule. If you are working almost every day, for a few hours each day, you are killing your resources. You are spending lots of resources to travel back and forth—mileage and gas for your car, plus time in traffic and at red lights. It would be better if you spent fewer days working for a greater number of hours. Then you would minimize the time and money you spend getting ready for work and maximize the number of hours you actually spend working.

The challenging aspect of resource management is thinking creatively about your day-to-day life. Most people are so bored or so tired with their daily life that they simply will not take one iota of time to think about changing anything unless it is absolutely essential. That philosophy of mental laziness will not lead you where you want to go. Make no mistake about it; should you stir up the minimal energy it takes to do some creative resource management, you will begin to find hidden profit.

OTHER WAYS TO PLAY DEFENSE

There are infinite ways to be defensive with your money, but you probably get the point. If you find ways to prevent the money you earn from slipping out all over the place, you are on the right track. This starts with good credit card awareness and self-control when it comes to lifestyle. The basic idea is that you must struggle to get money, so if you make it a habit to hold onto that money, you will not have to keep struggling harder and harder to get more of it.

TIP: One way you can save money is by taking college exams for credit and thus avoid paying full tuition cost. The cost of a CLEP (College Level Examination Program) exam is $46. The cost of an AP (Advanced Placement) exam is $77. The cost of an average freshman course ranges from $400–$800. Thus, you can save between $323 and $723 by taking the exams. CLEP and AP exams are available for various subjects. More information can be found at *www.collegeboard.com* or *www.ets.org*.

On the Offense

An offensive philosophy requires you to go out and find better in come than you currently have. Offense means looking for ways get *more* than the minimum hourly wage. Offense is where y unlimited potential, your creativeness, and your persistence bec important. The key to offense is one realization—there are ir ways to make more money.

SECRET #32

Offense is about increasing your income.

For instance, Bryan wanted to build an automatic necklace maker while he was in college. He needed money. He decided to start a small business—consulting—with two friends in order to make the money he needed to build the automatic necklace-making machine. To this day, he still does not have an automatic necklace-making machine. What he created, however, was a consulting company.

Julio has a talent for thinking up ways to make money. He could always spot something that people wanted. In middle school, he bought sheets of Plexiglas, cut them into small pieces, then sold them as "finger skateboards." They sold for between $5 and $20 each— and he could sell as many as he could make. When the finger skate- board fad died, he went to a wholesale store and bought pounds and pounds of candy at a bulk discount price. Then he sold the candy in individual packs. Not only did that bring him a fortune, it brought him fame. Even teachers bought candy!

THINK OUTSIDE THE BOX

There is no simple way to develop a complete offensive philosophy. It comes with a combination of creativity and practice. Such a com- bination is not an easy thing. In fact, the words *creative* and *practice* are nearly opposites. But they can be combined. Thinking creatively is merely seeing things in a new way, and if you practice doing this, you are essentially practicing creativity.

The man who first said, "Let's use the Internet for business instead of just research" was thinking creatively, as was the ancient man who said, "Let's use a wheel instead of dragging hundreds of pounds over the bare earth for miles and miles." Both of these insights seem rather obvious in retrospect, yet the Internet was around for a good twenty years before it began to be used as a business tool, and there is no telling how many tens of thousands of years it took for a man to finally develop the wheel.

SECRET #33

Find ways to earn more money with less effort.

When you spot a market or a need for something and think of a way to satisfy the need, then you will begin to think up ways to make money. This is not nearly as hard as you think. It does not have to be a business. Let's say you know a wealthy elderly lady who needs someone to take her cat to the vet every so often. If you proactively offered your services, you could probably make a tidy sum every so often. Thinking up ways to make money is not difficult, but it does require a little originality and a little marketing. If you can develop those two skills just a little, you can make it through college not only without debt, but with profit.

USE YOUR CONNECTIONS

Thinking up ways to make money is not difficult, but for most of us, it is like using a muscle we have never used—we have little control and endurance. Once you learn to give that muscle a good workout, you will have no limits to your ability to think up ways to make money. The danger is in never learning to use this muscle in the first place. The majority of people who have spent hundreds of hours in the weight room have probably not even spent one hour developing the muscle to think up money.

If you have a weakness in thinking up new ideas or marketing, make a few friends who have those talents. Just spend an hour or so with them every week and observe what they say, think, and do.

You will be using them as a crutch for your own thinking. You will begin to see new opportunities through them, and eventually, you will be able to find your own.

SECRET #34

Who you know can lead to what you know.

When you learn to see the value of your ideas, you will start to think up ways to make money much more easily. You can do more than sell your sweat. Your mind and its power will give you better returns than your back and your arms. The initial steps in using your mind are difficult. You have to think outside the lines and see things that everybody else does not see. It is something that is very difficult initially but which becomes easier with practice.

OVERCOME THE FEAR FACTOR

One of the biggest obstacles to thinking up money is *fear*. It is natural to have such a fear because putting yourself on the line does not always have a positive outcome. Yet if you never put yourself on the line, you will never end up with anything better than you currently have. If you do not believe, if you have no faith, then you will not have the stamina for financial offense. Putting yourself on the line can be scary whether or not it has to do with money. But for debt-free college, you have to be willing to try your hardest and to risk failure.

SECRET #35

Fear is a risk that you must take.

No one can say for sure if a new idea will work or not—that is a risk that drives many people crazy with fear. But not giving your ideas a try means failure for sure. Furthermore, if anyone tries to tell you that they have a foolproof idea, do not pay attention. Schemes do not work. Thinking works. If you will learn to think about opportunities, you will begin to find opportunities. Do not rely on other people if you want to think up money.

STACK THE CARDS IN YOUR FAVOR

Unfortunately, there are no guarantees in life. It is like the TV show *Wheel of Fortune*. Life makes each of us spin a giant wheel that has all kinds of opportunities—as well as many places to bust. There have been great minds who have ended up on bad slots, and people who were boneheads yet struck it big. Such inconsistencies are horrible to think about, but true. We do not always control our situations, but we often can.

We *do,* however, have the power to control something valuable. That is the ability to stack the cards in our favor. Life is a game in many ways. It is *not* like playing poker, where you are dealt a certain hand and you have to live and die by those cards. No, not at all. We can choose to exercise and deal ourselves the needed cards to avoid poor health and an early death. We can choose to study and deal ourselves a card to avoid ignorance. We can choose to manage our money and deal ourselves a card to avoid debt.

SECRET #36

Stack your own hand.

It is our ability to stack the cards in our favor that has the most profound affect on reaching the goal of debt-free college. Stacking cards allows you to have a small asset base yet still afford college. Stacking cards puts you on the path to success.

Stacking your cards requires endurance. You must invest time and energy. Apply for jobs you are not qualified for, use newspapers to advertise a service you can provide, start forming a bond with a professor whom you think might hire you to help him with his work. There are many seeds you can plant that could lead to something big. You must lay such seeds mercilessly and often without profit. You are only beaten when you stop seeing the possibilities around you and leave them for other people to find.

Do Not Throw in the Towel

It is easier to be a quitter than to be a believer and a hard worker. To avoid debt, you need to be both a believer and a hard worker. If you recognize the tendency in yourself to be a quitter, you must leave that habit behind if you wish to get an education and avoid debt. Once you learn not to quit, you will make big improvements not only in your finances, but in every aspect of your life.

If you find yourself breaking down, not measuring up, or hopelessly flailing, you will have to decide if it may be time to "give in." This does not mean "give up." It means restating your goal or changing your method. For instance, if you have entirely consumed your asset base by the time your freshman year is finished, it is time to decide one of three things:

- Are you going to reduce your expenses suddenly and drastically?

- Are you going to take some time off and rebuild your asset base?

- Are you willing to graduate with debt?

Unfortunately, there are some pursuits that you can sink unlimited effort and time into and still not achieve the desired result. Some people think of that as fate, others think of it as genetics, and some think of it as environment. There is no easy answer as to "why?" but there is an easy answer as to *what* to do about it.

SECRET #37

Be willing to change your plans—but only if you have to.

Knowing when to give in is a critical decision. For one thing, until you spend about two years trying to accomplish something, you really do not know if you can achieve it. Some people do not take that much time for major accomplishments; some take a bit longer. You might work for two long years and achieve something you want. Then, again, maybe you could have better spent those two years on a different goal. There is no easy answer. Nothing is set in stone. You must make the decision to continue heading across the desert or else change your course and look for an oasis.

One solution is to continue working on tough, slow-moving goals—like graduation—but learn to prioritize those bigger, slower goals with everyday, smaller goals—such as making good grades and working part-time. If you were to work on scholarship applications for only five minutes a day, you would still be moving in the right direction. Persistence is key.

SECRET #38

Persistence despite failure is key to financial success.

BILL

Bill grew up with all the advantages in life. His father owned a business that was highly profitable. Bill went to private schools, where clothes, backpacks, and jewelry were symbols of status. To attend the private schools that Bill did requires loads of money, and once you are in, the social pressure to look wealthy requires that you spend much more.

Ironically, he ended up going to a "mere" state university. His high school grades had not been sufficient to allow his entrance into higher-status schools. Bill did not have to work during college, yet he still had lots of money to spend. In addition to having all his bills and tuition paid by his family, he had a large cash allowance. He also had a seemingly unlimited line of credit, because his family wiped out any debts he accrued. He used the credit on things like clothes, colognes, fine liquors, gold jewelry, and vacations around Europe.

Whenever you were with Bill, you ended up spending more money yourself. It was embarrassing not to agree with his strong personality, which craved nice things, all of which were costly. If he liked you, then he would pick up the tab himself—compliments of the family.

Bill's spending pattern basically looked like this:

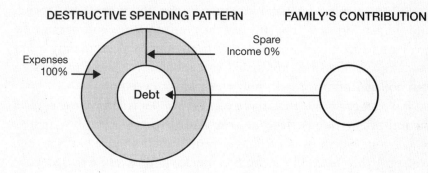

DESTRUCTIVE SPENDING PATTERN   FAMILY'S CONTRIBUTION

Spare Income 0%

Expenses 100%

Debt

Bill had such a talent for spending that no matter how great his allowances or how many lines of credit the family extended, his spending levels increased proportionally. Bill spent incessantly—even when it meant debt. Bill's family encouraged him to spend, directly and indirectly. Bill was socialized in the ranks of the wealthy, and he knew how to put on a show—people were amazed with his appearance and stories.

As Bill was finishing his undergraduate work, he decided not to pursue an MBA right away. Instead, he took a break from work and study. His parents did not approve of the break, however. An interesting thing happened at that point. Bill lost his allowance and credit line. If he were to have continued right along into graduate school, his parents would have gladly continued paying. Because he did not, they did not.

Bill's Lesson

Bill is now working for about $30,000. His parents have severed his allowance. He is learning to slow down his spending and says he still plans to go to graduate school eventually. Yet once again, he is paying the consequences for indulgence—poor college grades. Bill is learning a lesson that is more important than going to a fancy graduate school.

SECRET #39

Learn how to live within your means.

Bill is learning financial soberness—the ability to earn, spend, and (hopefully) save. He still has the tendency to spend because he has had a lifetime of practice in that art, but he occasionally looks for bargains and does not spend so capriciously. These are lessons that colleges do not teach, but which affect everyone.

Bill's story shows that there can be problems with wearing and buying pricey things. If you wear and drive your money, that is where your worth is. If you have spent $5,000 on nice clothes, then you probably *look* like a million bucks but have *decreased* your ability to pay next semester's tuition. Debt-free college doesn't care how you dress.

SECRET #40

Pursue something that leads to success—education—instead of acquiring "things."

Friends like Bill can be financially dangerous. They have nice things and lead interesting lives. They spend money seemingly without consequence, and by doing so, encourage their friends to do the same. It is difficult to see Bill's leather backpack, his new laptop, and the gold necklace he bought while in Italy and not want those things yourself—you deserve those things as much as him! And you could probably have some of them, too—by sacrificing debt-free college.

Practice What You Preach

You must play defense by getting a grip on your balance sheet and your income statement. Then you can build your offense. This means:

- Striking a balance between spending and saving

- Keeping the money you make

- Overcoming fear

- Stacking the cards in your favor

- Adopting Buddha-like and Amish-like qualities

- Using time and resources effectively

- Taking steps to accomplish your goal

- Continuing to try

Once you learn defense, you can start playing offense, which will take you straight to debt-free college. You must be willing to be a tyrant when it comes to defending your money and an encouraging ruler when it comes to thinking creatively about offense. Finally, the minute you quit trying is the minute you become trapped, unable to reach your goal.

CHAPTER FOUR

Stuck Luck:
How to Avoid the Waiting Place

It is said that everyone will have their fifteen minutes in the spotlight.
The same is true with luck. Luck meets everyone now and then. The
greedy disdain their luck and continue complaining that they have
none. The lazy ignore their luck and continue complaining that they
have none. The productive seize their luck, then continue doing what
they do well—*making* luck.

A Contingency Plan

Even if you have not one iota of luck, you can still avoid debt by
having a contingency plan. The key, however, is to develop one early
in the game so you are prepared should you need to use it. For
instance, a good contingency plan is to CLEP (College Level Examination Program) out of some basic classes to avoid expensive
class hours, or take classes for credit at an inexpensive community
college.

If you develop the skills of defense and offense discussed in chapter three, you will have an abundance of tricks to use in a financial
pinch. And if you master the college money game, chances are you
will never even need to use your contingency plan.

A contingency plan is not meant to be comfortable. Instead, it is
your parachute in case your plane's engine burns up unexpectedly

while you are thousands of feet in the air. The contingency plan is ground zero—it might be uncomfortable, yet it will help make ends meet.

SECRET #41

Develop a contingency plan in case your original plan doesn't work.

Part of budgeting is having a contingency plan to fall back on if your primary plan fails. This is why you do not struggle blindly after one single thing. You evaluate several possibilities you think you have a reasonable chance of attaining, then you begin stacking the cards in your favor to get those opportunities. Then, even if one opportunity fails, another one comes through.

The Waiting Place

There is an excellent book that helps illustrate the idea of "luck." You may know it—*Oh, the Places You'll Go!* by Dr. Seuss. Halfway through this book are two pages with many cartoon characters who all have wide eyes like zombies. They are all waiting for things to happen:

> *"The Waiting Place . . .*
> *. . . for people just waiting.*
> *Waiting for a train to go*
> *or a bus to come, or a plane to go*
> *or the mail to come, or the rain to go*
> *or the phone to ring, or the snow to snow*
> *or waiting around for a Yes or No*
> *or waiting for their hair to grow.*
> *Everyone is just waiting."*

The point that *Oh, the Places You'll Go!* makes so well is that you can expect to reach periods of your life when no major victories are in sight. During such times, the easy thing to do is become pacified, like a zombie, and just go on living in your Waiting Place. Dr. Seuss's hero in the book, a boy, frees himself from his Waiting Place and then goes on to move mountains—literally. The boy *makes* his luck by choosing to leave his Waiting Place.

There are different types of Waiting Places. Some of them are self-imposed, and some of them are entirely out of our control. An example of a self-imposed Waiting Place would be waiting until you are entirely out of money before you look for work. An example of a Waiting Place that you have little or no control over is spending the time and money necessary to recover from strep throat.

The only thing you can do about random Waiting Places is do your best to get out of them as quickly as you can. They are bad cards that you have been dealt. The sooner you can get rid of them, the better. And the truth is that you will probably always have one or two such bad cards at any given time for the rest of your life. Everybody does. Just don't make it a point to collect them.

SECRET #42

Discard bad cards—and move on.

Self-imposed Waiting Places are the most destructive. This is because we do not *have* to live with them, but we *choose* to anyway. Many people are experts at imposing Waiting Places upon themselves. Such people are fantastic waiters—waiting for the right person to have a relationship with, waiting for the economy to pick up before they look for a job, waiting for new shoes before they start to exercise, waiting for *luck*.

The human mind is a champion at thinking up reasons to wait. Of course, everyone has some tendency to be afraid, lazy, or apathetic. But when we search inside ourselves, we know that it is better to have the energy to set ourselves free. Focus on that energy in order to achieve debt-free college.

There are many things you can do to avoid the Waiting Place:

- Get a better paying job

- Find a roommate and share costs

- Use your time more wisely

- Eat in an inexpensive cafeteria

- Open your own tutoring business

- Sell party ideas to fraternities

It is only when you rely upon other people to do your thinking and acting for you that you wind up in a Waiting Place. You can use other people to learn *how* to think or to gather ideas, but to get your ball rolling, you must stand up and roll it yourself.

There is risk involved in taking action to help yourself. You could even fail. You could possibly end up in debt. A far greater risk, however, is to stay locked away in your Waiting Place. When you are in that place, you are not really alive; you merely exist. It is far more rewarding to make a plan, take the risk, do the work, and conquer your Waiting Place.

CEO of Yourself

In business, there is a position that entails making all the tough decisions and doing the high level thinking. That position is Chief Executive Officer—CEO. And that is what you must be—the CEO of yourself. The sad truth is that if you do *not* become your own CEO, then other people will be all too happy to become CEO for you. Only those other people will not be thinking in *your* best interest, but their own. Learning to be a CEO takes three main things:

- Keep your options open

- Stick with what you start

- Farm diamonds in your own yard

1. *Keep Your Options Open*

You must be on the lookout for options because you are not only your own CEO, but also your own accounting, marketing, and finance department. You must look for ways to keep yourself in business both now and in the future. The main part of doing this is managing your income statement. Unless you have a gift for pressuring your family or friends into supporting you for nothing, you have to manage your expenses and work for an income.

As you progress in your financial thinking, you will learn to play offense. There are many ways to play offense:

- Find a good co-op and establish yourself there as a freshman. Get to know the owners and let them know you are interested in doing maintenance, collecting rent, etc. By the time your junior year comes around, they might be paying *you* to live there.

- Perhaps you are an outstanding physics student. If so, you could probably make fantastic cash by tutoring—many tutors are currently drawing more than $20 an hour. If you did this for only three hours a day, five days a week, you would be making more than $300 a week.

- Or if you are superbly industrious, you could get your rich aunt to help you with the down payment on a house in your college campus area. Then quickly rent out every room in the house (and teach those people not to abuse your home). By collecting rent, you reduce your own rent (the mortgage payment) to a few hundred dollars—or you might begin to *make* money if you are good at marketing to potential tenants.

When you do not keep your options open, you are not being a good CEO, which means your future potential is unnecessarily narrow. Many excellent opportunities are around us all the time, but if we are too busy waiting, we miss them, we get older, we get farther behind, and we increase our debt.

2. *Stick with What You Start*

This is another part of being your own CEO. Unfortunately, it also seems to be a natural opponent of keeping your options open. Just as CEOs of large corporations have to stick with their companies during economic downturns, you must stick with your decisions.

If you have applied for scholarships during your freshman and sophomore years but have not received any, you must take the time and energy to apply for them again before your junior year. If you have landed a fantastic internship, you must learn to corral a double dose of energy to be both a good student and a productive worker.

We are all pulled in a hundred different directions at once. We are students, brothers, daughters, athletes, Christians, Hindus, Muslims, employees, and friends. We are many things, all at once. Each of our roles takes energy, time, and, undoubtedly, money. Being pulled in so many directions makes it difficult to stick with even very small tasks over time. But sticking with small tasks over time is what leads to success.

SECRET #43

Find a routine that allows you to practice small things each and every day—looking for better opportunities, keeping track of money, and keeping high grades.

Many people have a natural tendency to abandon things when they become difficult. This is especially prevalent today because we are used to seeking the instant gratification society has conditioned in us. Research shows that the youth of America have solid attention spans of about thirty seconds, which is also the duration of an average TV commercial. Coincidence?

It is a powerful exercise to observe how destructive *not* sticking with decisions can be. If you do not stick with brushing your teeth, you are in for some rotten, painful teeth. Brushing your teeth does not take more than a few minutes of your time each day. The funny thing is that most people are in the habit of brushing their teeth for two minutes a day, yet they spend less than two minutes a month thinking about how to manage their money. If you will spend at least the same amount of time thinking about the path to debt-free college as you do brushing your teeth, you can reach your goal.

SECRET #44

Make debt-free college a tangible, measurable goal.

If you do not brush your teeth, you will soon have a toothache. If you choose not to think financially, however, there seems to be no negative consequences. In the short run, there often are not. You get the things you want, and you can simply pay the minimum required balance on your credit card. Over the long run, such a philosophy is devastating to your financial situation. By never learning to make small financial steps in the right direction each day, you end up plotting a course that ruins debt-free college and leads you straight to the poor farm. Of course, people in the poor farm still brush their teeth every day—they admit it would be harmful not to.

3. Farm Diamonds in Your Own Yard

In *Acres of Diamonds*, Russell Conwell writes of a legend about a farmer named Ali Hafed who desired great wealth. He consulted a priest, who advised him to seek a river among white sands. Ali sold his farm, left his family, and searched for the river with white sands for years. Finally, his spirit was broken and he took his own life. What Ali did not know is that after he sold his original farm, the new owner discovered a diamond in the little river that flowed across it. The farm turned out to be one of the largest diamond mines in the world. Ali had been too stuck in his Waiting Place to recognize his own amazing original situation. So remember, *opportunity is already near you.*

ALL THREE

Putting these ideas together is a rare thing. There are few people who manage to do all three things and become their own CEO. It is a real trick. People with great ideas often have no determination or endurance—they use all their energy for thinking. People with tons of determination often work harder instead of smarter.

There is no easy solution for fusing the ideas, but there is a productive way to approach the problem:

- Gear yourself to work consistently toward your goals each day.

- Use the time at the end of the day to evaluate new possibilities.

These actions require discipline. The problem is that after a day of school and work, few people want to think about anything else but eating dinner and relaxing. Thinking about new possibilities does not have to be an anguishing mental experience. With even two minutes of critical thinking a day, you will begin to fare better. Opportunities abound. It does not take a genius to find them, but it does require that you are not sleeping away in a Waiting Place. Some people are so asleep in their Waiting Place that when they are practically struck in the face with an opportunity, they still do not recognize it.

 TRIVIA: Gatorade was named after the University of Florida Gators, who developed it—*www.funtrivia.com*

Control the Environment

Environment plays a tremendous role in the way we feel, and thus the way we act. Our surroundings are not just limited to where we are, but also *who* is around and what *causes* are being taken up. These things, taken together, are powerful and influential in who we are and who we become. The influence of environment is not always obvious. In fact, it is often very quiet and subtle, which is what makes it so powerful.

Unless you are aware of where you stand in relation to your environment, you are already losing the debt-free college battle. If you are not disagreeing with your environment, then you are tacitly agreeing. And it may not be a bad thing to agree—as long as you know *where* you are being led.

There are several main categories of environment: people, places, and causes. If you cover these, you will cover 99 percent of controlling your environment.

People

It has been said, "You are what you eat." However, the following statement is far more accurate: "You are who you spend your time with." The people you spend your time with introduce their own thoughts and feelings to you, including opinions about money.

SECRET #45

The people you spend your time with are also the people you spend your money with.

If your friend thinks that money is easy to come by and he spends it like water, you will probably be encouraged to spend money casually, too. If your friend thinks money is scarce and tries to budget and spend wisely, you will be encouraged to take more precautions yourself. This is otherwise known as peer pressure. What other people do determines what is "normal" for the group. If you choose a different route, you are "weird." Unless you do an above-average job of resisting the pressure, you will begin to broadly resemble your peers in attitude and action.

The effect is even more pronounced with larger groups. When you associate with a group, there is much less tolerance for "weirdness." Groups have a strong definition of what is acceptable behavior and what is not. If you don't match up to your group's standards, you are either marked as weird or outcast altogether. Because we do not like to feel weird or outcast, groups have a lot of power over us financially.

If you are in a group that encourages you to be financially destructive, you are in trouble. It is time to get out of such groups if you want debt-free college. In short, it is easier to change your peers than it is to fight continual peer pressure and a slow financial demise.

Groups that encourage you to be financially destructive are all over the place. A group that likes to go out and spend money is not necessarily destructive, since every group under the sun likes to do that. However, a group that puts relentless pressure on you to "keep up" with the spending is a group that encourages financial destructiveness.

MENTORS

Finding mentors is an important part of any pursuit in life. A thousand years ago blacksmiths had apprentices, and today young people intern for businesses. No matter how many books you read or how well you develop your habits on your own, there is no substitute for mentors.

Mentors can be much more powerful than the indirect channels of radio, magazines, and TV. They can give you consistent direction and help channel your thoughts. A book *can* be a mentor, but you should also find a person who is a mentor. Find someone who has either made it through college without debt or is in the process of doing it, then find out if they can help you do the same thing. It can be as simple as a conversation or as involved as daily training. Any piece of direction is valuable.

Mentors are valuable because they have been through situations like those that you will face. They have been through thick and thin. They have developed the mental, emotional, and physical toughness to accomplish their goals. You can learn from their wisdom and experience. They can help you out of the traps you will face along the way.

You do not have to limit yourself to just one mentor. You could have a hundred different mentors. But it is best to have one, maybe two primary mentors—one for academics and one for finance. Following one person through many different situations is much better for uncovering a comprehensive philosophy. The mentor you choose may not deal with every situation perfectly, but what you are after is the general vein of thought. If you look toward too many people, you will find many veins of thought, which is likely to lead you in confusing directions.

It should not be too hard for you to find someone with good academic habits; just head for the nearest campus library and make a friend. Finding a financial mentor can be more challenging. For one thing, it is much more difficult to know what someone's financial habits are. It is difficult to know how much someone is worth, how much they spend, what their goals with money are, and what their level of self-control is. Those topics are taboo compared to uncovering someone's academic habits.

You will have to do some finagling to find the right person. You may have to evaluate their accomplishments, watch their behavior, and speculate about their motives. If you find a probable candidate, let them know you would like them to be your mentor. If that seems embarrassing, you are not alone. For most people, asking someone to be a mentor seems silly, weird, and embarrassing. But guess what—most people are honored to be a mentor and will take the request seriously.

Sometimes mentors don't have the answer or have no experience in an area you need help with. During such times, it is essential to tap into a larger body of knowledge—books and the Internet. With either medium, you should be able to find someone who will have the answer you seek. Learning not to reinvent the wheel will save you time, energy, stress, and money.

Places

Places are what most people think of when they think of environment. Places surround us all the time. They are highly influential on our attitudes about spending money, about looking for opportunity, and about completing an education. We cannot escape places, but we can choose how much time we spend in them. More important, we can choose to be aware of the financial influence they have.

SECRET #46

Find out how location is affecting your financial attitude.

If you live in a rich neighborhood, you will notice that not only do the people own nice big houses, but they also drive nice cars, have nice landscaping, and wear nice clothes. Any person who moves into a rich neighborhood will face expectations to spend money in similar ways. By choosing to live in a nice place, a person can be suddenly expected to also drive a nice car.

If you understand the financial peer pressure that comes with moving into a rich neighborhood, then you understand the importance of how environment affects us emotionally and financially. The effect of places can be even more subtle. It can be as simple as walking down Mulberry Street instead of Vance Street for lunch. Both streets have the same kind of food, but Mulberry Street *looks* better, and thus people are willing to spend more money to eat there. If you avoid Mulberry Street at noon, you would not face the peer pressure of eating at an expensive café, and thus you would manage your expenses respectably.

Make a habit of being aware of your environment's financial effect. Different locations encourage different values, and you will probably start to dress and live in a way that matches the area you spend most of your time in. In fact, that is how groups and cultures form. This is a powerful thing to know when it comes to your personal finance! You can greatly influence your path to debt-free college simply by associating with different groups and places.

Causes

Your causes make a big impact on your financial decisions. If your cause is to help save homeless dogs, you might tend to volunteer your time for free. If your cause is to be a skydiver, you probably tend to spend more money than someone who likes to jog. In short, every cause has an expense, but some have a much higher expense than others.

SECRET #47

Causes have a big impact on your financial decisions.

Because emotion is tied to causes, we are often very blind to the financial consequences of causes. If you "live to do something" or to make something happen, your checkbook probably becomes unimportant next to that cause. That's a good thing and a bad thing. It is a good thing because it could lead you to being an exciting and self-fulfilled person, totally dedicated to a worthwhile cause. It is a bad thing, however, for debt-free college when you begin to spend money you don't have in order to accomplish your cause. You will have to make the choice.

You must balance causes with finance. Everything has a cost, both in energy and in money. Even if something does not actually cost money, there is still *opportunity cost,* which can be summarized as "the value of your time." It is necessary to be fully aware of the cost of your causes. It is fine to live and die for your cause, but you must decide if it is worth going broke and accumulating debt for. If you destroy yourself financially, there will be no way for you to continue helping your cause.

TRIVIA: Each year, the *Princeton Review* conducts a survey given randomly to more than 60,000 students. The survey is completed by students at each campus on the consumption of alcohol, drugs, and other criteria.

Top Fifteen Party Schools for 2001

1. University of Tennessee
2. Louisiana State University
3. University of California (Santa Cruz)
4. Florida State University
5. University of Colorado
6. University of Alabama
7. St. Bonaventure University
8. Ohio State University
9. University of Wisconsin
10. University of Florida
11. University of New Hampshire
12. University of Georgia
13. University of Texas
14. Tulane University
15. Lehigh University

Reprinted with permission of the Associated Press.

Input Equals Output

Thinking and believing that you cannot avoid debt is poor input. So is thinking that because everyone else has debt, it must be okay for you to have debt, too. If you have enough wrong inputs, you will eventually succeed in believing the wrong things and marching yourself straight to the poor farm. If you instead focus on strong, positive input, you will develop your financial thinking and competitiveness and put yourself on the path to debt-free college.

CONTROL INPUT

Controlling your input is an important part of making your own luck. This not only means selecting dynamic peers and dynamic causes that change you positively, but also selecting books, tapes, radio stations, TV programs, and mentors that will help you learn. Whatever helps you expand your financial insight is the kind of input you want.

Our feelings determine how we act with our money. Our feelings are determined by our thoughts. Our thoughts are determined by input—what we talk about and read or what we watch on TV or hear on the radio. Thus, what TV station you choose to watch as you fall asleep may have a strong impact on what you think about, dream about, and grow to accept as personal truth.

Books are one crucial way of learning to manage thought and action. The things you are trying to accomplish now have already been done, studied, perfected, and written about. Surely, it is worth a few hours of your time to read the solutions that experts have written about.

PERCEPTION OF INPUT

If you believe you are poor and will not be able to avoid debt, you will begin to find evidence to support that theory and eventually end up making the theory true.

An interesting parallel is that if two students submit the same paper, one with clear handwriting and the other with poor handwriting, the one with good handwriting statistically receives a full letter grade higher than the one in bad handwriting. The professor likes the paper he can read more clearly and gives it a higher grade, proving that clear input has a tremendous impact on outcome.

CONTROL OUTPUT

Output is about achieving results. Output is (hopefully) the action you take to improve your situation. The decisions you make in day-to-day life are important because if you were to sum up many days of your output, you should see positive results. If you are not seeing positive results, then you are a victim of poor output—and very likely a victim of poor input as well.

The concept of output is a lot like trench warfare, which was practiced heavily during World War I. In trench warfare, opposing armies dug massive trenches for their men and then defended those trenches with barbed wire, land mines, machine guns, tanks, and many other harmful things. Each soldier had the responsibility of holing up in his trench and defending it.

For months and months, as each day passed, each soldier would see the same dirt, the same sky, the same barbed wire, the same machine gun, and the same lousy canned food. There would be times when he was discouraged, bored, and frustrated. However, it was only if each soldier defended his individual trench that the lines could be held. If the lines were not held, the war was lost.

Just like the trench warfare soldiers, you have to control your output. That means you have to sit in your trench and defend it every day. You may also have to see the same old sights and face the same old struggles, as well as overcome discouragement, boredom, and frustration. If you learn to stick with your trench though, you will win the war and find debt-free college.

SECRET #48

Controlling your trench will win the war.

If you choose to study every day, you will maintain good grades and secure a successful future. If you choose to make an affordable budget and stick with it, you will be able to escape debt. That may not sound difficult. The *idea* is not difficult; the application is. To do the smallest thing regularly over time is difficult. Developing your focus for studying and developing your self-control and sagacity for financial management are not easy. But they certainly pay off and will pay off for your entire life.

It is important to monitor your output. Monitoring can be done in many ways. A written self-audit is an excellent starting place. It is a good idea to actually keep a written journal of the details of your progress in avoiding debt and completing your education.

When you analyze the results of your output, you will know your amount of progress. Either you will be on the right track to avoid debt and finish your education or you will not be. Once you know the output, you can begin changing your input and your mental filters if you need to. Unless you keep records of your output, you will probably not really know where you stand.

Self-Audits

Self-audits are another crucial tool. They are a way to measure your progress toward a goal. These can be as simple as taking tabs of your asset base and projecting its survival, or as complicated as forecasting your budget or income statement over the next four years. Seeing your numbers on paper is like seeing your "stats," which will instantly reveal where work needs to be done. Self-audits outline goals and objectives. They also help you remember your goal and why you are working so hard to reach it.

Refreshing your goals is one of the most important, and most overlooked, aspects of winning your battles. Dreaming big is easy. The problem is that getting to where you want to be in five years is not as easy as dreaming it.

SECRET #49

It is important to refresh your goal of debt-free college along the way.

If you forget to work, you make no progress. If that happens, you will be right back to where you started, dreaming about success but facing the harsh reality of the poor farm. Likewise, if you stop reminding yourself of your goal of debt-free college, you will forget to work toward it.

It is bad to never revise your goals. Flexibility is necessary and good. But if you are thinking about revising your goals simply because the going is rough, you are making a negative move. If you do that, you are effectively abandoning your trench and risking the success of the entire war.

Risky Business

If you ever pick up a book on investing in the stock market or starting your own business, you will learn that both are risky businesses. You might have heard the notorious statistic that nine out of ten start-up businesses fail in the first five years of their existence; of those that succeed, another nine out of ten fail in the following five years. There are no guarantees, but for those that do succeed, times are often great.

Luckily, the number of students who graduate without debt is far greater than the number of start-up businesses that succeed. Getting through college debt-free is not nearly as risky or difficult, but there is some risk.

People have very different feelings about risk. For one thing, there are many different types of risk. There is physical risk, financial risk, academic risk, emotional risk, among others. Oftentimes, people who are risky in one area tend to be risky in other areas, too. Peoples' behavior toward risk seems to come in a package. It is good to know how risk-averse you are. This goes back to knowing your habits so that you can predict and control your actions. If you really like risk, you are going to have to look out for different pitfalls than if you really hate risk. The ideal attitude is somewhere in the middle.

The main risk you will be taking is with your talent and energy, which are both worth a lot of money. You should reach for positions or benefits that are over your head. In other words, you must put yourself on the line.

People take risks and learn perseverance in order to land opportunities. You must take the risk of using your time, energy, and talent to pursue options that are out of your reach. In other words, you must persevere despite disappointments. Some studies claim that the average job applicant must send a hundred résumés to land one interview, then have ten interviews to receive one job offer. As you learn to take the risk of selling yourself, these odds will improve greatly.

There are many risks you can take to find work during college. If you are good at physics, be bold and volunteer to tutor physics as a freshman—even if the people you will tutor are older and taking more difficult classes than you. If you are looking for a roommate, approach people and be willing to stand your ground on getting half, or more than half, of the rent from them.

Taking a stand also requires you to hold out when all indicators tell you to move on. Thomas Edison made hundreds of attempts before getting the light bulb to glow. Abraham Lincoln failed innumerable times before winning the presidency. Michael Jordan was cut from his high school basketball team. These greats moved past their barriers, carrying themselves straight to success. And there is plenty of room for you, too, as long as you get moving.

Continuing to apply for scholarships year after year is definitely a risk. You spend time to find out how to apply, how to write essays, how to proofread, and how to format and send off applications on time. Then you repeat the performance for a different scholarship, and another, and another—all while you are busy and tired. You could be doing other things with your time, but you choose to bet your time on getting something better. This is a huge risk of your time because it is likely that nothing will ever come of 99 percent of your effort. But the 1 percent payoff is sweet. That 1 percent frees you from your Waiting Place.

It is easy to feel like no lucky breaks ever come your way. It is hard to know whether to stick around and hope for a promotion or a lucrative internship, or move to a different area and begin working toward something new. This is the kind of risk that can torment you if you think about it all the time. Make a good guess and be steadfast. Stay focused on the two or three possibilities that offer the best chance.

"The Love Song of J. Alfred Prufrock," by T.S. Eliot, is about a man avoiding risk. Do you think Prufrock is happy in the end? Here are a couple of lines:

> *And indeed there will be time*
> *To wonder, "Do I dare?" and, "Do I dare?"*

If you are like Prufrock, asking "Do I dare? Do I dare?" then do not expect to go far. Do not expect to achieve debt-free college. Debt-free college takes guts and endurance.

Motivation

In order to control your future and move past your Waiting Place, you need to stay motivated. Don't worry, motivation is not just something you are born with. Motivation will come as you learn to set goals and work toward them. Seeing your progress toward a debt-free education will motivate you to continue budgeting, working, saving, and learning.

The idea of debt is a powerful motivator. Having debt keeps you on the poor farm, keeps you owing your time and talent to others. That is no way to survive, much less accomplish your goals. It is better to earn money and use it as you wish instead of using it to pay interest to a creditor.

You may be on your way to moving mountains, but mountains are not moved in one day. Setting the long-term goal of beating debt is vital, but day-to-day operations are the way to get there. Each day represents a challenge to study, work, and follow your budget. It is slow, but over time, it moves you directly to your goal.

It is important to tie the knot between your everyday tasks and your long-term goal. Failing to see the connection between working and learning will devastate your goal. Instead, when you are burned out, tempted, and bored, remember that each little step is taking you closer to completing your journey.

Following is a little test—read what is in the triangle.

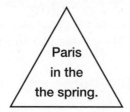

Does it say "Paris in the spring," or does it say "Paris in the the spring"? The majority of people read the contents with only one "the," whereas there are actually two. This little illusion demonstrates just how easy it is to fall into the seductive rhythm of a false pattern and miss the big picture.

To avoid false patterns that will lead you away from debt-free college, you have to be careful with the small details. When you learn to manage the small things, the big goals will come naturally and easily.

Luck Is Just Another Calculation

You do not have to count on luck. In fact, you should not. If you count on luck, there is a certain law you should investigate before you make any big decisions. That law is Murphy's Law.

If you will learn to think in terms of goals instead of luck, you will begin to find a lot more luck than you ever had before. If you learn to *act* in terms of your goals, you will really begin to have luck. Refreshing your desire every day will help in overcoming the necessary drudgery in goal achievement. When you have set your good patterns and done your work, you will find that life is filled with luck.

When a magician pulls a white rabbit from his black hat, he knows exactly how to make it look like magic. That magician is not just a lucky fellow. He has spent hundreds of hours perfecting each aspect of his routine. If he is a good magician, he has planned for every contingency in the book. He has planned for a sick rabbit, a noisy rabbit, a big rabbit, an excited rabbit, and a dirty rabbit. A good magician leaves no variables, and thus a good magician seems full of luck and magic. But good magicians do not count on luck or magic. They count on skill—just as you should for debt-free college.

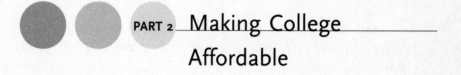

PART 2 Making College Affordable

CHAPTER FIVE

Reduce the Cost of College

In order to reach debt-free college, you must first understand what makes up "cost." This chapter focuses on analyzing the cost of college, the five cost components, and how to make college affordable. You will learn about:

- Fear factors
- Cost trends
- Cost components
- Affordability

Fear Factors

You've heard it all before—the myths about financing an education:

"I can't get any financial aid because my parents make too much money."

"Ivy League universities and private universities are only for rich kids."

"You have to be Einstein to get college scholarships."

These myths and many others like them are exaggerations. The key to understanding college finance is to recognize that these misconceptions are based upon fear.

> SECRET #50
>
> *To conquer debt, you have to overcome the fear factors.*

"Millions in scholarship money goes unclaimed every year."
Scholarship money is not play money. Colleges and scholarship sponsors make every effort to distribute all that has been allocated for that year, especially to deserving students. If scholarships are not awarded, it is because there are restrictions or specific qualifications that applicants did not meet.

"I can't get any financial aid because my parents make too much money."
Parents' income and your personal income is only one of the many criteria that the government uses to grant aid. Whether you qualify for aid depends less on your parents' personal income and more on their ability to use the income to pay for educational costs. The formula used by the federal government and colleges is based on other factors, including the cost of education and the number of college-attendees in your family. Ultimately, your financial aid is determined by your expected contribution and the cost of the college you are attending.

"You have to be Einstein to get aid."
Financial aid isn't based on your grade point average (GPA) or academic achievements. It is strictly based on need analysis. It is given to students because it is part of the government's duty to educate citizens. As long as you make satisfactory progress and maintain student status, you will remain eligible for support.

"The more you save, the less you get from financial aid."
Savings can only hurt students if they are substantial or if they are in the student's name. For instance, if a savings account was

opened on your behalf but actually resides under your parents' name, it is counted as part of their contribution, not yours. In part three of this book, we will discuss ways to save that will not directly affect your financial aid possibilities.

"Ivy League universities and private universities are only for rich kids."

Over the past few years, several studies have shown that most students at Ivy League or private universities receive more support from their colleges than students at public universities. Private universities have more to offer in the way scholarships because of private endowments.

"Only minorities or special ethnic groups receive aid."

Financial aid is geared toward those who need it most. You have to remember that you are combined into a pool of students. In that pool, you may have better financial standing than some of the others, meaning you have a reduced chance of receiving aid. Aid is given based on demonstrated need. It may be true, however, that some colleges allow minority standing to be a factor.

"The financial aid process is too complicated."

Thanks to the Internet and the web, the application process has been streamlined. The government has opened venues for students and parents to limit the processing time for applications. Much of the information requested on the application comes directly from your tax returns. There is more about the application process in part three.

Cost Trends

The cost of college education has risen steadily over the past decade and is expected to continue climbing for another decade. The figures are astounding. In fact, the cost of education has risen at an average of 3 percent more than the inflation rate and almost two-fold since the 1980s. By 2004, it will cost $30,000 to attend a private university and $15,000 to attend a public university annually—in tuition and fees only. The following graph displays the expected cost of college, with an inflation rate of 4 percent, for the next decade.

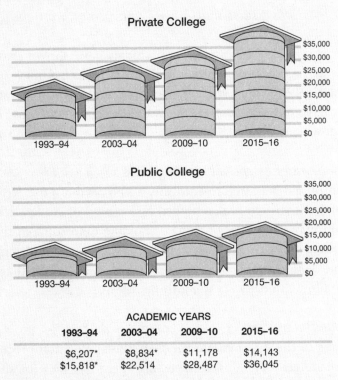

ACADEMIC YEARS			
1993–94	**2003–04**	**2009–10**	**2015–16**
$6,207*	$8,834*	$11,178	$14,143
$15,818*	$22,514	$28,487	$36,045

This graph from Masters Financial Group shows the 1997 College Board estimates for the next decade.

Sources: www.mastersfinancialgroup.com and the College Board.

Furthermore, a comparison of the Consumer Price Index (CPI) and the Independent College index (IC) reinforces that the price of education has remained higher than even the cost of living. The IC is the College Board's measure of the annual increase in the cost of education. The CPI measures the median household income and inflation. On average, the IC index has remained at 2 to 3 percent higher than the CPI.

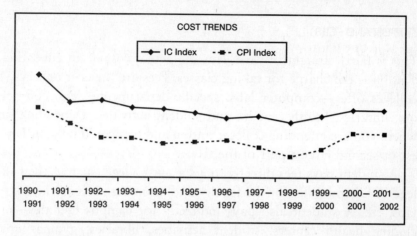

The IC Index, which measures the cost of college, has remained 2 to 3 percent higher than the CPI Index, which tracks average household income.

Source: Independent College 500 Index ®. Copyright © 2002 by collegeboard.com, Inc. Reproduced with permission. All rights reserved. www.collegeboard.com.

All these numbers and graphs mean that the incoming college student is expected to already have an asset base just to *begin* college. They also mean that without a few simple tools, a college student is doomed to debt, even before he begins.

Cost Components

The cost of attendance (COA) at universities (private or public), community colleges, and technical colleges is a combination of five individual costs. When determining your cost for a degree, you should include all components. The five main components of cost are:

- Tuition and fees
- Room and board
- Books and supplies
- Transportation
- Personal expenses

TUITION AND FEES

This is fairly straightforward. It is the actual cost of an education. Tuition is the charge for taking classes. Fees are the cost of services colleges offer—computer labs, specific departmental fees, counselors, libraries, health centers, and student activities. Depending on where you are attending college, tuition and fees could be your largest or second largest part of the COA.

A student pays fees directly to a specific college (such as the College of Liberal Arts) for the faculty and resources such as chemistry labs, etc. A student also pays indirectly for campus facilities—including health centers, student activities, libraries, gymnasiums, campus maintenance, etc.

Tuition and fees are nonnegotiable—every student must pay. Colleges are aware of the expenses and, thus, offer incentives to attract students. Colleges are willing to take on some of the cost by awarding financial aid, scholarships, and grants.

ROOM AND BOARD

Room and board is a controllable cost. Room is where you live. Board is food. Generally, when the costs are estimated, they are based on campus housing such as dormitories. Meals are combined with the cost of the room. There is usually a cafeteria within each dorm and a variety of meal programs you can choose from. A fraternity or a sorority house generally costs more than the average dormitory, so if you plan to be in one of these organizations, you should anticipate the additional cost in your budget.

TRIVIA: The top three factors accounting for tuition and fee growth at independent colleges and universities during the last three years were:

- Technological improvements on campus
- Institutionally provided student financial aid
- Faculty salaries and benefits

BOOKS AND SUPPLIES

Books and supplies are another big cost. This cost can be minimized through planning and smart shopping. For instance, buying used books for all your classes can reduce expenses by almost half. Many colleges also require that students have a PC or a laptop. As a result, you may have costs such as networking fees, connection fees, and software license fees. Purchasing a refurbished computer or simply using the university's computer lab can help reduce computing costs.

TRANSPORTATION

Some students attend out-of-state or distant in-state colleges. For these students, traveling home once a month or during holidays is expensive. If you have a car, or if you commute to campus every day, you have car management expenses such as parking permits and car maintenance. Transportation costs can be minimized with a few simple tactics and some forethought. Bus transportation or carpooling with friends are also good ways to reduce cost.

PERSONAL EXPENSES

This category includes the cost of clothes, shoes, toiletries, and entertainment. Because this category depends on your preferences, the total expenditure varies for each person. This category could be as small as 5 percent of your COA or as high as 50 percent. The key to keeping this piece small is being *self-disciplined*.

In your pursuit of self-discipline, remember that the truly eternal things in life are free—the things that people actually have enduring fun with. Exercise and sports, visiting parks, and getting involved in the community are examples. Eating can be inexpensive, reading and independent learning are not costly, and talking is free. There are thousands of small pursuits that people spend their entire life having fun at yet spend very little money on. Society can be misguiding and instruct you that small, inexpensive things like exercise or reading are a waste of your time—not worth your income or your sexiness. Such bull lets advertisers sell more of their product but keeps you from debt-free college.

Once you take hold of your financial situation and put yourself on the road to beating the cycle of debt, your definition of what is fun might change a little. You may start to focus on having the type of fun that does not break your back later on down the road. In doing so, there is a great chance that you will also learn to find fun in meaningful pursuits that will increase your health, spirituality, and talent.

Once you attain your degree and have a higher income, you will be able to have your fun with knick-knacks. Later on, you will be able to finance a car or take a vacation as a reasonable percentage of your income. Until then, you will stay on the path to debt-free college by finding financially harmless ways to have fun.

Affordability

Now that we have discussed what cost is and what it is made of, you are probably wondering how you are ever going to afford college. Here is how.

The cost of college is similar to the sticker price of a car. The dealer knows that his customers will not pay the full cost. The sticker price is merely a starting point for bargaining. Like the purchase of a car, the purchase of education can be discounted through financial aid. Statistics show that:

- Nearly *60 percent* of students at four-year public institutions receive some type of financial aid.

- Nearly *75 percent* of students at four-year private institutions receive some form of financial aid. (*Source: the College Board*)

The COA as estimated by colleges is based on a very generous income. When you break the cost into pieces, you will recognize where the burden lies—and you can begin negotiating luxuries and necessities. Ultimately, with good financial management skills, you can reduce your COA by 20 to 30 percent of the sticker price before you even begin college. Simply put:

SECRET #51

Cost is an estimated expense needed to cover business. Affordability is the negotiated price.

If you stick with the debt-free equation and choose a college that fits your budget, you are winning the college money game.

College can be *made* affordable for a couple reasons:

- Higher education is a business.
- Colleges need students.

Higher education, like corporations, is a business. Colleges are nonprofit organizations, but they are still in the "business" of education. Without students, they cannot survive. Moreover, colleges compete amongst themselves to lure students. Colleges use all sorts of gimmicks to attract a diversity of students in order to increase their academic standing and strengthen their student bodies.

Let's take a look at how college can be affordable. Kyle is a traditional student who is planning to attend a private university within his state. Kyle is dependent on his parents—his financial aid is based on their demonstrated need. Kyle also has two other siblings, one of whom is already attending college. If Kyle saves his asset base, receives financial aid, and seeks scholarships, he would need only $1,700 for the first year. This sum can easily be achieved with cash gifts, a job, and expense management.

COA	ASSET BASE	FINANCIAL AID	SCHOOL SCHOLARSHIPS	OUTSIDE SCHOLARSHIPS	PART-TIME WORK	REMAINING BALANCE
$23,000	$8,500	$4,800	$2,000	$2,000	$4,000	$1,700

FINANCIAL AID		SCHOLARSHIPS	
Pell	$1,500	Business school	$2,000
Federal grant (FSEOG)	$ 500	Community/church	$1,100
State	$ 300	High school merit	$ 500
Work-study	$2,500	Parents' employer	$ 400
Total	$4,800	Total	$4,000

Furthermore, Kyle has not even begun to tap into all available resources. There are grants from volunteer organizations and state guaranty agencies, tax credits, and jobs that offer housing perks. These options and many others will be discussed in the following chapters.

ASL

To make college affordable, you have to understand two concepts:

- Analysis

- Streamlining

Analysis is the process of validating and reinforcing the reason for a purchase *before* it takes place. It is the process of validating luxuries and necessities. If you are seeking debt-free college, then a *necessity* is your tuition and a *luxury* is a two-week vacation to Cancun. The analysis process makes you justify purchases in terms of debt-free college.

Streamlining is the process of identifying cost factors that impact the purchase. Cost factors are unnoticeable expenses that slip into the buying process and impact the total cost. For instance, brand names are cost factors. The Chevrolet Prizm, a small sedan, is manufactured with the same design as the Toyota Corolla. But the Corolla is $4,000 more expensive than the Prizm. In this situation, the sneaky cost factor is the manufacturer's name. The name "Toyota" demands extra dough although the car is the same. Similarly, the purchase of higher education is surrounded by cost factors that increase the sticker price—location, renowned faculty, prestige, rank, and size.

Together, these ideas—analysis and streamlining—reinforce the goal to identify cost factors and make debt-free college possible. The **Analysis and Streamlining (ASL)** process sharpens your vision and defines a financially feasible path. Take a look at how ASL helped Bryan save money.

Bryan is twenty-two years old and is completing his second year of college. He is offered a summer internship at a local corporation. That means he needs a car. Before rushing out to buy the latest convertible, he decides to use ASL. First, Bryan must validate that the car is a necessity. He tries to find a cheaper form of transportation—the public metro. After some hours on the phone, he realizes that the metro is not an option because it does not go north. Carpooling will not work, as his parents work on the south side of the town. With no other options, and the internship being valuable to his education, Bryan analyzes the purchase. He decides on a type of car, make and model, amenities, and a price range. For the next three weeks, he conducts thorough research and finds a suitable dealership. Bryan looks at the car, likes it, and negotiates a price. As he is walking to the counter, the dealer presents some enticements—an option package, expensive hubcaps, a sunroof, etc. Bryan is interested, but he realizes that adding options would defeat his financial goal of debt-free college. So he streamlines the cost factors and walks away with what he can handle financially. Bryan saves $3,500.

MORE PIE

Before you rush off and arm yourself with a fork and knife, you might want to stop and note that this is an Expense PIE (EP), no relation to an apple pie. An apple pie may offer the best remedy to a salivating mouth, but it does fall short of appeasing the pangs of a financial crisis.

The Expense PIE, introduced in chapter 2, demonstrates the ASL process in a visual manner. The EP represents the purchase total; each piece of the EP represents a cost component. Cost components are the individual expenses that comprise overall cost. In higher education, cost components are tuition and fees, room and board, books and supplies, transportation, and personal expenses.

Each separate piece of the PIE is evaluated by size (percentage of whole) and contribution to overall cost. As each cost component is analyzed, streamlining takes effect and excess cost factors are eliminated. The EP channels your energy on specific pieces of the PIE and allows you to identify problem areas.

The following table shows the estimated COA for the academic year 2001–2002 for different types of institutions. According to the College Board, an additional estimated $5,764 should be added to public four-year colleges for out-of-state students.

CATEGORY/ INSTITUTION	PUBLIC (IN STATE)	PUBLIC (OUT OF STATE)	PRIVATE	COMMUNITY COLLEGES
Tuition and Fees	$ 3,754	$ 9,518	$17,123	$1,877
Room and Board	$ 5,254	$ 5,254	$ 6,455	*
Books and Supplies	$ 736	$ 736	$ 765	$ 736
Personal Expenses	$ 1,564	$ 1,564	$ 1,127	$1,837
Transportation	$ 668	$ 668	$ 600	$ 974
Total Cost	$11,976	$17,740	$26,070	$5,424

*The College Board assumes that the average community college student will not have room and board expense, but instead have increased transportation expenses.

Source: "Table 1. Average Fixed Charges for Undergraduate, 2001–2002 (Enrollment-weighted)." *Trends in College Pricing 2001*: 5. Copyright © 2001 by College Entrance Examination Board. Reprinted with permission. All rights reserved. www.collegeboard.com.

Source: "Table 2. Average Expenses in Nonfixed Budget Components, 2001–2002 (Enrollment-Weighted)." *Trends in College Pricing 2001*: 5. Copyright © 2001 by College Entrance Examination Board. Reprinted with permission. All rights reserved. www.collegeboard.com.

The EPs on page 116 represent the cost for each type of institution. In fact, these EPs should be used as a standard for comparison against the PIEs that you create for your selected college(s). To graduate debt-free, aiming *below* the estimated averages offers the best solution. Remember, the average student has debt! By spending less than the average cost, you reduce your COA and move ahead financially.

The College Board uses a traditional student's profile. Thus, not all costs are considered in the estimates. An independent/adult student may have to add other costs such as day care or lost earning power (lower income), which could impact their ability to pay for college. If you are an international student, your total cost of education will most likely increase by an average of 10 to 20 percent because you are not a U.S. citizen or a state resident. An international student should add more for transportation and miscellaneous expenses because of costs such as airfare, telephone calls, and currency exchange rates. Similarly, all students should include additional costs that might affect their COA.

Remember that each college evaluates the COA differently. Some colleges don't consider all five cost components in their estimates. This will directly impact your PIE and may leave an unexpected need for which you have to plan.

TIP: If an institution does not provide you with all five cost components, you can do some quick research by:

- Contacting the college's financial aid office

- Using the reference books at the local library

- Estimating based on the Expense PIE

The Next Step

By using the elements of affordability, you should have a clearer picture of your financial position. You should know where your burden lies and what part of the COA affects you the most. If you don't, go ahead and take some time to do so before moving on.

PUBLIC (IN STATE)

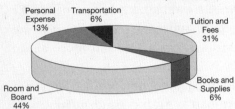

Personal Expense 13%
Transportation 6%
Tuition and Fees 31%
Books and Supplies 6%
Room and Board 44%

The biggest piece of a public, in-state tuition PIE is room and board, which is based on campus housing. This could be managed by taking on the position of a resident advisor or looking for less-expensive housing such as co-ops.

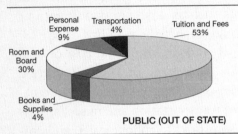

Personal Expense 9%
Transportation 4%
Tuition and Fees 53%
Room and Board 30%
Books and Supplies 4%

PUBLIC (OUT OF STATE)

The biggest piece of a public, out-of-state PIE is tuition and fees, which is more than half of the COA. This piece could be managed by selecting a college that meets both your needs and your wallet. The debt-free equation and the grading system are two tools to help with the college selection process.

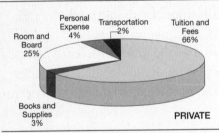

Personal Expense 4%
Transportation 2%
Tuition and Fees 66%
Room and Board 25%
Books and Supplies 3%

PRIVATE

The biggest piece of a private college PIE is tuition and fees, which is almost two-thirds of the COA. This piece could be managed by selecting a college that meets both your needs and your wallet. The debt-free equation and the grading system are two tools to help with the college selection process.

COMMUNITY COLLEGE

Transportation 18%
Tuition and Fees 34%
Books and Supplies 14%
Personal Expense 34%
Room and Board 0%

The biggest pieces of the community college PIE are personal expenses, tuition, and fees. You can reduce your tuition and fees with financial aid. You can reduce your personal expenses by playing financial defense.

- Gather data about your selected college(s).

- Make a COA table with the individual components.

- Create Expense PIEs.

- Use ASL to eliminate and trim costs (needs vs. wants).

- Use the Debt-Free Equation and the grading system.

Using the elements of affordability will help you focus on your goal. By understanding where you are on the road to debt-free college, you will be able to better utilize the upcoming strategies. If you don't have a clear idea, or try to implement strategies without focus, don't expect debt-free college. Whatever you do, avoid procrastination, as that is a debt-free college killer.

CHAPTER SIX

Twelve Quick-Hit Strategies

In this chapter, we lay out twelve strategies that can reduce cost of attendance (COA). The solutions are organized into four categories and address cost at four different stages:

- College pre-planning
- College selection
- College enrollment
- College in action

College Pre-Planning

Going to college doesn't have to exactly follow the traditional, four-year college route. Not everyone enjoys doing that. You can always ease into college life at a more comfortable—and affordable—pace.

COMMUNITY COLLEGE

The first two years of college curriculum are similar whether you go to a private or public school. Everyone is required to take basic English, math, and science courses. While meeting these basic requirements, everyone is also required to pay a hefty sum. Community colleges are an inexpensive way to handle the first two years. Until recently, the primary offerings at community colleges included associate degrees, certificate programs, and technical training. Now, most community colleges have expanded their focus to include two-year transfer programs as well. These programs allow students to meet the standard curriculum requirements of the first two years and continue the latter two years at a four-year institution. As of 1997, there were an estimated 1,100 community colleges supporting 9.3 million students nationwide.

Like bigger institutions, community colleges provide cultural diversity, high-quality faculty and resources, financial aid, and a high post-graduation success rate. In fact, the American Association of Community Colleges (AACC) reports that in the past five years, enrollment at community colleges has risen steadily. In addition, community colleges provide other advantages such as:

- *Open admission:* Open admission allows anyone who has a high school diploma (or the equivalent) to enroll. There are no requirements for grade point average (GPA), academic achievements, or extracurricular activities. In fact, most community colleges do not even require college admission test scores like the Scholastic Aptitude Test (SAT) or the American College Test (ACT).

- *Smaller classes:* Depending on the size of the university, a course section can hold between 20 to 500 students. For instance, a freshman attending the University of Texas at Austin can expect an average class size of 200 to 300 students in a biology course. Moreover, some classes are led by teaching assistants rather than senior faculty members. At smaller community colleges, faculty generally teach all classes. A strong benefit of small class sizes is more personal interaction with instructors.

- *Convenience:* Community colleges take pride in offering flexibility. If you are an adult or an independent student with outside obligations, flexibility is good. Community colleges offer classes during the day, at night, and in the afternoon. They also offer most courses in subsequent semesters, so you don't have to sit around waiting for a particular class and thereby delay graduation.

- *Campus life:* Contrary to public opinion, community colleges are not just for students planning to commute. There are 37 states with more than 500 community colleges that support on-campus lifestyles. Dormitories are available for students who have the desire to live away from home and experience independence. Although living away from home increases overall cost, community college housing is still less expensive than most university housing.

- *Low cost:* If you don't know which field of study to pursue or you just can't afford four years, starting out at a community college could be the key to success. With the average cost of tuition per semester totaling only $1,500 and with a 33 percent chance of receiving federal aid, the odds of beating debt are higher.

In addition, community colleges offer the opportunity to prepare for a four-year institution. For instance, if you did poorly in previous years—college or high school—community college is an opportunity to strengthen your GPA. Once you increase your GPA, you increase your chance for core admissions at a four-year institution. This also shows motivation and initiative to the admissions team.

In order to be successful, though, you must give considerable effort and work for good grades. If you want to transfer to a university, you have to investigate the feasibility and get the advice of the counselors at both the community college and the targeted college. If you decide to transfer from a community college to a four-year institution, here are a few steps you should take:

- *Find one counselor at both the community college and the four-year institution.* This reduces admission policy confusion—

ASSOCIATE DEGREES	CERTIFICATES
Liberal/General Studies and Humanities	Health Professions and Related Sciences
Health Professions and Related Sciences	Business Management and Administration Services
Business Management and Administration Services	Mechanics and Repairers
Engineering-Related Technologies	Protective Services
Protective Services	Precision Production Trades
Mechanics and Repairers	Vocational Home Economics
Education	Personal and Miscellaneous Services
Visual and Performing Arts	Engineering-Related Technologies
Multi/Interdisciplinary Studies	Construction Trades
Computer and Information Sciences	Transportation and Material Moving Workers

This table lists the different types of degrees and certificates that community colleges have offered in the past. Source: American Association of Community Colleges.

plus you will have *one* consistent point of contact at each institution. This also gives you the chance to keep both counselors aware of your plight and shows that you are dedicated.

- *Check for transferability of courses.* Degree requirements and curriculum changes happen all the time. Sometimes they are small, but sometimes they are huge. So at the beginning of each semester, always check to make sure your current and previous courses still have transferability. As a precautionary step, you should always save documentation from both colleges so that you can prove your status.

- *Research support agreements.* Most community colleges and universities have agreements with each academic department to make transferability easy. For instance, if you have an associate degree in teaching, you may receive unconditional entry into the university's teaching program. For this reason, you should always check with the colleges to see if such agreements are in place for your field of study.

For more details on community colleges, refer to these websites:

MORE INFORMATION
www.collegeboard.com
www.aacc.nche.edu
www.ed.gov

THE U.S. DEFENSE

The U.S. government strongly encourages all students to further their personal development. To make this easier, it offers to pay for any level of education (post high school) to anyone who devotes time to upholding the security of the nation. The government offers three choices—the Academy, the Reserve Officer Training Corps (ROTC), and the College Fund Program.

The Academies

The Military Academy (West Point, NY), the Naval Academy (Annapolis, MD), the Air Force Academy (Colorado Springs, CO), and the Coast Guard Academy (New London, CT) are top-notch U.S. military establishments. These four educational institutions are the most difficult and competitive military institutions in the nation. And they offer the most enticing deals for students.

Academy participants receive full scholarships throughout their undergraduate degree—including room, board, tuition, and fees. Academy students also receive monthly stipends for books, other incidental expenses, and full medical care. Applicants must have a high school diploma, excellent SAT scores, good academic standing, extracurricular activity, community involvement, and work experience. They must also pass a physical health test, demonstrate aptitude for morality, and obtain a recommendation letter from a State Representative or Senator.

Upon completion, graduates receive an undergraduate degree and a commissioned leadership job as a junior officer in the related branch of service. Graduates repay the government with a minimum of five years of active military service. For additional information, contact the academies directly or refer to the following websites:

	ARMY	NAVY	AIR FORCE	COAST GUARD
Website	www.usma.edu	www.usna.edu	www.usafa.ag.mil	www.cga.edu
Phone Number	914-938-4041	410-293-4361	719-333-3070	1-800-883-8724

The Reserve Officer Training Corps (ROTC)

The Reserve Officer Training Corps program is offered at 600 colleges and universities and trains students to serve in one of the military branches. It is a four-year program divided into basic and advanced courses. The first two years are basic and can be completed by anyone with no further obligation. If you find that ROTC is not for you, you can choose to receive academic or physical education credit for the first two years.

The ROTC program is available to high school students or previously active military members. If you have previous experience, you can skip the basic courses and move directly to the advanced courses. While you are in the program, you are required to take one ROTC course each semester as part of the curriculum. You are required to wear a uniform and participate in military drills, labs, and other activities.

ROTC scholarships are awarded on merit, good SAT scores, extracurricular activities, and other achievements. Scholarship awards range from $5,000 to $12,000 per year for up to four years. In addition, scholarship winners receive a $200 stipend for each academic month plus an allowance for books and other items. If you are a nonscholarship student, you receive the stipend and book allowance during the last two years only.

Following graduation, award recipients are expected to serve in the Army, the Army National Guard (ARNG), or the U.S. Army Reserve (USAR) for a minimum of eight years. This obligation may be completed either by serving either:

- Two to four years of active duty and four to six years of service as a citizen-soldier in the ARNG or USAR

- Eight years in the ARNG or USAR "preceded by a period necessary to complete the active component resident Officer Basic Course (OBC)" *(Source: www.rotc.org)*

Nonscholarship graduates may elect to fulfill their obligation entirely as citizen-soldiers or serve three years of active duty and five years as citizen-soldiers. For more information on ROTC, visit *www.armyrotc.com* or call one of these numbers:

ARMY	NAVY	AIR FORCE	MARINES
1-800-USA-ROTC	1-800-USA-NAVY	1-800-522-0033, x2091	1-800-MARINES

 TIP: The Simultaneous Membership Program (SMP) is another alternative for ROTC members. Under the SMP, you can sign up for the Army National Guard (ARNG), U.S. Army Reserve (USAR), or the Army while you are in school. As part of the program, you receive officer pay and the advanced ROTC stipend. Upon completion, you can choose to serve in the Army or continue as an ARNG or an USAR officer.

Other Programs

If neither the ROTC nor the Academy route suits you, you can try the Montgomery GI Bill Program (MGIB), the College Fund Program, or the Community College Air Force (CCAF) program. Under the MGIB program, you can receive either part-time ($9,180) or full-time ($19,296) benefits, provided you meet eligibility requirements. The program provides up to thirty-six months of educational benefits, which can be used for:

- Degree and certificate programs
- Flight training
- Apprenticeship/on-the-job training
- Correspondence courses

The College Fund Program is supported by the individual defense services and can be combined with the MGIB program. The College Fund Program awards are competitive and are based on academic merit. The Air Force does not have a fund program, but it does have CCAF. CCAF is a two-year college open only to Air Force members. It offers seventy different associate degrees in science and technical fields. Also, CCAF accepts credit by examination. (Details about credit by examination are discussed later in the chapter.) Additional information on the military can be found at:

MORE INFORMATION
www.myfuture.com
www.wiredscholar.com
www.finaid.com
www.todaysmilitary.com

DISTANCE LEARNING

The rapidity of technological development in recent years has spurred the growth of distance education (DE). DE, or distance learning (DL), is a form of education in which traditional face-to-face teaching is replaced with interactive multimedia. DE participants are physically separated from the classroom, the instructor, and the institution. As a result, three out of the five cost components are eliminated—you pay only for tuition, fees, books, and supplies—and overall COA is reduced.

Currently 1,500 public (62 percent), four-year institutions offer DL. There are more than 700 programs for undergraduate and graduate degrees, and within the next two years, 85 percent of two-year and four-year colleges will offer DE. DL is taught over the Internet using a variety of multimedia methods including email, video-conferencing, chat rooms, discussion boards, online bulletin boards, video and audio tape, computer based training (CBT), and print. DE is optimal for students with:

• Full-time jobs, families, and little spare time

• Disabilities

• Inappropriate access to schools (living in remote areas)

• A need to broaden job skills

DL can help students fit education into their busy schedules by allowing them to set their own hours. It offers flexibility, shortens time to degree completion, and, with smaller class sizes, makes learning effective. If used efficiently, it can minimize the time necessary to complete a degree. Classes are generally six to eight weeks long and run over a two-year period. Consequently, you need money for only two years of college, thus cutting your COA by half.

TIP: Even with the rapid growth of DL enrollment, financial aid does not regard DL students the same as regular students. Nonetheless, students should still investigate the possibility of obtaining aid with each school. Note that financial aid does not include scholarships, grants, or other aid.

DE is not easy, however, and requires unrelenting commitment—usually four to fifteen hours per week per course. DE students must be self-disciplined, self-motivated, proactive, and able to communicate well in writing. They must recognize their own learning strengths and weaknesses. Participants must also have the correct equipment such as a personal computer with high-speed Internet access and a printer. In order to succeed, you must contact each college individually and conduct thorough research. You should ask questions about:

? Where textbooks should be purchased

? What additional equipment is necessary

? Where the course information will be kept

? How late the help desk is open

? Who you should contact if technical problems arise

? Where and how you complete exams

? Will distance learning be effective for you

The last of these questions is the most important. Because DE uses nontraditional teaching methods, you may find that DE is not right for you. If you are not good at written communication, a web-based discussion course might prove disastrous.

Prior to taking any DE courses or pursing DE degrees, contact the school counselor and discuss options that match your learning style. You should also confirm that the college is an accredited institution with the authority to grant a degree online. For additional information about DE and related accredited institutions, refer to the following websites:

Regional Accreditation Institution	Contact Information
Middle States Association of Colleges and Schools	*www.msache.org* 215-662-5606
New England Association of Schools and Colleges	*www.neasc.org* 781-271-0022
North Central Association of Colleges and Schools	*www.nca.asu.edu* 312-263-0456 or 1-800-621-7440
Northwest Association of Schools and Colleges	*www.cocnasc.org* 425-827-2005

Regional Accreditation Institution	Contact Information
Southern Association of Colleges and Schools	*www.sacs.org* 404-679-4501, ext. 512, or 1-800-248-7701
Western Association of Schools and Colleges	*www.wascweb.org* 707-569-9177

College Selection

While selecting your ideal college, financial aspects must be balanced against nonfinancial aspects. Although characteristics like location, academia, faculty, resources, diversity, and prestige are valuable, it is important to note that some of these characteristics can dramatically increase cost.

TYPE OF INSTITUTION

The type of institution you choose directly impacts your COA.

SECRET #52

Choose an institution that meets your personality, your needs, and your wallet.

Below is a brief discussion of the types of schools in the United States.

- *Universities:* A university is the biggest type of institution. They have 40,000 to 60,000 students and offer many areas of study and extensive facilities. But they are also more expensive. Class sizes are usually larger, and graduate students teach some courses.

- *Colleges:* A college is smaller and less expensive than a university with minor modifications in the facilities and the resources offered.

- *Private/public institutions:* Public institutions are funded by the state and federal government and are less expensive than private schools. Private colleges are smaller and funded by private endowments. They follow strict guidelines and are more expensive than public institutions.

- *Community/junior colleges:* These schools offer associate degrees, technical degrees, and two-year transfer programs. The cost of attending a community college is about one half the cost of a four-year public institution.

- *Special interest institutions:* Special interest institutions serve a select group of students. They include single-sex colleges, religiously affiliated colleges, historically black colleges, and Hispanic colleges.

- *Upper division schools:* These schools offer the last two years of undergraduate study, provided that you have completed an associate degree or two years at a four-year college. They specialize only in certain programs.

TIP: One way to choose an affordable college is to talk to each college's financial aid office to find out the average student debt level. This may help you decide if the COA is worth its return.

LIFESTYLE

By now, you are familiar with the Expense PIE. Part of the EP includes a personal expense category. This category is an estimated cost for entertainment, personal toiletries, and outside activities. As your goal is to have below-average expenses, you must seek balance between your social life and debt-free college.

SECRET #53

Adopt a lifestyle that meets both your social needs and your goal of debt-free college.

As tempting as it may be, don't try to outdo your pals by throwing extravagant parties and spending gobs of money. Likewise, don't be a hermit, unless you prefer such a lifestyle. Find a median between the two. The college student activity center is a good place for weekend entertainment. After all, you paid for it. Almost every college has a student activity center that is funded by student fees. Student fees are also used to pay for intramurals, gaming centers, student theater, and community parties. The student activity center is not the only option, though. When going out, use your student status to your advantage for discounts at movie theaters, campus stores, and even grocery stores.

Remember, try to live within your means. If you don't, it leads to a destructive spending pattern and away from debt-free college.

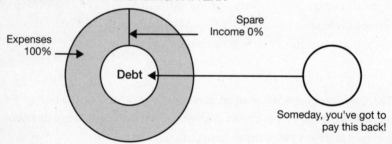

DESTRUCTIVE SPENDING PATTERN

Spare Income 0%

Expenses 100%

Debt

Someday, you've got to pay this back!

RANK AND VALUE

Rank is a measure of position, dignity, and excellence. Value is a relative measure of monetary worth. When selecting schools, both rank and value should be evaluated. A high-ranking institution might not necessarily be the best value for your money.

SECRET #54

While selecting colleges, keep value in the foreground and rank in the background.

Avoid paying an arm and a leg for a ranked college when you can get a comparable education for a lower cost. The following example shows why a "best-ranked" university is not necessarily the best value for your money.

RANK vs. VALUE

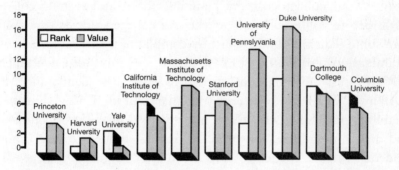

This graph is an example of rank versus value; the rankings are not based upon the actual rankings of these schools. The lower the rank and value numbers the better the school. You want to be number one!

In this example, ten schools have been arbitrarily ranked and valued for their cost of attendance. For instance, Harvard has a better rank than value, meaning you pay for more than you get. Columbia University has a better value than rank, meaning you get a good deal for your money. By comparing your selected college against their rank and their value, you will get a better understanding of your choices. When you make your decision, don't just settle for the best-ranked school. Instead, use this and the point system developed in part one to meet both financial and educational needs. For more information about annual ranks, values, and other statistics, visit *www.usnews.com* or *www.review.com*.

College Enrollment

The strategies listed in this category are most valuable when applied during the first two years. By adopting these ahead of time, you minimize future roadblocks. If you use them effectively, you may even increase your student level—freshman, sophomore, junior, or senior.

A-B-C-D-E YOUR START

Reduce your college costs by planning ahead and earning college credit before you even begin college. All college students can eliminate some required course work by completing either College Level Examination Program (CLEP*) exams or Advanced Placement (AP*) exams. CLEP* exams, geared toward all students, and AP* (*AP and *CLEP are registered trademarks of the College Entrance Examination Board, which was not involved in the production of, and does not endorse, this product.) exams, limited to high school students, offer a chance to skip a semester or more of expensive college tuition. Taking these exams can increase your class standing and shorten your time to graduation—you may only have to pay for three or four years instead of four or five. Ultimately, you save both time and money.

College Level Examination Program Exam
CLEP exams can be taken by students of all ages. Upon successful completion of a CLEP exam, you can earn between three to twelve hours of credit toward your degree. There is no limit on the number of CLEP exams you can take. However, CLEP policies vary between schools. Some schools may not accept CLEP credits, and others may require two CLEP exams for the same subject before awarding any credit. CLEP exams bring you closer to debt-free college by advancing you to core courses more quickly.

Advanced Placement Exam
AP exams are directed toward high school students. High school students can take AP courses as part of the curriculum. At the end of the school year, they can take an AP exam and receive credit. Students who do exceptionally well on AP exams are recognized for their efforts and are eligible for scholarships. Some schools limit the number of AP exam credits a student can receive. Other colleges

recognize the completion and let you advance early, but require you to take additional courses to replace the credits. By passing AP exams, you increase your student level, save time and money, and are automatically eligible for special awards—those given only to AP scholars.

International Exams

The Test of English as a Foreign Language (TOEFL) and the Advanced Placement International English Language (APIEL*) (*APIEL is a registered trademark of the College Entrance Examination Board which was not involved in the production of, and does not endorse, this product.) are two exams that international students should take. The TOEFL allows foreign students to pursue an undergraduate degree. However, depending on the test score, colleges may require additional English as a Second Language (ESL) courses.

This does increase your COA since ESL courses are not part of the basic college curriculum, but it is required for international students who want to study in American universities. On the other hand, successful completion of the APIEL allows you to advance and skip ESL courses.

With careful planning, all or one of the above exams can increase your student standing. Additional details on the exams, fees, and testing centers can be found at the following locations:

MORE INFORMATION
www.collegeboard.com
www.ets.org
www.ap.edu

SHORTEN YOUR STAY

An average college semester is twelve hours. Depending on the field of study you plan to pursue, this could take four to five years. Each extra year adds to your COA and forces you into debt. As a solution, consider making your average semester fifteen to seventeen hours during the first two years and bringing it back to twelve hours during the last two years, when you focus on core classes. If you do increase your hours early on, balance your strengths with your weaknesses.

If English and history are your strengths and math is your difficult subject, strategize so that you take these courses in the same semester. By balancing your curriculum, you can successfully complete math, English, and the other subjects while maintaining higher grades. This also cuts your length of stay at college, and thus the overall cost.

GRADUATE WITH A MASTER'S

Colleges and universities offer academic programs that combine undergraduate and graduate programs into a five-year, joint bachelor's and master's degree. If you are considering a master's degree in the future, a college that offers a joint program will reduce your COA. Joint programs reduce the cost of tuition, room and board, and other college expenses to five years instead of six.

The Professional Program in Accounting (PPA) is an example of a joint degree program. With the PPA, students receive a Bachelor's of Business Administration (BBA) in Accounting and a Master's in Professional Accounting (MPA), as well as a Certified Public Accountant (CPA) license, provided you pass the CPA exam. If you are interested in teaching, a similar option is available for future teachers.

Degree plans at each institution vary, so the best way to start is to contact your selected colleges and seek opportunities to minimize your stay in order to minimize cost.

College in Action

Once you enter college, branch out and broaden your horizons. In addition to studying and getting high grades, challenge yourself.

COOPERATIVE EDUCATION

According to Rothstein and Associates (a corporation of CPAs and financial consultants), approximately 900 colleges and universities nationwide offer **cooperative education programs (co-ops)**. Co-op programs allow students to work and study full-time. They offer students the opportunity to gain experience in their chosen field of study. With co-ops, you can earn money to pay for tuition and fees while attending college. Moreover, participation in a co-op does not make you ineligible for financial aid. However, completing a co-op takes additional time, thus you may take five years to graduate instead of four. Some major advocates of co-ops include:

- American University, Washington, D.C.

- Drexel University, Philadelphia, PA

- Georgia Institute of Technology, Atlanta, GA

- Purdue University, Lafayette, IN

- University of Cincinnati, Cincinnati, OH

INTERNSHIPS

Unlike co-ops, where students continue their development with one company that generally hires them after graduation, an internship is a temporary professional job in your career path. Companies usually hire interns to make their presence known, to stay in contact with potential employees, and to measure the quality of the students from a university. Internships may or may not count as course credit. Nonetheless, (paid) internships move you ahead financially and increase your chances of being hired following graduation.

A good starting point is Kaplan's *Yale Daily News Guide to Internships, 2000 Edition*. This book organizes internships by field of study and geographic location. Additionally, it includes tips for internship résumés. The best places to look for an internship, however, are college career centers and individual academic departments.

STUDY ABROAD

Studying abroad may be a viable option for you. In fact, studying abroad can help reduce your COA, especially if you plan to complete two or more years abroad. When you apply to study abroad, there are certain associated costs that automatically increase your COA. Consequently, your demonstrated need for financial aid increases, but your expected family contribution (EFC) does not. Your EFC does not increase because the formula—federal methodology—used to determine your EFC does not change. This means that you may receive more aid to help you pay for the COA. (The financial aid process will be discussed in more detail in part three.)

Also, you are automatically eligible for special study abroad scholarships that are off-limits to other students. This reduces your competition and increases your odds for more aid. To make it sweeter, the college you plan to attend might choose to offer additional assistance if you qualify. Moreover, with a favorable exchange rate, you may not need as much money to study abroad as you would to study in the United States. Furthermore, you get the benefits of learning about a different culture, making new friends, and having fun.

When I spent six months in Bangkok, Thailand, I received three scholarships totaling $3,325 as well as financial aid. With those sources of income, I was able to fly around the world, spend six months in a low-cost college, learn a different language, travel around the country, receive college course credit (twelve hours), make new friends, and buy souvenirs—all for "free."

For more information, take a look at Arco's *The Unofficial Guide to Study Abroad* and *www.allabroad.com*.

CHAPTER SEVEN

Reaching Success in Two Years

Roots are the perfect symbol of what is required to stand the test of time and conquer goals. Financial roots are what you will need to grow in order to graduate debt-free.

Obstacles

Obstacles to debt-free college are practically everywhere in our society. Most people are brought up to encourage them. Debt is treated lightly, and credit cards are promoted.

It is common for freshmen to fall prey to obstacles. Many freshmen charge into college like samurai warriors but within months are whimpering with debt. There is a big difference between independence and *financial* independence. Most students are independent, or on their own. However, most students are wobbly when it comes to financial independence. They rely on parents, credit cards, loans, or low-paying jobs to support their lifestyle. The problem is that their lifestyle often does not match their income statement (cash inflow and outflow), which means they are eventually choked by debt.

Most people carry around obstacles to debt-free college in their wallets or purses. They are small, thin, and made of plastic. They are otherwise known as credit cards, and they are frequently abused.

They make it very easy to swipe your way into a comfortable life-style—a lifestyle that you are not ready to support as a student. Credit cards give you *temporary* happiness, asking only a minimum payment while your debt turns into Mount Everest.

SECRET #55

Avoid financial obstacles through self-control.

As an underclassman, if you let a few obstacles choke you at the beginning, then your financial roots will start to die. It is easy to overlook while it is happening. To prevent this, focus on playing good financial defense.

AS A FRESHMAN

It is critical to have debt-free college in mind while you are starting out, for this is when you are planting roots. You have to be mentally strong to avoid the temptations of overspending. You must protect your asset base so you will have the money for future tuition. Self-discipline, a financial plan, and motivation will lead you to success.

SECRET #56

For a good start, find balance early on.

Finding balance is difficult because of the initial preparation. It takes strength, intelligence, foresight, and endurance to stay on track. Such qualities are in stark opposition to our instant-gratification, high-consumption society. In fact, such qualities can even seem unpatriotic and strange. Don't worry, they are not. All the founding fathers of this country had such qualities.

OPEN AND HUMBLE MIND

You may have the financial know-how to get through the first few months of college debt-free, but you may not have enough knowledge to get you through all four years. By not being proactive and seeking education, you become complacent and stop expanding your roots. It is essential to continue progress by examining new options and viewpoints. This will allow you to eventually control your financial situation.

Remember to stay humble during your financial learning. Don't get yourself into expensive catfights because of pride. If you keep the humility to continue playing good defense, then you will eventually succeed. You will have control of your financial situation, and you will be able to focus on grades instead of dollars.

Recognizing and Overcoming Obstacles

There are many obstacles to debt-free college. They often take the shape of things we are familiar and comfortable with, which is why they are so difficult to avoid.

PEER PRESSURE

During college, there is pressure to use drugs, to have sex, to drink, and to let your grades slip. One pressure, however, that people seldom think about is the pressure to spend. Spending money can make you popular—a nice car, stylish clothes, and throwing parties are attractive. There is a big price to pay for this "popularity," though. That price is debt-free college. You will be like a shooting star—catching everyone's attention, but burning yourself out along the way. Separating *your* financial situation from your peers' situations is essential.

SECRET #57

Develop your own opinions about money management—and stick by them.

Once you have your own rules to the game, you will be able to avoid the pressure other people exert on you. More important, you will be able to chart your progress toward debt-free college.

Naysayers

Naysayers abound everywhere. They encourage you to outspend yourself. And they have an arsenal of persuasion:

"You only go around once."
"We're young."
"Just put in more hours at work next week."
"It's not going to matter."
"Who cares?"
"Just this once."
"You know your parents will cover it."
"Screw it."

The common thought in these statements is the idea of sacrificing tomorrow for the sake of today. You might be able to make a "philosophical" argument for doing so, but the truth is that many great philosophers have died deeply in debt.

SECRET #58

What you do today will either benefit or harm you tomorrow.

Spending money is a lot like using drugs—the immediate high from the drug thrills people, but several years later, when users are broke, addicted, and have permanent organ damage, they are not so quick to defend the value of the drugs.

Naysayers usually end up with massive credit card debt. They do not know how to plan for their future or make the choices that would benefit themselves. They are impulsive, and they choose to take everything they can get today for the sake of tomorrow. If they had to cross a hot desert and had only a few gallons of water, they would be the ones who drank all their water in the first few hours.

You must learn to *separate* your thoughts from the mainstream and make choices that will be good for you in the long term. You want to make it through the big, dry desert; you want to graduate debt-free.

HOBBIES

Few people think of it, but those little extras that you accumulate can be a destructive financial habit. As a kid, I probably spent $1,500 on baseball cards with money I earned by mowing lawns and washing dishes in a laboratory. Those cards could probably only be sold today for about $500. Most baseball cards have been over-priced, overproduced, and overmarketed, and thus have little poten-tial of ever becoming really valuable. It was a fun hobby but lousy as far as money goes.

There is a wide range of what hobbies can cost. Model plane building and flying is surely expensive, as are hot air ballooning and traveling. Swimming is often free, rock collecting is free, and reading is practically free. There is no need to give up a hobby because it costs money, but there is surely a need to slow down if it is costing you an arm and a leg.

SECRET #59

Budget forecast for hobbies.

Hobbies should be written into your budget. If you know you will want to spend $700 on renovating a car over the course of a year, mark that down as a forecasted expense. Maybe you could still pursue the hobby and make it profitable—renovate the car for $700 and sell it for $3,000. Most people who are successful claim that they reached their success because they enjoy their jobs. In that sense, their jobs are nothing more than intensive hobbies.

DATING

In college, one hobby that many people have is dating. Dating can be a very expensive hobby! Flowers, expensive meals, anniversary gifts—all these small items of affection add up quickly. Dating doesn't have to overtake your goal of debt-free college, though. For instance, if you feel the need to give flowers, consider one rose ($3), instead of a bouquet ($50).

Another way to save is to consider lunch dates. Lunch is usually less expensive than dinner, and you can top it off with a matinee instead of a full-price movie. There are many other ways to organize an inexpensive date:

- Visit a museum or an aquarium

- Talk at a coffeehouse or bookstore

- Attend a high school or college play

- Cook dinner together

- Rent a video and pop your own popcorn

- Play a board game

- Study together

- Take a walk in a scenic area

- Party at a local festival

- Volunteer for community service projects

CREDIT CARDS

This is not the first time credit cards are being mentioned. Those small rectangles of plastic are pretty to look at—holograms, colors, and silver numbers. Credit cards themselves are not bad. They are safer and more convenient than carrying wads of cash around. The problem is that they allow you to spend more money than you actually have. If you had $6.50 in your pocket and asked a jeweler to let you buy a diamond because you'll have $150 cash in your pocket next week, what do you think she would say?

SECRET #60

Managing credit cards is managing debt.

In addition to the hundreds of lessons you will learn during college, you should also learn to manage your credit cards and balance ~~book. College is one of the most difficult times to avoid~~ ~~can learn to avoid debt while you are in college, finding~~ ~~void debt will be easier for the rest of your life. Even~~ ~~t work from a budget, albeit a large one.~~

non

~~fore~~ applying for a credit card, there are a few basic questions you should ask that will help you avoid debt:

1. What is the introductory rate, how long does it last, and after that period, what is the new rate?
2. Are there any application fees? Processing fees? Annual fees? Late fees? Over-the-limit fees? Account termination fees? Balance transfer fees?
3. What is the grace period before interest begins accumulating?
4. Will you get notification if you near your limit? If you go over, what happens?
5. What options do you have in paying off your balance?

By having these questions answered, you will have a better idea of what owning a credit card can mean to debt-free college.

TAXES

At the income level that most students have, they usually do not worry about taxes because they earn so little. But taxes impact paychecks, and thus they impact debt-free college.

Instead of thinking "I make $8 an hour," you should be thinking, "I make about $6.80 an hour." Even in the lowest tax bracket, you still pay about 15 percent tax. When you realize that you are not making even close to your "stated" salary, you will begin to change the way you think about money.

An $8 pizza suddenly takes more than an hour of your time to pay off. Add sales tax and a tip for the deliveryman and it probably takes close to two hours of your time to buy that "$8 pizza."

No one can avoid taxes—not federal or state or property or municipal. You may be able to avoid one or two, or pay less because of where you live, how you invest, or how much you earn, but you cannot avoid taxes. What you can control, however, is how you think about your income and expenses.

SECRET #61

Think about your finances after taxes.

In other words, think "Pizza costs $11 after tax and tip, and I make $6.80 an hour after taxes." You don't have to give up pizza! But you should get in the habit of thinking about your finances at an after-tax level. Once you are able to do this, you will have a more accurate idea of your true income statement, and you will not be fooled by the taxman into spending more money than you actually have.

SOCIETY

All the obstacles that were just listed are the cause of many students' downfalls. Financial obstacles assert their influence every day. It is like one lump attack, encouraging you to forget about debt-free college. The easy thing is to give in. Once you give in on one point, it becomes easy to give in on other points. You quickly become numb and don't even notice your goal slipping away.

Two-thirds of the American economy comes from consumer spending. If you have ever walked down Broadway in Manhattan, you know it is a great symbol of materialism. There is glamour, jewelry and perfumes, fine food, and fancy shows. There is nothing like it! It is fun, but it desensitizes you to spending. There is a price to pay for the kind of fun that costs a lot of money—what you spend now diminishes what you have later.

SECRET **#62**

Society will tempt you to overspend; you must overcome the "lump attack."

A wise thing to do is to not let the lump attack overtake you all at once; sort through the different influences that encourage you to be extravagant. Figure out if your peers are encouraging poor financial habits. Understand how much of your buying is related to advertising and branding. For instance, magazines are consumerism adrenaline. Magazines make money by trying to convince readers to continually spend more money to "improve" themselves. Magazines try to dictate how you should look and feel and act. If you try to keep up with the models in magazines, you will only drive yourself into debt imitating Cindy Crawford or Brad Pitt.

If you break things down, there will not be a confusing lump attack and you will have an easier time defending your financial goal.

 TRIVIA: A poll of U.S. college students revealed that 48 percent have bounced a check, 71 percent have a negative credit card balance, and 72 percent have called home for cash—*www.uselessknowledge.com*

STATUS SYMBOLS

Luxury is a costly symbol of status. A friend who recently graduated from college now works for a law firm. She works with other recent graduates with high salaries. You would think that they would have enough to pay off their debt right away, wouldn't you? Wrong. They are going into even deeper debt!

With the high salaries, they buy $80 towels and $600 suits and pay $150 to get their hair done in salons every other weekend. They are the culmination of the cycle of debt—people with educations and high salaries who still have increasing debt. They may have great jobs, but because of poor financial habits, they may have to work until they are eighty.

SECRET #63

Education and a high salary have nothing to do with avoiding debt. Avoid debt by making good decisions.

Most lawyers are intelligent and interesting people. Most have higher salaries than the typical American worker. But there is something else that many lawyers also have more of—debt. With people who lack financial discipline, high salaries only lead to higher spending, which leads to higher debt.

There are two key facts to help you avoid status symbols and the debt that comes with acquiring them:

- It is not income that controls debt.

- Ability to make good financial decisions controls debt.

It is not your income that controls whether or not you go into debt; it is your ability to make good financial decisions. Maybe your bath towels cost less than $5 each. You can bet the farm they dry just as well as the $80 towels.

Living costs money. No one can argue with that. Yet people are still able to finish college without debt and without regret. This is because the things that are truly valuable in life are seldom expensive. Materialism can be fulfilling for a while, but accomplishing debt-free college is fulfilling for the rest of your life.

STEADY GUARD

One way to stay on track for debt-free college is to avoid consumer debt. If you remember the debt-free equation, you already know the four primary tactics for avoiding debt—choosing a school and housing you can afford, working, saving money before college, and keeping what you have.

The point is to get yourself a budget and start focusing on the major obstacles you know are hitting you in the face every month. If you have no financial control, you will get hit quite a bit. With self-control, you will have a steady guard against those hits. As long as you continue borrowing money or using your credit card, you have no steady guard—you are a debtor.

As a student, you have more than enough opportunities to become a debtor but few opportunities to be a creditor. One way to get used to the idea of being a creditor is to establish the philosophy on a simple level. If you are going around borrowing two bucks from one friend, three bucks from another and a dollar from someone down the hall, you are a debtor. Granted, you are not taking on serious debt by borrowing a few dollars, but the fact that you are comfortable with accumulating small debts is a bad thing.

SECRET #64

Be a creditor, not a debtor.

You can quit being a debtor by paying off small debts and revising your budget until you are living within your means. Doing this will prevent your creditor friends from cringing when you enter the room. Besides, it is good training for dealing with debt in the big picture. Statistics show that if you let yourself become a debtor— even if it is to your parents—then you are likely to stay in that negative cycle for the rest of your life.

Success in Two Years

Many things in life work in two-year chunks of time. In high school, for the first two years you are classified as an underclassman, then for the next two years you are an upperclassman. The same classification applies in college. Then, in the working world, many people work for two years before they get a promotion or find a better job.

Two years is the *approximate* amount of time that most people take to reach a significant accomplishment. More important, two years is also the approximate amount of time that *society* tells us it takes to achieve something significant.

You can apply the two-year philosophy to any pursuit in life, and though some pursuits take longer than two years, it will still be true. Accomplishing a goal can take longer than two years, but you should still be able to make significant, measurable progress in two years. You should be able to see results after two years in college. Unless you wish to build an asset base to cover all four years of college (i.e., lots and lots of work for low pay), then this realization should make you happy.

IMPACT OF THE TWO-YEAR RULE

Before you begin college, you do not know what college is going to be like. You have only ideas about what is going to happen in your life. If you are anything like most people, there is excitement, anticipation, and some fear. You do not know what you will be doing or who your friends will be.

What most people do not realize is that they actually have more data about how things will be than they realize—especially about money. For instance, you should be able to get a reasonable estimate of your tuition, housing, and food costs. Using the estimates, you should be able to build a reasonable asset base. At that point, it is simply a matter of following through. Take a look at what two years can do.

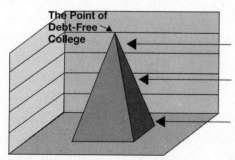

The Point of Debt-Free College

Senior Year: By your final year, you are playing good defense and hardly cutting into your savings at all.

Two-Year Point: This is where the pyramid goes from big to small.

First Year in College: During your financial learning process, you waste the biggest part of your asset base (savings).

The pyramid represents your spending pattern in college. At first, when you are learning to play offense and defense, you use a big chunk of your savings, the bottom of the pyramid. Then, when your financial defense is honed, you pursue your goal without cutting into your resources (asset base)—this is the point of the pyramid. The pyramid shows that during the first two years, your spending pattern gets adjusted to meet the needs of debt-free college.

The balance sheet is an ideal tool to help you predict your financial future. If you have learned the basics of your balance sheet, if you have developed some roots, and if you have tried consistently, you will have something going for you in two years. That is the way of life. Other people move on and you inherit their positions and their treasures. As long as you have faith in yourself and a good work ethic, you do not have to worry about finding opportunity within two years. You will learn to look for openings, and you will discover that opportunity was surrounding you the entire time.

STAY CONSISTENT

To reach the point of debt-free college, you have to be consistent. If you learn to think financially and work consistently, you will have something going for you after the first two years of college. If you keep your possibilities open and stick with two or three goals, those goals will start to materialize after a few years.

It is easy to be negative and think that good things won't happen while you struggle from day-to-day. For instance, many students are so reactive that they will not work on anything unless it is due the following day. That philosophy will lower your grades substantially over time; that same philosophy when dealing with finance will leave you with a lot of debt. It is easy to write things off after the first signs of resistance or the first hints of failure. Two years can seem like a long time. But if you think about where you were two years ago, two years will probably start to seem like quite a *short* amount of time.

Good things happen after two years of consistent work. Society *wants* to help you after two years. All the people with good things right now must eventually move on and leave their treasures behind.

Those treasures will be yours if you will simply stand in line. It is not difficult, but you have to stick with your plan.

SECRET **#65**

Consistency is crucial; it leads to treasure.

If you are following your budget and consistently seeking opportunity, you will get some breaks after your first two years in college. In two years time, you will simply outlast much of your competition—all the people who give up when resistance begins. In fact, for many people, good things happen before the first two years. But on the average, it takes two years of consistent effort for the big goals to start materializing.

CONTROL SPIRALS

Along with consistency, if you set your habits early, you will gain both a positive spiral when it comes to cutting costs (defense), as well as increasing income (offense). You should have continuous improvement over all four years, but because of the two-year rule, there should be a big jump between your second and third year.

DECREASING COSTS: FOUR YEARS OF FINANCIAL DEFENSE

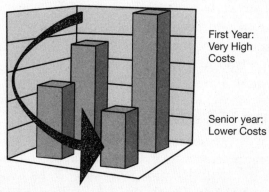

First Year:
Very High
Costs

Senior year:
Lower Costs

Because of the two-year rule, expect a good-size **decrease in your costs** *between year two and year three.*

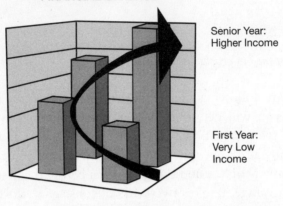

INCREASING INCOME: FOUR YEARS OF
FINANCIAL OFFENSE

Senior Year:
Higher Income

First Year:
Very Low
Income

Because of the two-year rule, expect a good-size **increase in your income** *between year two and year three.*

Align Actions to Goals

If you wish to beat debt, it is highly important that you are pursuing something that you know has the potential to help you financially—not socially, not mentally, not physically, but financially. To get bigger muscles, you work out. To get smarter, you focus and study. To make more friends, you go out and meet people. To achieve debt-free college, you form a plan and learn money management.

If you struggle for two years at community service and expect you will run into some miraculous financial windfall, you are making a mistake. Hopefully, you will work at community service and, hopefully, you will make lots of friends, but don't expect such pursuits to make you money! If you expect community service to help you avoid debt, you are crazy.

Being a nice person and getting an education while staying financially independent are two different things. You should not confuse one pursuit with the other. You need to be working on both pursuits. The financial side begins with setting your goal early, developing the know-how, and growing roots like crazy.

THE HARD PART

The two-year rule can be applied to other types of progress—winning an office in a campus organization, leading service projects, or making it halfway through college. Unfortunately, it is impossible to say *what* you will have in two years. You can only assume that if you work consistently for your stated goal, something powerful will happen for you.

If you have a hard time believing this, you will have a hard time making it happen. Don't waste time wondering if your goal will come; it will. Applying the rule to other parts of life is a good idea, but make sure you apply it financially, too. Good financial habits and beating debt will not jump into your lap on their own; you've got to do some planning and coaxing.

MARY

For example, Mary's parents were able to contribute portions of her state college tuition—about 40 percent of the entire cost. For the first two years, Mary lived in a dormitory. Living in a dormitory allowed her to reduce her costs as much as she possibly could. Mary was an avid saver and a shrewd spender.

Mary's family was middle class, and they immigrated to America when she was eleven.Throughout her early life, her hard-working and hard-saving parents taught Mary how to make a lot from just a little. While her friends were wearing Doc Martens or carrying Gucci purses, Mary learned to buy imitation styles at about 10 percent the cost. This is not to say that Mary looked bad. On the contrary, she successfully fooled most of the people around her into believing she spent a lot on her personal effects.

Throughout her first two years in college, Mary chose not to work. She wanted time for other things. Unfortunately, when it came to time management, Mary did not have the same keen sense as she did with saving money. At the end of two years, she ended up switching majors because her grades had sunk into an abyss.

In her junior year, Mary realized that her saving habits were not cutting it. She was gaining debt faster than she had anticipated. Unhappy with her poor grades and ballooning debt, Mary made a few sweeping changes in her lifestyle. She began working part-time in a campus store and also began studying more. Within a single semester, she managed to both slow down her debt and increase her grades. Happy with her performance, she quit her job. Though Mary retained her improved grades, her time management skills slipped. She tried hard to fight back, but her saving habits could make little difference. Without any income, it did not matter how well she saved—debt was unavoidable.

Confused and frustrated, Mary found another job. This time she worked part-time as a secretary at a downtown company and spent a lot of time commuting. Eventually, she quit the job. Mary graduated with $20,000 of debt.

Mary's Lesson

It was not Mary's spending habits that got her into trouble. Her defensive philosophy worked great. Had Mary not been frugal, she probably would have finished college with $40,000 of debt. Mary's problem was twofold: inadequate working habits and poor self-marketing.

SECRET #66

Manage resources with good work habits.
Think offensively—self-market.

Mary made a number of critical errors in the way she went about finding work. Her first error was not finding a job sooner. She should have been working part-time the entire way through her college career. Also, she should have sought work that would help accomplish her goal of maximizing social time and study time. By working in the campus store, she tied herself to a cash register that was often busy. This left her neither time to study nor time to socialize. As a secretary, she fared no better, plus she had to spend time commuting.

Mary indulged herself between jobs. Additionally, she quit a job without having another job already lined up. Had she not allowed herself such generous grace periods, she would have earned quite a bit more cash over time. Mary failed to work consistently during college. *She did not follow the two-year rule and work steadfastly toward a financial goal.*

SECRET #67

Slow and steady wins the race.

Finally, Mary failed to successfully market herself. She did not apply for scholarships, and she did not apply for internships. She was in an ethnic group and socioeconomic class that increased her chances for receiving scholarships, but she never bothered to apply. Likewise, by not seeking internships, she gave up an opportunity for increased experience and income.

It does not really matter that Mary plays above-average defense . . .

EXPENSE LEVELS

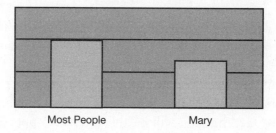

Most People   Mary

if she does a poor job of playing any offense . . .

INCOME LEVELS

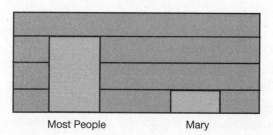

Most People   Mary

Mary's end result is an ugly cycle of debt. In Mary's case, it is caused by a destructive "earning" pattern.

PLANT MANY SEEDS

If you are not really trying to accomplish your goals, you cannot expect good things to happen after two years. You must *make* them happen. They will not happen unless you plant seeds. Planting seeds means going out and taking consistent chances at something better than you currently have—something that will further your goal of making it through college and being financially independent. You need to plant a lot of seeds. What if you plant only one seed, and that seed is a dud? You would not be in an enviable position then.

If you only try for one year, you cannot count on anything. If you only apply for scholarships for the first year then get lazy and give up, you are not trying. You are not planting a seed, and you are not guarding your place in line for debt-free college.

EXPECT NOTHING, BUT PREDICT SUCCESS

If you are a dedicated person, you should plan for the fact that you will get a few opportunities by your junior year that you did not have when you first started. At the increased cost of your energy, you can capitalize on those opportunities. If you are risking going into some small debt because your asset base is not big and powerful, then the fact that you will be able to create opportunity within a period of approximately two years should be a consideration for you.

PLOW THROUGH PROBLEMS

In the movie *The Shawshank Redemption,* Andy Dufresne is wrongfully imprisoned for life and wrongfully retained by a warden who knows he is innocent. But Andy never gives up hope. He discovers that he can chip away at the prison walls, piece by piece, tunneling his way to freedom. More than a decade later, he makes his great escape.

Andy is a fantastic example of someone who keeps his options open. His one option was to keep chipping away at the wall of his cell, piece by agonizing piece. Many years later, Andy had what he wanted—freedom. Andy's perseverance shows that you can move mountains by sticking with a small plan over a long period of time.

To keep digging your hole can be the most difficult thing in the world. It is the reason that people give up their diets after a few weeks, quit reading books as soon as they are out of school, or find it so difficult to exercise more or eat less. Most people really do have good intentions, and possibly even a plan, but they cannot, however, make themselves follow it. These people are just like the naysayers—they act for today at the expense of tomorrow.

TRIVIA: At an annual 6 percent college cost increase, a freshman in 2012 will need $112,250 to $235,000 to cover four years of college—*www.funtrivia.com*

THE LAW OF INERTIA

Initially, sticking with a new pursuit—such as getting your finances in order—takes a huge effort that makes you uncomfortable and tired. But the Law of Inertia says that once the big ball is moving, it stays moving with little energy. If all those people who quit their diet after only two weeks could have just stuck with their diets for two months, they probably would have been able to continue dieting for as long as they needed.

The nice thing about keeping the ball rolling, so to speak, is that you hardly notice your own effort after a while. It becomes a lot easier. If you ask someone who is used to spending $1,500 a month to spend only $900 the next month, they will have an extremely difficult time doing it. To do so would probably be just as difficult as committing a senior citizen to skydiving.

While those first few months of spending only $900 will be very challenging, six months later it will be relatively easy—a year later, it will be completely natural. Even better, after one year of spending

$900 instead of $1,500, that person will be closer to their long-term goal yet feel none of the pain of a financial "diet" that was so overwhelming at first. Suddenly, there is reason to feel great—both long-term and short-term finances are in order, which leads straight to debt-free college.

The Right Mindset

You cannot just think about growing roots if you want success. You must *want* to grow them, then you must *do* it. You must have the mindset that you are not going to quit. If you spend a year on the right track then let one small slip overpower you and sweep you away, it would be a tragic thing. All the world loves a winner and has no time for a loser. You shouldn't have time for losing either, which means you cannot get discouraged and quit because of small things.

If you feel tired and wish to quit your job, it is time to start focusing on your goal. You must keep your goal in mind at all times so you will have the energy to make it happen. This is why growing roots is emotional. It is not something that can be done overnight, but something that must be planned for and carried out every day. To plan and execute, you need more than just the know-how. You need desire. Desire for debt-free college will help you make it a reality.

ANOTHER LEVEL DEEPER

Once you have grown financial roots, you will be ready to stick with the work of getting your degree and remaining financially independent. But do not think that you have reached the limit of growth. That is impossible. There is always room to grow.

If you are on track to graduate debt-free, you have a great opportunity to contribute. One way to do this is to become a mentor to someone else. If you find someone who is looking for a mentor, you will have a chance to pass on your knowledge. Not only will this help someone to reach their potential, but it will sharpen your own skill. By guiding someone else, you will develop, too.

Another valuable pursuit once you have established your roots is to think farther ahead. One way to do this is by making contributions to a retirement account such as an individual retirement account (IRA). When you do financially positive things like contribute to an IRA, you are fertilizing the ground for your financial freedom. The more ways you can find to keep your roots strong and growing, the more success you will eventually have.

A POWERFUL LIFE

Throughout Abraham Lincoln's life, he suffered enough defeats to discourage ten men, but because he never, ever gave up, he won the highest office of the land.

Age 22	failed in business
Age 23	ran for legislature and was defeated
Age 24	failed again in business
Age 26	sweetheart died
Age 27	had a nervous breakdown
Age 29	defeated for speaker
Age 31	defeated for elector
Age 34	defeated for Congress
Age 37	elected to Congress
Age 39	defeated for Congress
Age 46	defeated for Senate
Age 47	defeated for vice president
Age 49	defeated for Senate
Age 51	elected president of the United States

Abraham Lincoln was a man of powerful roots. He developed a moral consciousness far ahead of his time, but the real reason he changed the course of history is because he stuck to his goal. Relax, your roots don't have to save America—they only need to get you through college, debt-free.

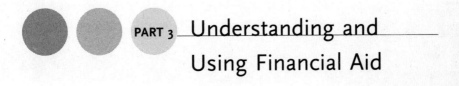

PART 3 Understanding and
Using Financial Aid

CHAPTER EIGHT

The Financial Aid Process

Financial aid is similar to using a coupon in a store—your cost is lowered. Today, approximately 75 percent of full-time students receive some form of financial aid—federal, state, school, or private. As a student, the amount of aid you receive depends on your financial situation, the school you attend, and the policies and regulations your selected college follows. This chapter covers the intricacies of the financial aid process, including:

- The process
- Financial aid requirements
- Aid appropriation
- The forms

A Note About Financial Aid

Financial aid, also referred to as aid or fin aid, is money that colleges distribute to students to help them pay for the cost of education. Students must demonstrate financial need in order to get financial aid. Fin aid is the most direct method of obtaining college money; however, it is a fast-paced, time-consuming process driven by quick deadlines and cryptic forms. The process requires patience and re-search, because each university has its own standard. After analyzing your COA, identifying the major components of your EP, and using some of the quick-hit strategies, financial aid should be your focal point.

Before we move forward, a few financial aid myths must be dispelled. Financial aid:

- **Is *not* all free money**—A financial aid package includes grants, scholarships, federal work-study, and loans. As each college attempts to meet the financial gap, it compiles a package depending on student status, demonstrated need, academic and extracurricular achievements, and current Satisfactory Academic Progress (SAP) standing. As a result, the aid package may consist mostly of loans or mostly of grants and may vary significantly for each student.

- ***Is* used to attract new college students**—Higher education is a business; it needs students to stay alive. Therefore, colleges give fin aid to attract students. This is especially true for public institutions, as they try to keep as many in-state students as possible. This is a significant point to note, as this affects COA and the EP.

- ***Is* process driven**—The fin aid process is cumbersome, and a high degree of self-discipline is essential in dealing with the repetitiveness and frustration inherent in the necessary bureaucracy. In order to receive aid—and receive as much as possible—applications must be submitted on time and without flaws. Inaccurate information could cause processing delays—and when your turn comes, colleges may have no money left to award.

The Process

Financial aid bridges the gap between the retail price (college expenses) and your bank account (what you can afford). It helps you obtain debt-free college. The fin aid process begins when you submit the *Free Application for Federal Student Aid* (*FAFSA*) form. The FAFSA is the primary tool that the federal government uses to ascertain your expected family contribution (EFC), which is the key to awarding aid. The formula, noted below, describes the aid process in a nutshell.

Total cost of attendance (COA)

− Expected family contribution (EFC)

= FINANCIAL AID/DEMONSTRATED NEED

The last line of the formula shows that financial aid and demonstrated need are synonymous. The demonstrated need for money is the financial aid that colleges and the government attempt to meet. This is crucial during the aid appropriation process when the package is consolidated.

When you submit a FAFSA, you report all your personal financial information as well as a list of colleges that you would like to receive your information. The government is mainly interested in your personal finance information because it is used to determine the main component of the aid formula—the EFC.

EFC is what the government ascertains that you and/or your financial supporter should contribute to your education. To do this, the financial data you provide on the FAFSA is entered into a government database, where it is applied to a predefined formula. (The formula and its components will be discussed later in this chapter.) After two weeks of churning, the database spits out a number. This result is your EFC. At this point, the first step of aid appropriation begins.

The federal government has certain standards dictating that if a student's EFC is below the standard mark, then the student automatically receives the Federal Pell Grant. The *Federal Pell Grant* is a need-basis award that is one of the most generous awards a student can receive. In addition, the student becomes eligible for the *Federal Supplemental Educational Opportunity Grant* (*FSEOG*). The EFC is then sent to your selected colleges, which compile the remaining portion of the aid package.

As each college receives your FAFSA, your account is assigned to a financial aid counselor/administrator. This assigned counselor then becomes your financial guardian and handles your requests, whether you choose to attend the college or not. As your financial guardian, the counselor's first task is to calculate your COA for that college. The administrator is bound by that college's rules and regulations and estimates your COA on several factors.

Each college uses different criteria for their estimates and may or may not include all five cost components of the Expense PIE. Some colleges empower administrators to use "professional judgment"— allowing them to adjust the estimated EFC in order to compute your award. The counselors then compile a package to match your need according to their standards.

The package is then forwarded to you, and you are required to either accept or decline. The aid package is comprised of several types of aid, some of which can benefit you and some of which can be harmful to debt-free college. The contents of the aid package will be discussed in the next chapter. In summary, the financial aid process looks like this:

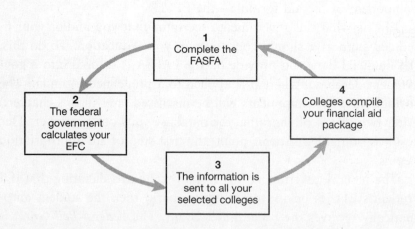

Each year, the process must be repeated so the college and the government are aware of your continued need. Also, the previous year's reported information must be updated. As a reminder, at the beginning of each academic year, a FAFSA renewal form is sent to all *participating* students. (Participating students are students who submitted a FAFSA at the beginning of the college academic year.)

The renewal form is prefilled with the information from the previous year, and you validate it against your current circumstances, then mail it back. You may or may not have changes; regardless, you have to do your part by completing the form every year.

TIP: The biggest source of financial aid is the Department of Education. But student aid is also available from other federal agencies—U.S. Public Health Service, U.S. Department of Veteran Affairs, and state governments. Remember to include these in your search.

Financial Aid Requirements

To receive any federal, state, or private aid as a student, you must meet the eligibility test, qualify for student aid, and demonstrate need.

ELIGIBILITY TEST

Meeting eligibility is the first step in the process. Eligibility gets your foot in the door and allows you to take your place in line. *All students* must meet *one* of the following criteria:

- Be a U.S. citizen

- Be a U.S. national (includes natives of American Samoa or Swain's Island)

- Be a U.S. permanent resident with an Alien Registration Card

If you don't fit in any of these categories, then you must present proper documentation from the U.S. Immigration and Naturalization Services (INS) showing **one** of the following:

- Be a refugee

- Have granted asylum

- Be a Cuban-Haitian entrant, status pending

- Be a conditional entrant (valid only if issued before April 1, 1980)

- Be on indefinite parole and/or humanitarian parole

As of July 1, 2000, the government issued a new law that affects eligibility. The law states that students convicted under federal or state law for sale or possession of drugs are *suspended* for aid eligibility. If you were convicted of *drug possession,* you are deferred from eligibility for one year from the date of your conviction on your first offense, two years on your second offense, and indefinitely after your third offense. If you are convicted for the *sale of drugs,* you are ineligible for aid for two years from the date of your conviction for the first offense, and indefinitely afterward. However, eligibility can be regained earlier by successfully completing a state-approved drug rehabilitation program. Although the law was implemented in July 2000, a conviction prior to July 2000 could affect your eligibility status. It is important to remember that a conviction may suspend you from federal aid, but you may still be eligible for state or private aid.

Students who are *not eligible* for federal student aid include:

- F1 or F2 visa holders

- J1 or J2 exchange visitor visa holders

- G series visa holders

Misunderstanding the eligibility requirements or drawing unwarranted conclusions could make you liable for any federal aid you might receive and/or have received. If you have any questions regarding your eligibility status, visit *www.fafsa.ed.gov,* or contact one of the fin aid service lines listed in the resource guide at the end of the book.

QUALIFICATION TEST

The second step in the requirements process is to qualify for financial aid. To qualify for fin aid, you must:

- Have a valid Social Security number

- Have completed a high school diploma or a General Education Development (GED) certificate or passed a similar test approved by the U.S. Department of Education

- Be enrolled or accepted for enrollment as a regular student in an eligible institution in an eligible program working toward an associate, bachelor's, or graduate degree program (Federal aid is not provided for correspondence or telecommunication courses unless they are directly part of an associate, bachelor's, or graduate degree program.)

- Must show Satisfactory Academic Progress (SAP) toward a degree or a certificate while being enrolled

- Must be enrolled in an institution, at a minimum, half-time (Half-time is defined differently for each university. Generally, a six-hour semester or the equivalent is considered half-time.)

- Register with the Selective Services if you are a male student (If you are an eighteen- to twenty-five-year-old male and have not registered with the Selective Services, you can give the Selective Services program permission to do so by checking a box on the FAFSA form or register directly at *www.sss.gov.*)

- Must not be in default on a federal education loan or owe a refund on a federal grant

The list above is for all students, and in most circumstances, all you will ever need to show if you are a traditional college student (eighteen to twenty-two). However, if you are a nontraditional or an independent student and support yourself financially, you must also meet **one** of the following requirements:

- Be born before January 1, 1977

- Be married

- Have legal dependencies other than a spouse

- Be an orphan or a ward of the court/state, or have been the ward of the court until age eighteen

- Be a veteran of the U.S. armed forces without dishonorable release (includes students who attended a U.S. military academy)

Independent students must submit evidence of their claimed status prior to being considered for student aid. Generally, independent students and those with dependents are given favorable treatment by federal programs; however, as an offset, they are scrutinized heavily by institutional programs. If you have unusual circumstances that would make you independent but you do not meet the above criteria, consult your fin aid counselor. They may be able to adjust your EFC and increase your federal aid at their discretion.

Unfortunately, international students receive little or no help from the federal student aid process because of their ineligibility. However, state or individual colleges may offer aid to foreign students or others who do not qualify for federal aid. Part-time students, although eligible, might receive less aid because of their part-time status.

TIP: Although international students are not eligible for federal aid, they may still be eligible for special grants and discount loans. For more information on foreign student grants and aid, visit *www.iefa.org.*

DEMONSTRATE NEED

The third step in the requirement process is to demonstrate need. The concept of need has a very specific and particular meaning in the realm of college financial aid. Your need to pay off credit cards or buy the latest designer wear is not the same as your need to meet the COA. Need is the difference between COA and EFC and is determined through the financial aid formula. Remember, financial aid and demonstrated need are synonymous.

Total cost of attendance (COA)
− Expected family contribution (EFC)
= FINANCIAL AID/DEMONSTRATED NEED

In essence, fin aid is the amount of your financial need. The more you exhibit a need for money, the more you will receive. Remember, when the aid appropriation process takes place, your demonstrated need is weighted against other students and their demonstrated need. You may need $2,500, but there may be another student who needs $8,000. In this case, you may receive a partial grant and the difference in student loans.

Aid Appropriation

When you apply for aid from any of the student financial aid programs, the U.S. Department of Education validates the information on the FAFSA and other forms with the following agencies:

- **Social Security Administration**—to verify Social Security number and citizenship status (permanent resident, visa)

- **Selective Services System**—to verify registration, if applicable

- **Immigration and Naturalization Service**—to verify noncitizenship status

- **Department of Justice**—to verify court suspensions or criminal record as a result of drug-related offenses

- **Department of Veterans Affairs**—to verify veteran status, if applicable

It is very important that you report all your financial information accurately. If there are any perpetrated discrepancies between your reported status and your actual status, you may face legal implications. Provided that the information on the FAFSA form is accurate, it is used to determine EFC. EFC determines the contents and the size of your aid package.

TRIVIA: Princeton was the first noted college in history to use the word *campus* to refer to its college grounds—*www.uselessknowledge.com*

CALCULATING EFC

One of two methods is used to determine EFC—Federal Methodology (FM), or Institutional Methodology (IM). The FM is a set of formulas created by Congress to "equally" allocate government funds among students. It is applied to the FAFSA and all the funds that it supports (work-study, federal grants, and loans). FM is used to award federal and some state funds as well. The IM is used by colleges to award aid from the institution's private funds such as donations and endowments. IM is applied primarily to the CSS Profile forms and other state and institutional forms.

The two methods are similar in that they consider the assets and income of parents, stepparents, and students. The methodologies look at the age of the parents, age of the student, number of family members, and number of dependent students attending college. As of 2001, the FM formula no longer allows being a student-parent to reduce EFC.

The two formulas use your reported financial data differently. For instance, FM does not count home equity, family farms, or the assets of independent students whose income is below $50,000 (Sim-

FEDERAL METHODOLOGY	INSTITUTIONAL METHODOLOGY
Focuses on income	Focuses on equity—home, retirement
Considers both the number of children in college and the number of parents supporting the children	Considers only the number of children; ignores the number of parents supporting the children
Does not require student contribution	Requires a minimum student contribution
Relies heavily on the established rules in distributing contributions	Relies heavily on professional judgment and circumstantial events

This table shows the main differences between the two methodologies used to grant aid.

plified Needs Test). FM does not expect family contribution if income is below $12,000 (Zero EFC). IM, however, includes home equity and retirement savings, requires minimum contribution from students, and inquires into the finances of noncustodial parents.

To get a better understanding of the factors in the decision-making process and how the methodologies are used, check the Department of Education and College Scholarship Service (College Board) websites:

MORE INFORMATION
www.collegeboard.com
www.ed.gov
www.fafsa.edu

STUDENT AID REPORT

The Student Aid Report (SAR) is the intermediary step between the application process and the acceptance process. Following your FAFSA submission, you will receive a SAR (usually within four weeks). The purpose of the SAR is to validate that all the reported data is accurate before the EFC is sent to colleges for package consolidation.

The SAR comes in three colors—pink, green, and blue—and has two parts. The first part details everything you submitted on the original FAFSA. The second part allows you to make any revisions from the original FAFSA. You should read the SAR carefully, checking everything twice.

The SAR shows the calculated EFC for the academic year and reveals whether a Pell Grant was awarded to you. The calculated EFC is located at the upper-right-hand corner of the SAR and looks like a serial number. The first character of the five-digit number should be read as a dollar sign. This tells you how much your EFC should be—**the lower the number, the better.**

If the EFC number is marked with an asterisk, you have been selected for verification. A verification process is required—if it is not completed, you will not receive any aid. The process involves providing forms and documentation to support the reported information.

Your corrected SAR must be available to your school by the last day of enrollment in the academic year or by August 31—whichever is earlier. A tardy submission might limit the amount of aid you receive. If you do not receive your SAR within four to six weeks of the FAFSA submission, or if you would like to check on the progress, contact the fin aid service lines for additional detail.

THE FORMS

In order to successfully apply for aid, you need the correct application forms:

- Free Application for Federal Student Aid (FAFSA)
- College Scholarship Services Profile (CSS)
- Institutional and state forms

TEN RULES

Before you complete the forms, you need to follow some basic rules. Following are ten rules that will aid you in the application process.

Rule 1—Assume Nothing

Always ask questions, and never jump to conclusions. If you have questions about your student status, eligibility, or special circumstances, contact the fin aid service center or the college you plan to attend. An ill-informed student is his own worst enemy.

Rule 2—Commit Time and Be Self-Disciplined

Deadlines and forms, both of which are side effects of bureaucracy, drive the fin aid process. As a result, you may be required to complete fifteen different forms—all of which report the same information. Keep in mind that there is no single set of funds or guidelines. Each form will scrutinize different portions of your personal finance.

Rule 3—Educate Thyself

The application process is cumbersome and complicated, and to win the game, you must know how it works. If you hit a dead end, use the information provided in this book or call the appropriate people. Spend the time, do the research, and find the answers to your questions. It could be worth thousands of dollars in aid.

Rule 4—Get to Know Your Financial Aid Counselor

Of all the steps you follow, this is one of the most important steps to complete. Meet with your counselor. Tell him about yourself and your position and find out what else you can do. The more interest and effort you show, the more likely he is to respond and ensure that you get aid. If this is your first time attending college or you are completing a transfer, call the college financial aid office and ask to speak with *your* assigned counselor.

Rule 5—Gather Data

Make sure you have all the information you need. Draft a checklist of all the background data you will need to complete the forms accurately. In fact, you should create folders to collect the research for each college. A typical financial aid checklist should include:

- High school transcript

- College transcripts (for transfer students)

- Recommendation letters (may be required for the Profile and other forms)

- Tax forms (1040, 1040EZ, 1040A)—yours and your parents'

- W2 forms—yours and your parents'

- Asset records (businesses, farms, stocks, bonds, investments)

Also, do your own research on state and private funds, such as need-based and merit-based scholarships. You may find that certain colleges request more information, requiring you to dig farther into your past.

Rule 6—Complete Forms Neatly, Accurately, and Timely

It is crucial that you read carefully and understand what numbers should be entered in which boxes. Inaccuracies could ruin your application. When completing your forms, follow these guidelines:

- Read instructions carefully. Pay special attention to any questions on income, because most errors occur in this area.

- Enter the information in the correct boxes. Don't enter a phone number when the line calls for a Social Security number.

- The FAFSA is arranged into sections. Each section asks for specific information about different people. Check to make sure that the correct data is entered in each section.

- Know the difference between a degree, a diploma, a GED, and certification. A high school graduation or certification is not an institutional degree. Students have been known to confuse the two and automatically exclude themselves from the biggest source of aid—the Pell Grant.

- Dependents are people for whom you provide financial support, including children and/or grandparents. To be a "dependent student" is not the same thing as having dependents.

- Marital status has a direct impact on the federal aid you receive. Separation, whether it is legalized or in the process, is important to note, as it reduces your supported income and may increase dependents—both of which increase your aid.

- Break your final goal into steps. If you plan on pursing medicine or law, your path probably includes a bachelor's degree in biology, psychology, English, or other liberal arts. By narrowing your focus to a special field of study, you might receive additional aid from a college.

When you've completed each application, make photocopies or save a copy on your computer before you submit the final version. Having proper documentation alleviates the future burden of the verification process.

Rule 7—Memorize the Deadlines

There is a calendar of important dates provided in the resources appendix. Do whatever it takes to keep yourself apprised of the days, the months, and the tools needed to complete the forms and submit them before the deadlines. But do not jump the gun and submit the forms too early. Early submission might actually eliminate you from the aid process. For instance, if you are attending college in the fall of 2002, do not send in an application while the summer selection process is taking place—your application will likely be misplaced, lost, or tossed.

Rule 8—Use Estimates

Do not wait until you complete your tax forms to get actual income and tax payments. Aid processors understand and expect some of the numbers you provide to be estimates. In fact, the sole purpose of the SAR is to validate that the information you originally reported is indeed accurate. So estimate intelligently and move on to the next free money application process.

Rule 9—Reapply for Aid

Whether your personal situation changes or whether it is the beginning of a new year, the aid renewal process is important. If a sudden financial trauma hits your life—you or your parents lose a job, someone in the family dies, etc.—during the middle of a year, contact your aid counselor immediately. Your counselor will help reassess the upcoming semester and maybe even scrounge some aid that other students didn't accept.

Rule 10—Pay Your Dues

As suffocating as it may be for your budget, dole out the necessary application processing fees. The CSS Profile and other institutional forms require a small processing fee. That minimal fee could lead to a debt-free future.

FREE APPLICATION FOR FEDERAL STUDENT AID

The Free Application for Federal Student Aid (FAFSA) is a non-self-renewing federal form that must be completed by any student seeking federal aid or state scholarships. Ideally, the FAFSA should be completed in early January (and no later than March 15), and submitted at the same time you submit your college application. Some colleges have their own specific deadlines (which may be earlier than March). However, be careful not to apply too early, as it could work against you.

Most public, private, community, and vocational-technical colleges use the results from the FAFSA to determine the size of fin aid awards. FAFSA is a need-based form that concentrates strictly on income, academic accomplishments, and extracurricular activities. A separate form for each college is not required. On the form, there is a section where you select the colleges that you would like to participate in the financial aid process. The reported information is shared by all colleges and is used to determine your award money.

As a result of the Internet and other technologies, you can now submit the FAFSA in several formats, including:

- *FAFSA on the Web:* A free U.S. Department of Education website that allows you to complete the form and submit it via the

Internet. There is also a renewal version of FAFSA on the Web. The address is *www.fafsa.ed.gov.*

- *FAFSA Express:* A free software program you can use to apply for federal student aid from an Internet-ready computer. If you wish to apply using *FAFSA Express*, you can download a copy of the program at *www.ed.gov/offices/OSFAP/Students/apply/fexpress.html* or call 1-800-801-0576. There is no "renewal" version of *FAFSA Express,* so the same process must be followed to complete the FAFSA renewal process each year.

- *Electronic filing:* You can also submit your application directly to your selected college electronically. You must verify that the recipient school has electronic processing. With electronic filing, the same process must be followed to complete the FAFSA renewal process each year.

- *Postal mail:* The traditional and still most common form of submission is the hard-copy format. You can download the form from the Internet, pick one up at a high school, or get one from a college financial aid office. The renewal FAFSA is automatically mailed to you at the beginning of each academic year.

INSTITUTIONAL AND STATE FORMS

These forms are additional college-specific forms that some institutions require. They focus award distribution on special requirements. The purpose of these forms is to target exceptional students (need/nonneed) and channel money in that direction. Some merit awards are based on a student's field of study, physical qualities, and demonstrated need. Other special requirements may include arbitrary characteristics such as left-handedness, last name, sex (male/female), family ancestry, or special skills.

THE COLLEGE SCHOLARSHIP SERVICE PROFILE

The College Scholarship Service Profile Aid (CSS) form was created by the College Scholarship Services division of the College Board. The Profile form is customized to individual colleges and is more comprehensive. It focuses primarily on family assets such as home equity, retirement accounts, and insurance policy values. Unlike the FAFSA, which uses FM, the Profile uses IM, which adheres to harsher guidelines and expects more parent and student contribution. This form is also guided by nonstandardization and plenty of "professional judgment." Copies of the application can be obtained online at the College Board (*www.collegeboard.com*) for a minimal fee.

The Last Phase

Once you receive your financial aid package, read it carefully and understand what is being offered. Consider the ratio of the gift aid against other aid. Compare the ratios and gap against any financial aid packages from other colleges.

Be sure to add in other cost components that were not initially considered when determining your COA. Your main goal in the acceptance phase is to find the best deal from each college and then compare deals.

You may accept or reject all or part of an aid package. Unless your circumstances prevent you from accepting gift aid, you should accept all federal and state gift aid. We strongly suggest that you decline loans. Stay focused and remember your goal—debt-free college.

Not all students have the capacity to use all types of aid. A part-time student who is already employed might find that work-study aid helps little, as it leaves not much time for studying. To address special circumstances, part four of the book offers alternatives.

If you haven't decided on a college when you receive a fin aid offer, go ahead and accept the package so that you have time to compare the value of the award. But if you decline the aid, *do not hold onto it longer than you need to.* You should notify the college financial aid office immediately after making your decision so that other needy students like yourself can be considered.

CHAPTER NINE

Federal Aid, State Aid, Private Aid, and More

If you complete the financial aid process and submit the application before the deadline, you will receive a financial aid package four weeks following the SAR submission. When you receive the package or the award letter, it will contain a combination of aid—grants, scholarships, loans, and other federal aid. This chapter covers the elements of the award letter and its role in debt-free college.

- The aid package

- Federal, state and private aid

- Maximizing financial aid (ten rules)

- Loans

The Aid Package

The financial aid package consists of merit scholarships, grants, loans, federal work-study (on- and off-campus jobs), athletic scholarships, tuition waivers, and military aid. Merit scholarships, athletic scholarships, and grants are gifts that students do not have to pay back to the school or to the government. Federal work-study allows students to earn income—while enrolled—to pay for all or part of the COA. Loans are debts that must be repaid to lenders regardless of your financial situation after college. A financial aid package/award letter might look like this:

FINANCIAL AID NOTIFICATION

Cost of Education:	Student Name: Jane Doe
$9580	Student SSN: 111-22-3333
Expected Family Contribution:	Date: 01-01-2001
$1146	
Financial Need:	
$8434	

Counselor: Jack-in-the-Box   **Accept/Decline**

Federal Pell Grant	$ 400
Federal Supplemental Grant	$ 250
University Grant	$ 100
Federal Work-Study Program	$1500
Federal Subsidized Stafford Loan	$3500
Federal Perkins Loan	$2750

Your appointed financial aid counselor determines your aid package. Not all colleges are able to provide the full amount you might need. There might be an aid "gap" for which you have to look elsewhere. If the package does meet your need and you are later awarded "outside" scholarships, the college will retract a similar amount from the award letter.

Outside scholarships are additional awards that are not associated with the aid package. For instance, a scholarship from a religious community or a special talent contest is considered an outside award. The three primary forms of aid associated with the package are:

- Federal aid
- State aid
- Private aid

Federal Aid

The federal government provides 70 percent of all financial aid and participates in four programs:

- Federal Pell Grant

- Federal Supplemental Educational Opportunity Grant

- Federal Work-Study

- Federal Perkins Loan

The Federal Pell Grant is the largest of the federal programs funded by Congress and administered by the government. Under the Federal Pell Grant, colleges are required to award the maximum Pell amount to every eligible student. There are no limits to the amount a college can distribute, but there is a limit to the amount a student can receive. The other federal programs are part of the federal campus-based programs, which are jointly administered by the university and the government. These programs have limited grant money and issue awards in different methods. However, they do share some common characteristics:

- Neither entity makes guarantees to provide funds to all eligible students.

- Limited funds are distributed by the college's financial aid office at the office's discretion.

- Once the appropriated money is gone, no more awards can be made for the year.

- Each college sets its own deadlines for the application process—usually earlier than federal deadlines.

Aside from the grants, the government participates in loan-assistance programs. These programs let students borrow at low interest rates.

FEDERAL PELL GRANT

The Federal Pell Grant program awards money to more than four million students across the nation. Federal Pell Grant recipients must be undergraduate students who have not completed a bachelor's or professional degree. A professional degree is typically earned after an undergraduate degree such as an MBA, MD, or JD. The Pell Grant also excludes students who are attempting to complete a second bachelor's degree in another area.

Anyone can receive a Pell Grant, provided they meet the eligibility criteria, complete the FAFSA, and submit it before the deadline. The amount of the grant you receive depends on:

- Your demonstrated need

- The COA at your selected institution

- The length of the program you enroll in

- Your student status (full-time or part-time)

If you are a part-time student, you will not receive as much as a full-time student. For the 2001–2002 academic year, the grant award ranges from $400 to $3,750. If you receive $3,750, you have reached the ceiling—congratulations!

A student can receive only one Pell Grant in an award year. The grant can be spread over two or three semesters—fall, spring, and summer. Because the grant program is a federal program and the process is universal, you cannot receive a Pell Grant from more than one school at a time.

At the beginning of each academic year, universities notify students of their financial aid package and give instructions for package distribution. The university can credit the funds directly to your school account, pay you via check, or combine these methods to your preference. The university can also electronically transfer your funds directly to your checking account—a free service that makes computing balances easy. Typically, a university will wait until the twelfth class day of the semester, when all the scheduling ends. Then they deduct the amount you owe from the awarded amount for tuition, fees, and room and board. Any remaining balance is transmitted via check.

FEDERAL SUPPLEMENTAL EDUCATIONAL OPPORTUNITY GRANT (FSEOG)

The FSEOG program is a campus-based program with limited grant money whose recipients must show exceptional need. Students with exceptional need are those who have the lowest EFC in that college. The program gives priority to students who have received a Pell Grant and demonstrate additional need. There is no guarantee that an eligible student will receive a FSEOG award, because the funds are limited and are not backed by the U.S. Department of Education.

To qualify for a FSEOG award, you must be an undergraduate student enrolled at least part-time at an accredited institution. Like the Pell, the award amount depends on when you apply, your level of need, the funding available at the school, and the financial aid office policies. The FSEOG award ranges from $100 to $4,000 a year. The chance that you might receive $4,000 is rare—an award of $1,000 to $1,500 is generally considered the maximum payout. About one million students qualify for this desperately needed money, which makes it difficult to receive the full amount. The FSEOG award is also included in the aid package and can be credited directly to your account, paid via check or EFT (electronic funds transfer).

FEDERAL WORK-STUDY

The college work-study program is supported by both federal and state governments, and provides students a chance to wage-earn additional aid. The work-study money is included in the package and is distributed across the number of semesters you plan to attend. To receive work-study, you must be enrolled at least half-time at an undergraduate school, demonstrate need, and qualify for the posted jobs. Usually, work-study positions are profiled for college students, require basic skills, and offer flexible work hours. Students are paid current federal minimum wage or higher, depending on their level of experience.

Most work-study positions are on campus; however, some off-campus positions with community service organizations do exist. Examples of on-campus positions include assisting professors or other personnel in administration, college housing, cafeterias, laboratories, and libraries. Off-campus positions are usually administrative positions in hospitals or in social offices.

Students are encouraged to work the minimum number of hours required to earn the assigned award money, because they cannot earn more than is awarded—unless the employer expresses a need and is willing to pay from personal funds. Work-study employers pay according to their payroll (semi-monthly or monthly) and accommodate for transferring your wages.

TIP: College career centers and financial aid centers are the primary sources that list work-study positions. You should check here first. Also, participating employers are urged to wait a reasonable amount of time before hiring non-work-study students. This makes job hunting easier for aid participants.

State Aid

In 1998, Congress revised the State Student Incentive Grant program and renamed it the Leveraging Educational Assistance Partnership program (LEAP). LEAP is jointly funded by federal and state governments. LEAP money can be used to award grants or to assist student activities. The flexibility of this program allows states to set their own standards for award limits, student qualifications, need requirements, and calculation methods for award issuance.

State aid is primarily offered in the form of subsidized tuition. Subsidized tuition is reduced tuition and fees for in-state residents who attend in-state colleges/universities. This is done to encourage state residents to stay at home. Subsidized tuition can save you $8,000 to $10,000 each academic year—a total of $32,000 to $40,000 over four years.

Another form of state aid is grant money, which may be issued based on merit or need. The standards used to determine need-distribution vary significantly among states, as do the standards for merit-distribution. State aid is also provided through special arrangements with neighboring states to equalize tuition payments. The neighboring state policy allows students to attend regional out-of-state colleges but pay in-state tuition. This policy was instituted so that state colleges that do not offer a specific field of study can help students afford education in a neighboring state. A few of these states include California, Florida, Wisconsin, Minnesota, Maine, Ohio, and Pennsylvania.

Finally, state aid is issued as part of the federal work-study program and state savings plans. As of 1997, state plans allow students and parents to save money for college expenses with no tax penalties until the money is withdrawn. As soon as the money is withdrawn, it is considered income and is taxed at the recipient's tax rate. To find out more about these benefits and others, contact your state agencies using the information provided in the appendix at the back of the book.

Private Aid

Private aid is the most unpredictable form of aid. It is used primarily to lure freshmen and retain talented students. For this reason, private aid can be issued as grant money, specific talent or merit scholarships, work-study, or a combination thereof. A difficult aspect of private aid is identifying the exact criteria for eligibility, which is generally not disclosed to the public. If you are aiming to qualify for this aid—as you should be—you need to conduct research and seek assistance from your assigned financial aid counselor.

Private aid is funded by endowments and a combination of do-nations, investments, and corporate contributions. The bigger the share of the endowments, the more funds available to you and the less you pay for college. According to the National Association of College and University Business Officers, the top ten college endowments for 2001 included:

UNIVERSITY	AMOUNT
Harvard University	$17,950,843,000
Yale University	$10,700,000,000
University of Texas System	$ 9,363,588,000
Princeton University	$ 8,359,000,000
Stanford University	$ 8,249,551,000
Massachusetts Institute of Technology	$ 6,134,712,000
University of California	$ 4,702,729,000
Emory University	$ 4,315,998,000
Columbia University	$ 4,292,793,000
The Texas A&M University System and Foundations	$ 4,030,881,000

While you are selecting a college, keep this in mind, because it could mean more opportunities for you to receive additional aid.

Institutional Aid

Many schools provide their own institutional awards based on ac-ademic record, extracurricular activities, or ethnic background. Most of these scholarships are awarded automatically when you enroll, provided you meet the requirements. All you have to do is complete the institution-specific application form.

MAJOR-SPECIFIC SCHOLARSHIPS

These scholarships are awarded to students who have performed particularly well in a certain field of study or have shown an aptitude in a certain area. These awards are issued to encourage excellence and specialization.

FELLOWSHIPS

Fellowships are granted to students to pursue certain projects. For example, a student interested in performing research in chemistry may be awarded a fellowship to carry on ongoing research under the supervision of a faculty member. Fellowships can help pay for all, or part, of academics. They are commonly issued to graduate students and undergraduate students with exceptional situations.

ATHLETIC SCHOLARSHIPS

Athletic scholarships are one of the better-known types of merit aid. The amount of your scholarship depends on your skill and how the college views your particular sport. The bigger scholarships usually go to athletes in "major" sports such as football, basketball, or baseball. Regardless of the size of the award, if you have athletic ability, this arena is a gold mine. Depending on your choice of sport, your COA may be reduced by half or more.

TRIVIA: In 1997, Harvard University granted a degree to eighty-nine-year-old Mary Fasano—*www.uselessknowledge.com*

Maximizing Financial Aid

Students who receive the most aid are those who exhibit an undeniable need for assistance. In order to maximize your aid, you must *demonstrate a greater need than your peers and prove that your earning potential is lower.* This does not mean that you should falsify records or report untrue circumstances. Remember that the financial aid process supports more than two million students and attempts to support as many qualified individuals as possible. Also, remember that your honesty affects other needy students.

Below are ten steps you can take to maximize your aid potential:

1. Reduce Base Year Income

In order to determine your aid, the government uses the year prior to college enrollment known as the *base year*. The base year starts in January and ends in December of the year previous to college attendance. For instance, if you are planning on attending in fall 2002, the base year begins in January 2001 and ends in December 2001. This is important because the size of your award is based on your EFC, which is determined by the base year income and the circumstances that surround the base year. If your base year is financially unstable, your EFC is lowered and financial aid is increased. The bottom line:

SECRET **#68**

The lower your EFC in your base year, the more you receive in financial aid.

In order to maximize your aid potential, during your base year, make all the necessary large purchases (a computer or car, for example) that you know you must have for college. While making these purchases, you should deplete any of your assets first (trust funds, cash awards, etc.) because student assets count more heavily than parents' assets.

If you or your parents are self-employed, consider reducing your salary the year before you plan to enter college. If you are self-employed, hire your children as employees. A reasonable wage for normal office work will provide you with tax benefits and reduce your base year income.

Another option is to pay taxes early. Paying taxes early reduces income in your current checking or savings account and could increase your need for aid. Avoid receiving refunds from the IRS. Refunds suggest additional income, thus lowering aid potential. If you have questions about determining the exact tax amount, use the IRS tables at *www.irs.gov* to estimate your tax withholdings.

Finally, you should consider paying off any debt that you have been accumulating. For instance, if you have credit card debt, pay it off during the base year using savings, as this reduces your income.

2. ALWAYS APPLY FOR AID

Never make assumptions or convince yourself that you are ineligible. If you are ineligible, you won't receive any money. But if you *are* eligible, you miss the opportunity to reach debt-free college. Moreover, if you are rejected the first year, you will still receive a renewal FAFSA, at which point your circumstances might have changed, making you eligible.

3. GET PARENTS (AND SPOUSE) INVOLVED

According to the *Guide to College Financial Aid 2001,* aid administrators will not accept a statement that parents are unwilling to help financially. Too many families would make that claim. So at a minimum, get your parents/spouse to assist in the application process and help report accurate information.

4. TRANSFER AT THE START OF FALL SEMESTERS

If you are planning to transfer colleges, consider doing so at the beginning of a fall semester. The academic year begins in September, and college treasuries are most full at the beginning of the academic year. Moreover, the award money is best allocated and distributed at this time. If you transfer during the spring or summer semesters, colleges may have no funds left to distribute, leaving you in the cold.

5. SAVE MONEY IN YOUR PARENTS' NAME

Regardless of which methodology is used to determine aid, parents' income and savings are a key part of the formula. In the IM formula, both the parents' income and the student's income are included. As a rule of thumb, several private institutions expect a minimum student contribution. If a student has any form of passive income, it is included in the EFC—which ultimately reduces the financial aid award. During your college years, consider transferring your money to a tax-sheltered investment under your parents' name. If you are an independent student, consider saving money under your children's names. This reduces your personal income and EFC but increases your financial aid.

6. MINIMIZE OUTSIDE INCOME

The less income you receive from outside sources, the more your aid eligibility increases. Capital gains are a good example. Capital gains are profits made on investments such as stocks, bonds, or other securities. If you, your parents, or your spouse currently owns such investments, convert them to non-income-generating assets. If you plan on selling them, wait until *after* you file the last FAFSA application, just before graduation. Selling them during the base year or during college might yield capital gains and, thus, reduce your eligibility.

7. SIMPLIFIED NEEDS TEST (SNT)

The Simplified Needs Test (SNT) states that if the combined income of the parents or an independent student and their spouse is less than $50,000 and both file the IRS1040A or 1040EZ, any existing assets are disregarded. If your income range is close to (or slightly above) $50,000, try to reduce your income by making larger contributions to retirement funds and postponing bonuses until after the base year.

8. ESTIMATE CONSERVATIVELY

If you overestimate your income or tax payments, you may present an inaccurate picture of your financial situation. For instance, if your parents (or you and your spouse) have a combined income of $49,000 and you overestimate by $2,000, you just made yourself ineligible for the SNT. So look over the previous year's income and estimate conservatively. If you need help estimating, visit one of the college websites presented in the book.

9. REDUCE ASSET HOLDINGS

Gifts of love from grandparents and other relatives made directly to the student are considered assets and are included in need analysis. For this reason, delay receiving gifts until after graduation. You can use them at college graduation to pay any loans you might have incurred. Another option is to have the gift money directed to your parents and have them use it to pay for college expenses. Even better, speak to the aid counselor and have your grandparents make direct contributions to the EFC instead.

10. ART OF NEGOTIATION

Even if you have done all of the above, you may find that you are still short of funds. There is one last opportunity—negotiation. A majority of institutions offer students the opportunity to present their case. However, if you are interested in attending an elite or top-tier school, don't bother. These schools can conjure students with parents who are willing to pay and, thus, don't even consider bargaining an option.

If you are planning to appeal to a college, a feasibility analysis should be conducted. The analysis should answer the questions:

  ? Is your case legitimate

  ? Are negotiations possible with the college

  ? Are they part of the fin aid process

You can get this kind of information by reading brochures or by calling the college financial aid office.

The best way to make an appeal is to communicate directly with the counselor face-to-face. Once you are there, ease into the negotiations. *Don't threaten or give ultimatums to your aid counselor.* He is trying to help you—demanding money from him will only be harmful. Present new information and have valid reasons for an upgrade. "I can't afford to" or "I just need more money" are *not* good reasons. Also, do some research and find information about historical enrollment and aid distribution. Identify the number of students that should be enrolled—if the college is shy of enrollment figures, it may be able to help you meet the gap. This would benefit you *and* the college.

Also, check to see if the college is bound by special arrangements. Most colleges have to meet a minimum enrollment for minorities, cultural diversity, and ethnic background. If your background can add to this cause, your appeal may prove easier.

Another alternative is financial aid distribution. Historically, if the college meets student aid at 100 percent but only meets 75 percent of your need, you may have an edge. Other options include special talents such as sports, arts, music, computer skills, or being a merit finalist. Colleges especially like to attract merit scholars and students with special talents.

A more difficult path is to appeal based on personal situations. For instance, you or your parents may have special financial circumstances such as illness in the family that generates huge medical bills, relatives who receive personal care, or certain costly disabilities. Bad credit ratings, excessive debt that impedes taking on loans, job displacement, or retiring parents can assist an appeal process. But for whatever claims you make, you must be ready to show documentation.

Throughout the entire process, it is important to remember that you *appeal with just cause and relevancy.* Appealing to an all-minority college on your minority basis will most likely not improve your situation. Neither will intentional competition between colleges when the colleges are not interested in enrolling more students.

The underlying theme of negotiation is to do research and identify potential leverage to help the process.

A Note About Loans

If you were reading carefully, you probably noticed that we have delayed reference to loans. This is because loans do not help achieve debt-free college. However, some students may take on loans to complete their education. The following two letters reveal what the burden of loan debt is doing to two former students.

Dear Susan & Co.,

My wife and I have combined our student loans. Our current balance is $45,000. I was curious to know if there are any grants that will pay off some or all of your student loan. We can't afford the $380/month payment, and if we don't pay they keep adding interest. **Eddie**

Dear Susan & Co.,

I am getting married next September. I have a defaulted student loan of about 25,000, and have not made a payment in a couple years, because it really overwhelmed me to think about it. Now, I do not want it to become a source of tension, so help me to get on the right track with this. How much do I pay each month, etc. Thank you, **Dan H.**
Source: http://www.cccsintl.org/susan/cd.htm

This short section shows how to *minimize borrowing* by understanding a few basics. However, you should still read the rest of the book for more options prior to taking on loans.

LOAN BASICS

A loan is an agreed-upon amount of money—*principal*—that is lent to a borrower—*you*—by a *creditor*. A creditor can be a bank, a financial institution, or a university. In return for providing you money, creditors want a reward—*interest*. For example, if Jim wants to borrow $1,000 at 10 percent, he would repay the creditor $1,100. The $100 is interest reward for the money lent.

Unfortunately, loan interest is not that simple. Loan interest can be accrued in various forms—variable, compound, or annual percentage rate (APR). Each type of interest accrual can turn $100 into thousands of dollars of debt. In addition, there are origination, back-end, and other supplemental fees associated with loans. These fees are included as part of repayment schedules and increase your overall debt.

When you borrow a loan, you must sign a *promissory note*— promising the creditor that you will repay the amount. Repayment schedules are set at the same time you sign the promissory note.

TYPES OF LOANS

The most common student loans are federal, private, Parent Loan for Undergraduate Students (PLUS), and college-sponsored loans. Federal loans are generally the best option because they offer low-interest, better repayment options, and sometimes pay the interest for you. The next best option is a college-sponsored loan, followed by PLUS and private loans. The best way to get low-interest loans is to complete the infamous FAFSA. Even though you may not receive any financial aid, you may be able to use the low-interest federal loans.

Federal

Federal loans come in two forms—subsidized and unsubsidized. A subsidized loan is a *need-based* (based on FAFSA guidelines) loan where the federal government pays the annual interest for you while you are in college (and during the grace period). An unsubsidized loan is not need-based and requires that you pay the interest for the life of the loan, but it offers an interest rate lower than other loans.

The table at the end of this section describes federal loans and their options.

College-Sponsored

College-sponsored loans are the next best option to federal loans. Because these are specifically directed at student borrowing, they have favorable interest rates. Most universities also use fixed rate, which means that there is no accrual.

Private

Private loans are available to both parents and students. These are issued by financial institutions and have higher interest rates and longer repayment schedules. The interest rates are generally variable and mirror bond market fluctuations, so *when* you take on the loan could be harmful. Private loans should be avoided at all costs.

CHOOSE CAREFULLY

The best way to avoid loans is to make sure that there are absolutely no other options—part-time work, taking time off to save, community college, etc. If those options don't work, make sure you choose a reasonable loan.

SECRET #69

Choose a loan with the lowest interest rate, no fees, and a quick repayment schedule.

With a low interest rate, you pay less for services. With no fees, you don't pay sales tax on your purchase. With a quick repayment schedule, you minimize interest and avoid costly mistakes. The five golden rules to borrowing are:

1. Go only two levels deep for borrowing. Federal Perkins first, then subsidized Stafford.

LOAN	REQUIREMENTS	AMOUNT	INTEREST AND FEES	REPAYMENT
Perkins	• At least part-time • Minimum 2.0 GPA • U.S. citizen or permanent resident	• Undergraduate $2,000 • Graduate $6,000	• Fixed interest • Capped at 5 percent • No fees	• Nine months after graduation • Up to ten years • Minimum of $480 per year per each loan
Subsidized Stafford Loan/Direct Loan	• At least part-time • U.S. citizen or permanent resident	• Freshman $2,625 • Sophomore $3,500 • Juniors and Seniors $5,500 • Graduates $8,500	• Capped at 8.25 percent • Variable interest rate • 4 percent origination fee	• Up to ten years • Minimum of $600 per year • Six months after graduation
Unsubsidized Stafford	• At least part-time • U.S. citizen or permanent resident • Non need-based	• Freshman $2,625–$6,625 • Sophomore $3,500–$7,500 • Juniors and Seniors $5,500–$10,500 • Graduates $18,500	• Capped at 8.25 percent • Variable interest rate • 4 percent origination fee	• Up to ten years • Minimum of $600 per year • Six months after graduation
PLUS	• U.S. citizen or permanent resident • Parent of full-/part-time undergraduate • No adverse credit history	• Expense need for COA	• Capped at 9.0 percent	• Sixty days after sign date • Interest payments up to four years

This table briefly shows the types of loans and their terms. Source: www.ed.gov, www.collegeboard.com, and www.finaid.com.

2. Borrow only what you need. Do not borrow for the future. If you need $4,500, borrow $4,000 and use some creative expense management for $500.

3. Always track your interest payments and loan tabs. Keeping organized records will make debt tangible and keep you motivated for debt-free college.

4. Consider other options prior to taking on loans (see the rest of the book).

5. Do not capitalize interest payments. When you capitalize interest, you are compounding interest upon interest and increasing your debt. Instead, try to make interest payments while you are in school. Generally, the first few interest payments are low.

Things to Remember

To benefit from the financial aid process, keep these following tips in mind and refer back to this list as often as you need.

• Gift aid and college scholarships are mostly given to state residents attending in-state colleges.

• If you receive outside aid that impacts your financial aid award, use bargaining skills to negotiate a median between loans and aid (scholarships and grants).

• Apply for aid no earlier than January 1 and no later than March 15. Remember that the FAFSA is not self-renewing and must be completed annually.

• Do not wait to apply for aid until after you are accepted for enrollment. A few bucks spent on scholarship applications could lead to a debt-free future.

• Read all instructions and complete your forms accurately. Little mistakes lead to big debts.

- Reapply even if you did not quality for aid the first time.

- Be friendly with your financial aid counselor.

- Never make assumptions. Always ask questions.

- Allocate time. Do research. Use self-discipline.

- Avoid applying at mid-year.

CHAPTER TEN

All About Scholarships

Next to financial aid, scholarships are the most abundant source of free money. The scholarship process mirrors the financial aid process; it requires time, patience, and self-discipline. But the most fundamental element is research. Research is the key to getting scholarships. In this chapter, we will discuss the key factors to obtaining scholarships.

- A strategy

- The quest

- Scholarship scams

- Starting points

A Note About Scholarships

To appreciate the world of scholarships, you have to understand what they are, why they exist, where they come from, who decides how much, and most important, how you can get your hands on one. Once the W's of scholarships are analyzed, navigating through the maze will not seem such an arduous task.

TRIVIA: Albright College in Reading, PA, is listed in the *Guinness Book of Records* as being on the only street in the United States on which you can spend your entire life. The road has neighborhoods, a hospital, an elementary school, a middle school, a high school, a college, a church, various businesses, and a cemetery.—*www.funtrivia.com*

THE WHAT

A scholarship is a defined sum of money awarded to a student to help finance his educational needs. A scholarship is given to a candidate who best meets the outlined criterion. Sometimes the specified criteria may have outlived its original purpose, but the foundation still continues to award money. Sometimes scholarships might have no rhyme or reason. In any case, they are a good source of aid.

THE WHO

Some common reasons for establishing scholarship funds are name recognition, college ties, public ties, tax credits, idea generation, camaraderie, and civic duty. The financiers are federal, state, and city governments; wealthy families who have ties to their alma mater; local communities that want to place their mark on society; corporations that need tax credits; and scientific organizations that want to attract potential candidates for their research.

THE WHY

A defining aspect of scholarships is competitiveness. Scholarships compete against each other, and they compete unselfishly for your benefit. They have been created with the mindset of giving money to students who—from the founder's perspective—are worthy of receiving it. Also, there are hundreds of thousands of them in existence. For instance, if you search the Internet for "scholarships," you will receive approximately 1,420,000 hits—give or take a few thousand. Scholarships help you obtain debt-free college because they are abundant and competitive.

THE HOW

In the scholarship game, there are no formulas, no standard rules or regulations, and no opportunities to bargain. The awards are issued strictly on a subjective basis. To receive money from a scholarship you must meet the defined criteria and meet it better than your competition. For instance, if the award calls for a student whose grandparents lived through the Great Depression, worked for the federal government as a postman, and earned between $3 and $3.25 a day, you must meet those exact requirements.

THE WHEN AND WHERE

There is no better time to apply for scholarships than now. With the use of the Internet and the multitude of resource databases, it has become easier to find scholarships and apply for them. All you have to do is learn some key rules in order to play the game successfully.

TIP: Scholarships have no age restriction—just merit, talent, and full-time status. If you are an adult or an independent student, substitute teacher's recommendations with employer's recommendations, update achievement test scores, and list recent accomplishments that show commitment, leadership, and motivation.

A Strategy

There is a scholarship for almost every human characteristic—race, ethnicity, religion, culture, sex, ancestry, historical evidence, intelligence, sports, common ideas, hobbies, skills, etc. Scholarships are even awarded to students who exhibit an interest in fruit breeding.

The educational market is saturated with scholarships, but without sufficient research, you may not be able to reap the benefits.

Although there are no hard-set rules about researching scholarships, the following tips will assist you in the hunt.

START EARLY

Don't wait until high school graduation or the summer before you enter college to apply or research scholarships. Regardless of where you plan to attend, most scholarships are *portable* and *transferable*. As soon as you decide to attend college, begin the process.

- **Develop your skills**—Join organizations, take on responsibility, and get involved in the community. Develop special skills that generally offer more money.

- **Focus on your goal**—To reach debt-free college, you have to be persistent. You have to concentrate and act accordingly. Despite opposition, keep in mind that your present efforts could eliminate years of loan payments.

- **Collect information**—Spend time asking for information from counselors, talking to teachers, and gathering information from books. One hour a day could lead to hundreds of dollars in aid.

BUILD A DATABASE

Knowing who you are makes it easier to focus on the types of scholarships you could be eligible for. So sit down for a few hours and collect the necessary facts.

Write down everything—academic achievements (GPA, honors, class rank), special awards and recognition, hobbies, interests, languages, community involvement, religion, intended college major and career path, citizenship status, and current involvement in organizations. The list should also include personality traits and characteristics—left-handedness, physical disabilities, sex, ethnicity, and religion. By creating an inventory, you are actually building a database of potential scholarships. For every item you identify, there are probably a great number of scholarships.

FILTER RESEARCH

The biggest disadvantage of scholarships is that they are numerous and they resemble stock tips. By the time a stock tip comes around to you, it is no longer a tip. "Hey, guess what? I have a tip for you . . ." is no longer profitable. By the time you get the tip, stock prices will have already skyrocketed and you have yet to make a trade.

All the famous and big-money scholarships are well publicized. The overlooked, undervalued, and unapplied-for scholarships, however, are readily available. Gather data, scholarship profiles, and the profiles of past recipients. Also, conduct a cost/benefit analysis. You may find that your time is best spent on rock sampling for a summer instead of seeking a National Merit Scholarship. Channel your research and energy to those scholarships that best resemble your situation, your skills, and your ability to get money.

FIND ADVOCATES

Several community service organizations have national projects such as homeless shelters, children's hospitals, and nursing home support. If you're interested in pursing a career related to these projects (pediatrics, geriatrics, or social work), share your goals and ask for sponsorship. Volunteer a few hours of your time, and you may reduce your COA a little each semester.

Moreover, contact the presidents of the organizations and ask for their advice. Ask them specific questions about similar opportunities. Let them know you have potential and that the award money will be well spent if it ends up going to you.

PREPARE AN ESSAY POOL

Almost all scholarships require a written essay. Essays are used to get a sense of how you measure up to the scholarship criteria. Generally, scholarships ask similar questions, although they may switch the idea around to meet specific needs.

The four common essays are personal essays, academic essays, marketing essays (why you are the perfect candidate), and future dreams/hopes essays. If you develop a template for these core essays, you can often reuse them for different scholarships. If you need help writing essays, *The Best College Admissions Essays*, by Mark Alan Stewart and Cynthia C. Muchnick, is a good start. This book includes tips and advice from experts and presents fifty example essays.

PREPARE A RECOMMENDATION POOL

Scholarships often require recommendation letters. Scholarship committees use recommendation letters to understand you and your abilities through what others have to say about you. Recommendations are crucial because they speak for you. Use caution when asking for a recommendation. Make sure the person knows you, your personality, and your potential. In fact, you should always provide a small bio with your request to help the writer.

FOLLOW THROUGH

Whether you receive a scholarship award or not, follow through. Keep track of all your applications and their status. If you speak with someone about the status, write down her name and phone number. As the deadline for announcement approaches, continue checking for news—good or bad. If you are not one of the finalists, find out why. Maybe they were missing part of your records, or maybe they never received your file. If you don't receive any sort of news, call the sponsor and find out what is happening or if the process has been delayed. Be persistent, but not annoying, in finding out why.

APPLY CONSISTENTLY, ACCURATELY, AND FACTUALLY

Because scholarships are so different and unique, you must approach each scholarship accordingly. The more you know about each scholarship, the organization, and the requirements, the better your chances for winning that scholarship. When applying for scholarships, keep the following tips in mind.

Completing the Application

When completing an application, use the same vigor and caution you did when you applied for financial aid.

- Do not exaggerate your grades, memberships, qualifications, achievements, characteristics, physical abilities, or finances. Dishonesty will only distance you from debt-free college.

- Follow all instructions to a T. There is a reason why there are limitations and requirements. Trying to overachieve or outdo the requirements will only harm you. If the application calls for a ten-word sentence, compose the tightest, truest *ten-word sentence* you can.

- Meet the specified deadline and, if possible, send the application early. Scholarship committee members have other obligations, and their time is as valuable as yours. The more time you give them to read about you, the better.

- Proofread the application several times. In fact, get someone in the family, a friend, or a close teacher to help with your application. They may catch errors that you didn't.

- Check that all pieces of the application are included—recommendation letters, personal essays, qualification proof (if necessary), financial information, etc.

Because there are often many applicants for scholarships, the smallest error in your application could put you out of contention. Always proceed with care.

Winning the Scholarship

In order to win a scholarship, you need to do more than complete the application and meet the requirements. You need to know a few things about the scholarship itself—history, sponsors, previous candidates, and the committee members.

- **Know the sponsor and the committee members**—Learning about the sponsor and the committee can help you understand the committee members and their backgrounds and why the scholarship was created. This knowledge may help you tailor your essays to the organization's purpose as well as appeal to individuals on the selection committee. Collecting the details also shows that you are a highly motivated individual, guaranteeing that your name will stick out.

- **Meet past recipients**—Scholarship foundations usually keep a list of past winners. If possible, use this list and contact previous winners. Find out their stories. In only a few minutes you will get a winner's profile, tips on interview techniques, and a feel for positive and negative attributes. You will benefit from their success. In this way, you will avoid pitfalls and overcome hurdles.

- **Show interest**—If you are applying for a fruit-breeding scholarship, know what it is about. Talking about the implications of rocket science will do you no good in an interview about mangoes and bananas. Spend some time and learn the facts about the scholarship's topic, foundation, goals, future, and mission.

TIP: Once you receive an award, be polite and draft a thank you letter. Make time to attend the finalist luncheon or dinner. Meet the sponsor and other candidates. Be gracious and avoid bragging. You will be surprised at how well you will be remembered by the sponsor and the committee members and what a huge impact it has. Remember, good words travel fast, but bad words travel even faster.

Interviewing Effectively

The scholarship game is about marketing yourself to a select committee and winning them over through forms, letters, essays, and interviews. This is why it is crucial that you do all of the above and prepare for interviews. Find creative ways to present the details about yourself to the committee. Arrive early, dress conservatively, and be modest. Brush up on current events. Show that you are a well-rounded person, worthy of receiving an award.

Interview questions are assembled to draw a complete picture of you and your abilities. Some of these questions might include:

? Where do you see yourself in five years

? Why did you choose to apply for this scholarship

? Why are you a better candidate than the rest

? Why should we choose you

? How do you plan to use the award money

These are just a sampling of the questions you might run into. At all times, you should be prepared to present yourself in a respectable manner.

The Quest

Earlier in this chapter, we noted that scholarships come in various sizes and forms. Scholarships are established for various reasons with specific purposes. In this section, some of the key establishments that offer scholarships are discussed.

PLACE OF EMPLOYMENT

One of the best places to begin the scholarship quest is right at home. Whether you are a traditional student or an independent student, an employer is a key resource. Most companies award money to their employees or their children to improve their skills and to support the community. Have your parents or your spouse ask their supervisors about company scholarships. If you, your spouse, or your parents are members of a union—the Pilot Association, for instance—you might be eligible for more scholarship money.

ETHNIC, RACIAL, AND MINORITY ORGANIZATIONS

There is a plethora of community organizations that award scholarships to support different cultures, races, and members of a community. The best way to learn about possible scholarships is to inquire to the president of the organization about opportunities. If none are available, propose sponsorship. As part of the proposal, offer to spend a few hours a week organizing events or collecting information for a limited amount of time.

RELIGIOUS ORGANIZATIONS

Most religious establishments offer money to the community. These scholarships do not always require that you be of a particular faith. Most base awards on your class rank. Other groups might focus on your dedication and involvement within the community, and some award money based solely on financial need. Check with your local church, temple, mosque, or other religious establishment for opportunities.

CORPORATIONS

Large corporations such as Wells Fargo, Chevron, Westinghouse, and Target, among others, also offer college scholarships. Smaller companies offer money in smaller amounts. The requirements for corporate scholarships vary and may focus on certain areas of study or people who demonstrate exceptional leadership.

CLUBS, PROFESSIONAL ORGANIZATIONS, AND GROUPS

Local civic groups and organizations, like Rotary Clubs and the Elks, offer scholarships as part of their community service. Sometimes such scholarships are only available to members or dependents of members. Nevertheless, check into any possible groups—especially those that someone you know belongs to.

Traditional students should also check into high school clubs such as the Latin Club, the National Honor Society, Chess Club, Athletics, etc. Adult or independent students should check with any professional organizations, local community organizations, civic groups, and philanthropic organizations. Examples of these groups are the National Press Club, the Parents Teachers Association, the Chamber of Commerce, or Goodwill.

SPECIAL SKILLS

Creativity has its rewards, including scholarship aid for higher education. If you are interested in a specific hobby or posses a talent, check to see if that hobby or talent supports any special contests with cash rewards. For instance, if you are interested in modeling, a small modeling job during the semester could provide some pocket change. Talent shows are also a good source of cash awards. Art, photography, surfing, writing, and bowling offer opportunities to win and receive extra cash.

MERIT SCHOLARSHIPS

Merit scholarships are the most known and advertised scholarships of all. They are awarded to students for outstanding academic achievement, athletic achievement, leadership abilities, class rank, GPA, and test scores (SAT and ACT). Depending on the college, some may also take into account the financial need of a student. Check with the colleges you wish to attend to see what factors they consider in awarding scholarships. Remember, the more attractive you are to a college, the better the chance you have of receiving such a scholarship.

One of the most widely known merit scholarships that traditional students are eligible for is the National Merit Scholarship. The National Merit Scholarship Program (NMSP) began in 1955 and is funded by the NMSP program as well as 600 sponsor organizations—businesses, professional associations, colleges, and universities. Any full-time high school student with U.S. citizenship planning to attend college the following semester who takes the PSAT exam before his senior year is automatically eligible for the scholarship. The process starts in September, and finalists are announced in March of the school year. Scholarships are awarded either through the corporate sponsored program, the college sponsored program, or the NMSP in the amount of $2,500. Each year 7,900 students receive a NMSP award.

Scholarship Scams

Each year, scholarship companies and telemarketers claiming to have the answer to free education approach students. Of those students who respond, an average of 30 percent are victims of scholarship fraud. In fact, the number of reported incidents over the years resulted in the enactment of the Scholarship Fraud Prevention Act of 2000. This law protects students and their families by increasing the penalties for perpetrators, acting on behalf of the student to retrieve any promised and unpaid money, and warning students against scams through websites and college brochures. To protect yourself from scholarship scams, here are some warning signs to look for.

"You can't find this information anywhere else."
Scholarship information is free and available to everyone. You can also get scholarship information from the sponsoring foundation, the financial aid office, your counselors, or the local library. If a company asks you to pay for free information, then they are probably illegitimate.

"It's guaranteed!"
A legitimate scholarship company would never guarantee students' success or promise students any amount of money. This is because the scholarship companies, or similar establishments, do not decide who gets the money—evaluation committees do. Evaluation committee members have no direct relation with fraudulent schol-

arship companies. Evaluation committees abide by strict regulations set by the sponsoring foundation. They don't just give money away because you applied. If a scholarship company offers guaranteed success, be assured they are a guaranteed bust.

"We'll do the work for you, for a fee."

Scholarship applications are hard work and require time. Most scholarships ask for information about you; you will do a better job of providing this than a company working for a fee. Companies that are willing to do the work for you—complete your application, write your essays, and gather your recommendations—are probably going to be around just long enough to collect your money and move on.

"Millions of scholarships go unclaimed each year."

This claim is usually made by scholarship search companies to lure clients hoping to find mysterious scholarships. The fact that scholarship money is still available does not mean that the scholarship company has the edge on information. If there is a scholarship that has not been awarded, it is because the colleges/sponsors have not found suitable candidates. Generally, the scholarship criterion deals with specific characteristics or unpopular topics such as fruit breeding. Students don't always meet such specific criteria.

OTHER

Not all scholarship companies are illegal, however. Some are actually quite productive. Although we recommend not using a scholarship search company, if you choose to hire a scholarship company, you should look for key elements:

- Government regulations ensure that legitimate companies buy licenses, register, and adhere to minimum standards. This means that legal companies have telephone numbers for questions and inquiries. They must have a business address, not a PO Box or residential address. When hiring a company, wait a few weeks, then call them back and see if they are still active.

- Legal companies do not dramatize their results or claim to have influence with sponsors.

- After you decide on a company, scrutinize it. If the company is acting on behalf of a nonprofit organization or a federal agency, use extreme caution. Either type of establishment does *not* solicit individuals, and the latter does not endorse private organizations.

- Company names that piggyback on the U.S. Department of Education or Chamber of Commerce are often fraudulent.

- Always ask the solicitor for evidence of their success and substantiated awards. Most legal organizations can provide you with contacts, actual scholarship recipients, addresses, and names.

- Check the Better Business Bureau and search for opinions on the Internet to assure the company does not have a foul reputation.

If the company demands an immediate response and insists that you are delaying the process, hang up or walk away. They are just bullying you into making a hasty purchase. Finally, ignore requests to have access to your bank accounts, credit card numbers, or other information about your personal belongings, assets, or properties. A scholarship company does not need to have access to this information.

Starting Points

Hopefully, you are ready to begin the scholarship search. The best places to start are the financial aid office at your selected college, local libraries, college libraries, community newsletters, guidance counselors, academic departments, and the city newspaper. To help you along your journey, here are a few starting points.

BOOKS

Sports Scholarships and Athletic Programs by the Peterson Learning Center is a good resource guide that lists thousands of scholarships for the athletically inclined.

How to Go to College for Almost Free: The Secrets of Winning Scholarship Money by Benjamin R. Kaplan is directed toward high school students and offers insight into obtaining scholarships.

Scholarships and Loans for Adult Students by the Peterson Learning Center provides direction and guidance to both under-graduate and graduate adult students.

The Scholarship Book 2002 by Daniel J. Cassidy is filled with various types of scholarships, fellowships, and grants.

SCHOLARSHIP DATABASES

If reading a book is not the way you like to do research, then you can go online and use scholarship databases. You enter résumé details into a database that matches you to possible scholarships. A word of caution—because database queries are specific, they often do not show potential scholarships. For instance, if a scholarship calls for a 3.5 GPA and you have a 3.48 GPA, the database might consider you ineligible.

A combination of books and online databases yields the most comprehensive results. A more complete listing of scholarship resources can be found at the back of this book.

ORGANIZATIONS

The following are well-noted academic/merit scholarship foundations:

- Coca-Cola

- National Merit

- Intel Science

- American Legion

- Rotary

- Robert C. Byrd Honors

- National Academies for Science and Engineering

- Fulbright Foundation

- Woodrow Wilson

The following are prominent ethnic, cultural, racial, and minority organizations:

- Japanese American Citizens' League

- National Hispanic Association

- Native American Associations

- African American Associations

- American Council for the Blind

- American Disabilities Association

A Few Hints

To get the most out of your scholarship hunt, here are a few hints:

- Apply for scholarships that match your skill set. By applying for scholarships that focus on your aptitudes, you have a higher chance of winning out.

- Apply for at least ten scholarships each college year. Although ten may seem like a lot of effort, this will increase your chances for receiving one.

- Read all instructions and complete your forms accurately. Incorrect or poorly entered information can result in your disqualification.

- Prioritize your scholarships. Make a list of your opportunities, then rank them according to your preferences. If possible, consider renewable scholarships first.

- Choose the right references. When you need a reference, ask someone you know will have something good to say about you.

- Keep trying. The scholarship process is a game—sometimes you win, sometimes you don't. But you have to always keep trying and remember your goal—debt-free college.

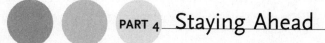

PART 4 Staying Ahead

CHAPTER ELEVEN

Eighteen Additional Strategies

Not all students start college on the same economic field. Traditional students generally have support from family and relatives, which makes it easier to maintain an asset base. Independent and adult students may not have the same size of an asset base as a traditional student due to other financial obligations. An international student may need a bigger asset base because of unfavorable currency exchange rates. To spend one dollar might mean four units of the student's home currency.

Because each student and their respective economic standing are different, some of the alternatives presented thus far may have applied to you; others may not. In fact, you may still feel stretched and have a COA gap to fill. Here are a few additional methods to drive away debt.

- Budget and money management

- Expense management

- Expense PIE management

- More alternatives

Budget and Money Management

In part one, we discussed financial defense and offense. The defensive philosophy focuses on keeping money, recognizing spending patterns, and finding good values. This section builds upon the defensive philosophy by presenting alternatives to help you keep your money and reach debt-free college.

BANKING

As a college student, you will have special banking needs that most banks do not offer. For instance, an average bank account requires a minimum checking balance, an ATM transaction processing fee, an electronic deposit fee, a customer service center call fee, and/or a bank teller assistance–processing fee. In addition, a bank might charge additional fees for online banking, money transfers, and monthly maintenance.

As a student, you may not be able to maintain a required minimum balance, pay a monthly banking fee, or other required fees. Thus, a student-friendly bank that caters to the needs of students is optimal. Most universities and colleges have local credit unions that specialize in student banking. These banks aim to please their primary clients—students. They frequently offer no-balance, no-fee checking accounts. Local credit unions usually do not charge monthly fees, require minimum balances greater than $0, or impose hefty check-processing fees. And because credit unions are local, you have access to credit union ATMs, thus reducing or eliminating ATM fees. By banking carefully, you can save up to $100 or more a month—that's $1,200 a year, or a semester's tuition, possibly.

Some ways to avoid banking fees and reduce daily cost management include:

- Not overdrawing on your account

- Keeping your checkbook balanced with your account

- Asking the bank before completing an unusual transaction—such as wiring money to a friend

- Writing checks only if needed—bouncing checks means a double fee—one from the bank and one from the vendor

PAY TUITION IN INSTALLMENTS

College tuition does not have to be paid as soon as you enroll. It's a lot like buying a refrigerator. You can go to the store and buy a refrigerator but make payments over a number of months—in installments. In a retail store, they charge you interest on the remaining balance. In universities, there is no interest on the balance.

Several colleges have tuition-installment programs where you can pay the tuition over the course of the entire academic year—ten to twelve months. Usually, once you make the necessary arrangements, there is a small grace period that allows you to do some quick budget shifting. This option delays the use of loans, alleviates the immediate burden of payment, and becomes part of your monthly expense.

For instance, if you have a $2,000 tuition bill, instead of borrowing a loan at 5 percent, you can budget to pay $167 each month for 12 months. This small amount can be easily managed by forfeiting a few luxuries—clothes, fine dining, and vacations. Also, this can save you $100 or more of loan interest.

SAVE WISELY

As you approach college, save as heavily as you can. In other words, build your asset base. If you save wisely and put your money in places that yield good returns, your asset base will be protected. To most people, the meaning of "good returns" varies. High risk can provide high returns. Low risk usually guarantees a return. Whatever you choose to do, remember to keep a balance between high-risk and low-risk investments in order to meet your economic needs. In other words, don't put all your eggs into one basket.

As you are saving, keep in mind that some savings accounts can count against you during the financial aid process. If you plan to be a financial aid applicant, avoid prepaid tuition plans. If you don't plan to be a financial aid applicant, choose the savings plan that best meets your needs. And remember that savings plans under your parents' names are treated less severely than those saved under your name. If you have any questions about how something is calculated, visit the websites listed in the appendix.

The key to saving successfully is to set a target savings amount. By setting a target, you can measure your progress and stay on track for debt-free college. The target amount you choose should be one half of the current tuition cost at your selected college. If you haven't decided on a college, then use the College Board's estimates.

For instance, if tuition currently averages $14,000 at private institutions and you are planning on attending a private institution, you should save $7,000 per year. Over four years, that is $28,000. Or go backward, starting at the four-year figure, and determine when and how much you need to contribute to your COA. If you can't build such an asset base, shoot for just the first two years— $7,000 to $14,000.

One savings option is to invest in a CollegeSure CD. The CollegeSure CD is benchmarked against the Independent College (IC) index. The IC index measures the inflationary cost of college tuition. For more information on this CD and others, visit *www. collegesavings.com.*

Other options include money-market funds, short-term U.S. Treasury bills, and bonds. Although these options are not the solution to all four years of college, they generally offer steady income and higher interest rates than a regular savings account. If you need more choices, consider Educational IRAs, Series EE bonds, and tax-deferral savings plans.

TRIVIA: In a science experiment, college students were matched against lab rats to see which one would learn to navigate through a maze faster. The experiment showed that rats learned three times faster than the students—*www.funtrivia.com*

Expense Management

Remember the balance sheet and the income statement? Well, the next few strategies will help you make your balance sheet and income statement look and feel better. The following options will decrease unexpected liabilities and increase your cash flow. In the long run, they will help keep you away from a destructive spending pattern.

PAY FOR NOTHING

As a student, your income is probably lower than your expenses. One way to reduce your expenses is to pay for nothing, except the five cost components—tuition and fees, room and board, books and supplies, transportation, and personal expenses. As a college student, all your expenses should focus foremost on the cost of attending college.

This means that accessories such as cell phones, pagers, and Palm Pilots should be avoided. A monthly cell phone bill is a liability that a college student's budget cannot support. The "necessity" of a Palm Pilot can be easily remedied with paper, a pencil, and some time management skills. Another example is finding ways to reduce transportation costs. If it will cost you less to use a city bus than to own a car, consider the possibility. If possible, avoid purchasing laptops, printers, and Internet services. Most of these requirements can be satisfied with the college resource centers.

AVOID CREDIT CARDS

Credit cards offer convenience and easy access to immediate cash. But as friendly as they may seem, they often lead to impulse-buying and can cloud your focus. In fact, *bankrate.com* reports that in the year 2000:

> 78 percent of college students had at least one credit card. The average credit card debt per student was $2,748.

Add interest to the balance over a few months and you have enough debt to keep you busy well into your mid-thirties!

If you are unfamiliar with the world of credit cards, educate yourself. It is important to know that "0% interest" does not truly exist, even if advertised, and that credit card companies use different accrual methods. Here are some hints to avoid credit card debt:

- Limit yourself to *one* low-interest rate card.

- Repress impulse buys.

- Use it only when needed—emergencies (Friday night beer tab is *not* an emergency).

- Educate yourself on how credit cards and their balance system works.

- Charge only what you can reasonably afford to pay.

- Avoid interest payments.

For additional details on managing credit cards or learning the basics of credit cards visit:

MORE INFORMATION

www.discovercard.com

www.americanexpress.com

www.mbna.com

www.capitalone.com

www.citibank.com

www.bankrate.com

TELEPHONE BILLS

An average of 350 million people use the Internet at any given time. In fact, for many people, the Internet is now the preferred method of communication. So join the bandwagon and use online chat rooms and email as an alternative to expensive, long-distance phone calls. Almost all major telephone companies offer Internet services for a monthly fee of $20, which is far below the average long-distance bill of $75 to $100 dollars a month. And if you use the university's resources, you don't even have to pay the $20.

If you must use long distance, avoid calling during normal business hours. Hold all long conversations after 8 P.M. (when rates are lower) and choose programs with no monthly fees. Telephone companies, like banks and credit card companies, impose monthly fees, late-payment fees, and other service fees. As you pay each bill, carefully review the charges, or you may end up like Ryan:

Ryan had a girlfriend in Australia. He just had to talk to her ever so often. So he worked out a deal with the telephone company to make international calls at $0.89 a minute. One month later, Ryan received an $810 bill in the mail. When he called to ask the telephone company, they explained to him that as part of the deal, there were other addendums that amounted to $405 in processing fees.

Instead of calling, Ryan could have written letters and spent only $2 per letter. Or he could have sent emails or instant messages from the campus computer lab for free.

Another option is to purchase prepaid calling cards. Prepaid calling cards can be bought for any denomination—$5, $10, $15, $20, etc.—and you don't have to pay telephone initiation or other monthly fees. With prepaid calling cards, you have the flexibility to spend money wisely.

You can also use web telephone companies to manage long-distance bills—*Onesuite.com* is one such Internet company that allows you to do this.

OUTFITTING YOUR PLACE OF RESIDENCE

As exciting as it may be to have your own place, apartment or otherwise, spend your rent money wisely. Avoid excessive decorating. Shy away from unnecessary purchases like lavish curtains or fine furniture. Over the course of their life, the average American moves around ten to fifteen times. You will have plenty of future opportunities to decorate and add a personal touch. But college is your time to save, protect your asset base, and graduate debt-free. Another way to reduce cost is to coordinate with your roommate(s).

For instance, if your roommate has a microwave, you can offer to buy a vacuum cleaner. This way, you reduce your cost *and* help your roommate.

Expense PIE Management

College debt comes from five cost components—tuition and fees, room and board, books, transportation, and personal expenses. Taken together, these costs can be viewed as your Expense PIE. For debt-free college, you have to manage your EP.

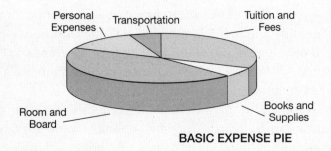

BASIC EXPENSE PIE

TUITION AND FEES

It is true that you cannot directly control the cost of tuition, but you can, however, minimize spending in this area. When you select your courses for the semester, make sure they are what you need. Avoid dropping courses in the middle of the semester or after classes begin.

Dropping classes increases cost in the short run *and* in the long run. In the short run, you lose the money you paid for the course. In the long run, you are forced to stay an extra semester or take summer classes—both of which increase your COA. Here are a few things you can do to avoid falling into the trap:

- Audit the course you plan to take. Most institutions allow students to sit in a class, observe the course material, and listen to the instructor for free. You are not included as part of the grading process, and you receive the benefit of enrolling only in the classes you need or like. In this manner, you avoid paying for an unnecessary course.

- Take only the classes you need. Even though you haven't decided on your specific field of study, try to focus on taking courses that are still transferable and credit-applicable. If you know you want to be a business major but you don't know what you like better—marketing or accounting—do some research. Check to see if accounting classes count as electives for marketing and vice versa. This allows you to take more classes without having to earn extra credit for other degree electives, thereby reducing your COA.

- If you must drop a course, do so quickly. By waiting till the first mid-term to see how you fare and then withdrawing, you waste valuable time, effort, and money. If you drop within the first two weeks, you can often collect an 80 percent refund of the initial course fee. You can use that money for the next semester.

- Avoid summer classes. Summer tuition at colleges/universities usually costs more than the fall/spring semesters. This is because it costs the universities more to hire faculty, keep resources open, and maintain facilities for a smaller pool of students. If you must take summer classes, consider correspondence or transferable community college courses. These fees are usually lower.

ROOM AND BOARD

Aside from tuition and fees, housing is the biggest piece of the EP. One way to maintain low-cost housing is to stay in college housing, where meals, utilities, and rent are lumped into a single payment. In addition, other costs such as decorating, obtaining furniture, and providing maintenance are negligible or nonexistent. In general, living in college housing is cost efficient.

If college housing is not an option for you, seek roommates to help reduce your rent and utilities costs. Or if you like the city, buy a house and rent part of it to help pay for the mortgage. Also, you can choose to rent a room in someone's house or live with a parent, relative, or a friend.

Also, remember that where the college is located can impact the cost of housing as well. The cost of living in some cities is more expensive than other cities. For instance, living in New York would cost almost two and a half times more than living in Dallas. So if you are attending college in an expensive city, take into consideration that the housing piece of the PIE just went from medium to large.

BOOKS AND SUPPLIES

Books are a critical part of your education, and so are supplies. New books are nice to have, but to reduce costs, buy used books; you can even buy them from friends who already took the course or upperclassmen who will sell their books for less than the bookstores. Consider sharing the cost of a textbook with another classmate and arrange it so you can both use the book when needed.

During my senior year, I took Aerospace Engineering, an upper-division elective, for which the book acted as a reference and lectures provided most of the education. Because my friend and I were taking this course together, we split the cost of the used book and swapped as needed. At the end of the course, we sold the book to another student and got back almost half of our original cost—and we both aced the course.

Aside from the basic school supplies, desktop and laptop computers have now become a vital part of the college curriculum. Unless it is required, however, you can save money by not purchasing a personal computer.

Colleges usually provide students with computer labs at no extra charge. As a graduate student, however, you may be forced to own a computer. In this situation, consider purchasing a refurbished computer. All major PC providers—Dell, Compaq, and Gateway—offer refurbished equipment. Refurbished computers can reduce the price tag and help you maintain a healthy EP.

TRANSPORTATION

This category varies significantly for each person and may or may not be a cost component. Some students choose to fly home every so often. If you are a frequent traveler, watch for bargains. Look for buy-one-get-one-free ticket deals and join one of the many frequent-flyer airline membership programs. Try to purchase your tickets well in advance, as this usually lowers the price. Also, travel during nonpeak seasons and use the lower-priced airlines—Southwest, Midway, or Kiwi. Also, watch for airline warfare, which usually happens at least once a year. Another option is to use bus lines. You can save money by riding the bus or local metro rail instead of flying. Finally, carpooling with a buddy who is traveling in the same direction is a cost-cutting approach.

PERSONAL EXPENSES

College becomes affordable by managing basic costs. By adopting the right mind-set and setting spending patterns, you can reduce the everyday cost of attending college. To manage cost effectively, you can:

- Bargain shop. Always look for sales. If you have a choice between spending $35 or $10 on a clothing item, take the lower price.

- Cut coupons. If you are smart and shop during double- or triple-coupon days, you can save even more.

- Inquire about student discounts—many businesses offer up to 10 percent off with a student ID.

- Give inexpensive gifts and avoid high-priced entertainment and food.

- Use resources that you already have. Resources include computers, libraries, cafeterias, and student activity centers. Almost all colleges and universities provide these resources for free. Instead of buying a computer, eating out all the time, or spending extra money to meet people, use what the college provides.

More Alternatives

The last few options are not applicable to the entire student body. Some options will benefit traditional students; others may benefit nontraditional students or parents of college students. With some thought and planning, they may be able to help you a lot.

A LITTLE WORK CAN GO A LONG WAY

A paycheck is a paycheck, whether it is $5 or $50 an hour. It is needed cash flow for your everyday needs. Generally, students do not experience difficulty in finding temporary employment such as waiting tables, retail store assistance, or filing papers in an office. Hopefully, you will seek employment that complements your education and offers higher pay. Some viable options include:

- Assisting a faculty member with research

- On-campus computer/science lab technician

- College librarian assistant

- Tutors (private and group)

- College tour guides

If you find that none of these jobs are suitable, focus on your extracurricular interests. If you are highly active or have special talents, seek employment that develops that special interest and provides cash flow. A few choices include:

- Student body president

- Newspaper editor

- Student organization leader

One of the more profitable and engaging jobs often overlooked is resident advisor. College dormitories need resident advisors to manage college housing, monitor student activity, and ensure that college rules are followed. For performing these duties, colleges pay for the cost of room and board—sometimes part of it, sometimes all of it. In addition, some colleges offer a monthly stipend for everyday expenses. This can eliminate 40 to 60 percent of your overall COA. To become a resident advisor, contact the campus-housing department at your selected college.

VOLUNTEER ORGANIZATIONS

Community service organizations are a wonderful way to receive scholarships, grants, and fellowships.

The Corporation of National Service (CNS) was initiated as early as 1910 to improve bad conditions in the community—illiteracy, poverty, crime, and the environment. As part of its mission, the CNS grants fellowships and other scholarships through its major initiatives—AmeriCorps, Learn and Serve America, and National Senior Service Corps—to volunteers.

Each organization is focused on specific items, and each has its own rules and regulations. This means the grants and fellowships have different requirements, and the amounts vary from one organization to another. The awards range from $100 to $4,500 and depend on the length of service, the type of service, and other achievements. Listed below are a few details about the organizations and the awards. Contact the organizations to learn more information.

- The Corporation of National Service offers internships in state offices and Washington, D.C., as well as fellowships in specific programs. For further details, visit *www.cns.gov.*

- AmeriCorps gives awards through AmeriCorps*VISTA (Volunteers in Service to America) and AmeriCorps*NCCC (the National Civilian Community Corps). AmeriCorps participants can receive up to $4,725 for their term of service. Participants can receive a maximum of two awards totaling $9,450. Visit *www.americorps.org* or *www.friendsofvista.org* for more details.

- Learn and Serve America promotes academic skills and awards grants and scholarships to volunteers. Visit *www.cns.gov* for more details.

Other service organizations include the Department of Veteran Affairs, which offers awards to veterans and their children. Visit *www.va.gov* for more details.

TUITION TAX CREDITS

Tax credits are one way to recover part of your COA costs. In the late 1990s, the government established the HOPE Scholarship and Lifetime Learning Tax Credit to help students and their families with tuition and fees. At the beginning of each year, participants can subtract a predetermined amount from their total federal income tax bill.

The two tax credits can be used in conjunction but can only be used once for each person. For instance, one student cannot claim both the HOPE Scholarship and the Lifetime Learning Tax Credit at the same time; it can only be one or the other. The following table compares the difference between the two options.

If you want to learn more about the tax credits and how they can be applied, visit *www.irs.ustreas.gov/prod/forms_pubs/pubs/p970toc.htm*.

	HOPE SCHOLARSHIP	LIFETIME-LEARNING TAX CREDIT
What is it?	—$1,500 maximum tax credit per year **per dependent student**	—$1,000 maximum tax credit **per family**
Who is eligible?	—Parents of a dependent student —Only undergraduate students	—Those who meet the requirements —Graduate and undergraduate students
When can it be applied?	—Only during the first two years of postsecondary education —More than one student —Limited to two years —After December 31, 1997	—Any time during the course of education —Once for entire family —No limit to the number of years it can be used —After June 30, 1998
Requirements	—Must use only one of the tax credits —Enrolled at least half-time —Enrolled in a program leading to a degree —No felony convictions	—Must use only one of the tax credits —Enrolled in one or more courses at an eligible institution —No felony convictions
Qualified expenses	—Only tuition and fees as noted by the IRS —Tax-free grants —Tax-free scholarships	—Only tuition and fees as noted by the IRS —Tax-free grants —Tax-free scholarships

PREPAID TUITION

One option directed toward parents is prepaid tuition plans. These plans allow parents to buy their children's education at current prices. Parents save from their present income for the upcoming years in an interest-bearing plan. The parents pay for the four-year college education either in monthly installments or in a one-time payment. As the student approaches college, the bills have already been paid. But keep in mind that investing in a prepaid plan does not guarantee college admission.

The advantage of a prepaid tuition plan is that it hedges the price of education against inflation and locks in current tuition and fee prices for future college attendee(s). Moreover, there is a huge tax benefit. The plans are often exempt from local and state taxes until redemption, at which point taxes apply to the person using the proceeds—the student. Because students are in a lower tax bracket, this is an added bonus.

However, a few words of caution are necessary. The plans are valuable only if the projected COA increases by 5 percent and future candidates are willing to attend in-state colleges. Prepaid plans can only be used at public institutions. If for any reason the attendee does not attend college or attends a nonparticipating institution, the parents may recover the original contribution, a portion of the interest, and if lucky, face no cancellation penalty.

Some state plans are generous and are transferable to other siblings. Also, prepaid plans reduce federal aid eligibility because they count the plans as expected contribution. The need formula treats the plan savings as a 100 percent contribution, and you may not receive any financial support. Also keep this in mind:

- Prepaid plans are reported as resources, not assets, thereby decreasing federal aid eligibility potential.

- Prepaid tuition plans are safe, low-risk, low-return (6 to 8 percent) tax-advantage investments.

- Prepaid tuition limits the student's college selection list.

- Taxes are due only upon redemption on the increase of share value.

DELAY THE NEXT STEP

After completing twelve years of education, many students are not quite ready for yet another four (or more) years of school. College doesn't necessarily have to follow high school. Taking some time off to consider other options—working, traveling, or starting a business—can be a great thing. Education is valuable, and it will be ready whenever you are. Work for a year to save money—spend a year working in an area that interests you before you start college. This way you will get an idea of what you like and what you don't. Deferred admission, meaning you apply now but start the following year, is another good option.

TURN HOBBIES INTO MONEY

There is no better way to make money than by doing what you like most. Hobbies and active interests are an effective way to make money—perhaps small amounts at first.

Laurie is a small-time artist. She enjoys painting. Since she started college, she has been using her talent to pay for her nights out on the town. She runs a small ad in the college newsletter and in the local city newspaper for a few dollars a month. As a result, she now paints portraits of people's pets for a small sum. This sum covers her advertising costs and pays for her entertainment, all the while increasing her talent.

John has played the piano for years. When he needed spending money for car maintenance, he decided to put his talent to work. He now makes money by playing the piano during college events such as graduation, initiations, and award ceremonies. He makes enough money to pay for his car expenses.

If you have any hobbies, think of creative ways to piggyback off your talent to make money for debt-free college. Such creativity helps you meet two goals at one time—debt-free college and developing your talent.

CHAPTER TWELVE

The Surprising Truth About Compound Interest

Jason had a new Nissan sports car. It was black, and it was the nicest car that anyone in the dorm drove. No one knew if he made the payments himself. Everyone assumed his parents did.

Everyone knew about Jason's car, but no one seemed to know about his individual retirement account (IRA). He had $6,000 in an IRA. None of my friends had ever made a financial investment besides a bank account or a certificate of deposit (CD). But no one ever stopped to tell Jason that "investing is for adults." Jason had more money than the others in the dorm, but his IRA was assurance that he was going to have a lot more in the future, too. He was already making moves on a game that everyone else had not even begun.

Filling the Tub

Mr. Stanley, a high school economics teacher, presents an analogy about accumulating wealth:

> Accumulating money is a lot like filling a tub. If your goal is to fill the tub up with water, there are several ways you can do it. The first way is to start early. If you do start early, then you just have to put a teaspoon in every week. Then, in twenty years, the bathtub

is almost full and the work in filling it seems inconsequential. If, instead, you choose to wait eighteen or twenty years, then during the last two years, you have to pour buckets and buckets of water to fill it up. That is a lot of work.

Mr. Stanley's scenario is intriguing. But there is one thing that does not make sense. In Mr. Stanley's scenario, whether you fill the tub slowly or quickly, you have to put in the same amount of water. Similarly, some students choose to study three or four nights in a row before a test, and some choose to pull all-nighters. Either way, they exert about the same amount of energy. Something is missing from Mr. Stanley's scenario.

MISSING ELEMENT

The part of the equation that the "filling the tub" scenario does not account for is the *time value of money,* or **compound interest.** Compound interest means that your money earns interest, then you earn interest on that interest. This is a better story:

Accumulating money is a lot like filling a tub. If your goal is to fill your tub with water, there are several ways you can do it. The first way is to start early. If you do start early, then put a teaspoon in every week. The nice thing is that the teaspoon has a special power. When you use the teaspoon, it charms the water so that the water reproduces on its own. So if you put a teaspoon in today, then in seven years' time, that teaspoon of water magically becomes two teaspoons of water—on its own.

This happens for each teaspoon you put in. In twenty years, the bathtub is overflowing, and your effort in filling it has been almost inconsequential. The other way to go about filling the tub is to wait. If you wait many years, then the only way you will be able to fill the tub is with a big bucket. The bucket, however, has no magic. You get the privilege of doing all the work of filling the tub instead of letting the water increase on its own. If you are lucky, you might be able to fill it to the top. End of story.

There are no such things as charmed spoons; however, time really *does* charm money. Time will, on the average, double your money every seven years if you make a decent financial investment. The effects of an IRA, sheltered from taxes, are even more powerful. Jason had already put 6,000 teaspoons into his tub, while everyone else had not even put one teaspoon into theirs.

SECRET #70

Time charms money.

When you build an IRA, you build financial independence. Because people are changing jobs more frequently these days, there is far less opportunity for lifelong pension plans. You might be heading straight for the poor farm if you *don't* have an IRA.

LEARN TO SEE THE FUTURE NOW

Most people, when they understand the concrete facts of an IRA, want to own one. The problem is being able to see into the future while living in the present. It is a lot easier to want to go to an exotic city in Spain right now than it is to invest money. However, you don't want to become old and poor!

SECRET #71

To be poor while you are young is an inconvenience. To be poor while you are old is a tragedy.

What you are doing today decides where you spend tomorrow. You are either getting closer to or farther from success every day.

TRIVIA: In 1994, ten-year-old Michael Kearney, the youngest college graduate ever, received a bachelor's from the University of South Alabama—
www.uselessknowledge.com

The Rate of Return

In case you are still unsure, the numerical justification of owning an IRA follows. Let's continue to use Jason as an example. Let's say he just had his twentieth birthday and ignore the $6,000 he already has invested. Let's also assume Jason contributes $2,000 a year to a Roth IRA every year until he is sixty years old, with an average interest rate of 5 percent.

That is forty years of contributing $2,000. This is a face value of $80,000 (40 × 2,000). The compound interest, however, makes the final account value $253,680. "Not bad," you say? Consider that 5 percent is quite a low return. If you are willing to take a bit of risk, you should have no problem getting a return that averages twice that amount—10 percent. Take a look at a variety of returns based on different average rates of interest.

Jason, twenty years old, invests $2,000 a year in a Roth IRA until he is sixty:

RATE OF RETURN	5%	7%	10%	12%
With Compound Interest	$253,680	$427,219	$973,704	$1,718,285

This assumes that Jason is in a 28 percent tax bracket. Unless you have a strong fear of the stock market, or unless America sputters over the next fifty years, you should be able to achieve an average of somewhere between 8 to 12 percent. The calculations were done using a Roth IRA calculator at the myFICO website, *www.myfico.com/MyFICO/CreditCentral/Calculators/Retirement/ RothIRA.htm.*

A nice thing about IRAs is that Jason actually gets to *keep* that money at the end. He doesn't have to pay half of it back to the government like many other people will be doing. IRAs are tax sheltered. Therein lies the profound advantage of the Roth IRA.

By now you are screaming, "What does this have to do with getting through college debt-free?!" Well, whereas it is true that there is seldom such a thing as spare money to invest in an IRA while you are in college, it is also true that you do not have to dedicate many thousands of dollars to an IRA. You can start simple—maybe give only $500 a year. The important thing is to begin playing the game as soon as possible. Even making a few simple moves now adds up to a big gain in the future.

THE PIE OF A FUTURE MILLIONAIRE

You do not have to kill yourself to become a millionaire. It is not a super-fast process, but it is straightforward. Sarah earns $40,000 after taxes, and faithfully invests $2,000 of that amount in an IRA every year. If she continues her contributions as Jason did, she will eventually become a millionaire by simply saving 5 percent of her income. Sarah's PIE would look like this:

THE PIE OF A MILLIONAIRE

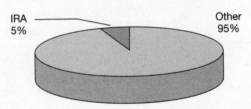

IRA
5%

Other
95%

By paying a small price over a number of years, Sarah achieves financial independence. You might argue that not everyone makes $40,000 after taxes, so it is not that easy to contribute $2,000 a year to an IRA. You would be right, but it is also true that if you have a lower income, you pay fewer dollars in taxes, which should allow you to find enough of your paycheck to secure your financial future.

Who Wants to Be a Millionaire?

College is generally four years, but there is a lot of life after that. You can set habits as a student that will lead to a debt-free life.

Since you have read this far, you and debt are probably not best friends. You can beat debt your entire life if you start early, and college is one of the first real chances for you to take a crack at it. Once you are beating debt, you may find yourself reaching for even more.

There is a fad show on TV called *Who Wants to Be a Millionaire?* The name of the show is attention-grabbing. Very few people ever become millionaires on the show, though. In truth, becoming a millionaire only takes a few teaspoons of money into your IRA and some time.

SECRET #72

Become a millionaire a few teaspoons at a time.

The effects of your IRA's tax-free growth are so powerful that if you actually have a low-interest college loan, you may come out ahead by going into debt—if you use the extra cash you have to invest. The positive benefits of your tax-free compound interest may outweigh the harm of a low-interest loan. Basically, if you are paying 5 percent in interest but are receiving 10 percent and keep it tax-free, you are still coming out ahead. This is one case where debt is not as harmful as failing to invest.

The Opposite of Equity

You have seen the power of interest accumulation with the IRA example. If we turn the tables and reverse the scenario above, you will see how destructive debt is. Instead of contributing $2,000, say Jason borrows $2,000 a year until he is sixty at 12 percent interest.

Jason can expect to pay more than $1,500,000 over time instead of the $80,000 face value that he borrowed. Simple credit card balances such as $500 have the same effect.

For many people, Jason's black Nissan would have been a point of jealously. Most people would not care about Jason's $6,000 in an IRA, but they would want his car. This is the type of thinking that debt-ridden people share. They focus on things that are fun and flashy instead of things that lead to economic health. Expensive things are generally luxuries—they count heavily against your financial health. Liabilities are always more than happy to chauffeur you straight to the poor farm.

FORGET THE JONESES

Not everyone plays on the same economic field. Jason probably came from a wealthy family, but most other dorm dwellers did not. Avoid the trap of comparing apples to oranges by learning not to compare your purchases with everyone else's.

It is true that those who buy nice things are glorified in our society, but it is not worth your personal debt to get that glorification. Nobody will be crowding around when you are too broke to buy a new pair of socks. You must know the consequences of your present actions—then you must take action.

If you know you will succumb to temptation, do not introduce it. If you are a window-shopper, stay away from windows. If you love expensive cars, do not tempt yourself by going to car shows. You will probably drive many nice cars later in your life, but as a student, it should be your last priority. If you are tempted, just think about how much better it will feel to buy a nice car after you graduate debt-free, making a lot more money than you made as a student.

SECRET #73

Deliver yourself from temptation.

Do not fret about keeping up with the Joneses. You will only run yourself ragged and break yourself down. If you ever keep up with the Joneses, you will only discover that there is a new set of richer Joneses to keep up with. You will never lead a satisfying life if you let yourself be dominated by an endless, financially destructive chase. Instead, take control of your possessions and do not worry about keeping up.

CHAPTER THIRTEEN

Moving Past the Finish Line

Congratulations! You now know how to achieve a quality education without a lifetime of debt. Assuming you have done your financial homework along the way, the solution to a debt-free education should seem straightforward. More important, you have the tools to make it happen.

Another Look at the Debt-Free Equation

Hopefully, this equation looks familiar. This is the same equation that was introduced in chapter one.

THE BASIC DEBT-FREE EQUATION

Four elements of debt-free college			
Choosing an affordable college	Saving money before entering college	Earning income during college	Keeping what you earn

You should feel differently about this equation, just like you will feel differently once you begin to put the concepts to work. The equation helps you develop a plan and reflect on your progress in segments. By now, you should have analyzed your circumstances using the tools provided throughout the book. If you haven't already, now is the time to act. Take a look at each piece of the equation, use the balance sheet and income statement, and begin mapping a route to your debt-free future.

"Thinking" about something does little good. Putting it down in a plan; using words, numbers, and forecasting does a lot of good. When you are *numerically* conscious of each box in the equation, you will learn to think in terms of what you need and what you can reasonably afford. After you evaluate the cost/benefit, you will realize that a private prestigious university, a fraternity house, or even the latest Nikes are not as crucial as a quality education and a debt-free future.

Getting Started

Now is the time to sit down and plan. You must start on your path. When you finally arrive, you will prove that completing an education without ending up in the poor house really is possible—even easy.

THE LIFE OF THE EQUATION

The debt-free equation will follow you even after graduation, but it will become more complex. When you are younger and unworried about retirement (and have fewer people depending on you), the planning process is simpler. There are fewer variables when you have only yourself to consider and a lifetime ahead of you.

This is why it is so important to master the equation while you are in college. Doing so will give you the opportunity to graduate in a good financial position. Then you can apply the same concepts in your working life and do even better. You will be able to find a financial balance and prosperity that habitual debtors will not have time to find, because they will be too busy paying off debts.

Your New Toolbox

As a student of geometry in high school, I had a teacher who used a metaphor throughout the year. The metaphor was a toolbox.

Does everybody remember how to find the area of a cone? *Remember,* all we have to do is take a tool from our toolbox and we can get the answer.

By the end of the year, everyone was storing lots of tools in their toolboxes. Whenever we were faced with a problem, we would sort through the tools in our minds until we could find the right tool to solve the problem. Thinking about solving problems by using tools from a toolbox helped us break things down into parts, analyze the parts, and use the correct formulas to solve the problem.

SECRET #74

Use your toolbox to make your budget fit your goal.

After you learn to live by a budget, you will have a powerful new tool in your toolbox. Not only will you be ahead of those who graduate with a lot of debt, you will be ready to get even farther ahead. And the habitual debtors with impressive salaries will still be floundering, not knowing how much they are earning after taxes, how much they are spending each month, how much they are saving, or even how much they need to save. They will not know any of those things, but they will be working harder and harder to pay off debt.

On the other hand, you will know where your money comes from and where it is spent. And with a college degree, you will have increased earning potential. You will feel more secure as you accumulate money faster and concentrate on the things that actually lead to happiness.

Emotional Learning

Though the idea of debt-free college is easy, the practice of good financial habits is an art. Debt-free principles are continually around us—but they are drowned by the loud consumerism that also surrounds us. Debt-free principles are easy to miss, which is exactly what most people do. As important as the logic and common sense behind the debt-avoiding philosophy is the **emotional learning.**

There is a big difference between passively reading something in the newspaper and actively evaluating something from a book. If you take the time to learn and think about a philosophy and to understand how it challenges your value system, you will begin not only to react *emotionally,* but in a different way than you have in the past. This is how beliefs are changed. Beliefs control our behavior.

Uncle Scrooge, Uncle Sam—a Balance

The ideas on finance that this book encourages are based on reevaluating what is necessary and what is luxury. If you must live in college housing that is old and smells of mildew when it rains, chances are you'll survive. And if you put up with a few faults such as those, you have the chance to beat debt.

Developing defense is crucial to beating debt. But if it is taken to an extreme, it will yield a negative effect—an unhappy life. You could become Ebenezer Scrooge, counting your money and thinking you are happy when you are actually miserable. In such a case, you will be a miser and you will chase people away, harming your personal growth. Or you could become Uncle Sam, an extravagant spender. If you are an extravagant spender and you have no extravagant source of income, you will quickly fall into the cycle of debt that so many other people have.

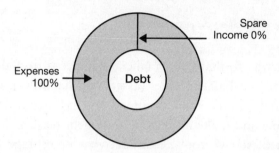

DESTRUCTIVE SPENDING PATTERN

As an extravagant spender, you will have material possessions but no time to enjoy them because you will be working your absolute hardest to pay the hefty bills that accompany your possessions. If you are Uncle Sam, money is controlling you because you are in a destructive spending pattern.

Being financially savvy comes from striking a balance between being Uncle Scrooge and Uncle Sam. It is not good to be either way, but to walk the thin line between the two is difficult. Everything in life is tied to money—going out with friends, traveling to see your family, traveling to see the world, pursuing hobbies, eating correctly, or buying a gift for your boyfriend or girlfriend on their birthday. But these are the kinds of things that make life important. If you were to give up these things entirely, you would not be a happy person. You might not miss them at first, but you would miss them later on.

If you find yourself becoming overprotective of your money like Uncle Scrooge or gambling your future away like Uncle Sam, stop and reevaluate your situation. It could be the difference between debt-free college and the poor farm.

ACHIEVING BALANCE

Balance is essential if you want to control yourself and not let money control you. The idea of balance is supported by history. The ancient Greeks valued balance above all else, and so did the Chinese, who adopted the idea of the yin-yang.

SECRET #75

Balance will make you prosperous.

The best way to find your financial balance is to make a budget. First, start with a balance sheet (assets and liabilities); this will determine which schools you can attend and still avoid debt. Second, get an income and make an income statement (cash inflow and outflow). With these two tools, estimate what percentage of your PIE must go to monthly bills, what percentage you should save for big expenses like tuition, and what percentage you can safely spend as you wish.

Remember, if you want to graduate debt-free, you should aim for a desirable spending pattern.

DESIRABLE SPENDING PATTERN

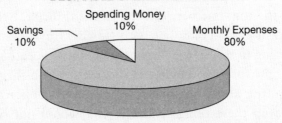

Spending Money 10%
Savings 10%
Monthly Expenses 80%

Then, after you graduate, you will be able to have a more flexible Expense PIE that looks like this:

DESIRABLE SPENDING PATTERN
(Post Graduation)

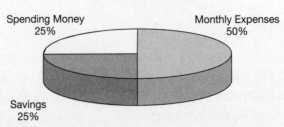

Spending Money 25%
Monthly Expenses 50%
Savings 25%

THE PURIFICATION EFFECT

There is an interesting side effect to learning good financial habits while in college. Good financial habits have the effect of taking the emphasis away from material goods. Whereas the ethics of materialism are for you to decide, the presence of materialism is definitely dangerous to debt-free college.

If you ask people, they will never admit to being materialistic. They will say that they have other values—education, family, religion, and health. As a freshman, I would have denied being materialistic, even though I was wearing Nikes, Gap Jeans, and Ray Ban sunglasses. But by the time I was a graduating senior, I was wearing unrecognizable shoes, generic jeans, and $5 sunglasses. Because I was my only source of income, I came to realize that every penny spent on luxuries was taking away from my ability to pay tuition. By graduation, I had a beat-up car and generic clothes—no one could accuse me of being materialistic.

Once you have aligned your goals and actions, you will find a new kind of balance and satisfaction. You will find your own process as you develop your independence and make room for other sentiments in life—self-denial and fortitude. Through self-denial and fortitude, you will eventually make yourself financially free. The more quickly you begin to develop your financial thinking, the faster you will progress. Correct mindset is the most important element to any undertaking.

By working toward debt-free college, you will experience a strong purification by setting a goal, establishing priorities, and laboring to accomplish. Through your purification, you will likely find that it makes you happy to save a portion of your income. Eventually, such saving will lead to your financial liberation.

Beyond Four Years

You will feel fantastic when you graduate without debt. You will not feel the pressure of having to find a job immediately; in fact, you will be able to take enough time to find an employer who will treat you well. You will not have to face the stress and pain of staying ahead of debt and bills from month to month. You will know that you can control your spending, and if you were to lose your job, you would be able to live for a long time without a paycheck. You will feel even better when you begin to move toward financial independence, which will be easier for you because you will not have the ball and chain of having to pay back enormous student loans.

More important, your years in college will be stepping-stones to a better financial position in life. When your friends ask how you are able to save money and accumulate wealth, you will be able to tell them just how naturally and easily you did it.

- Learned to shift financial thinking

- Learned to control your emotions

As you see many people slipping into debt while you lift yourself into wealth, you will feel proud. While debtors succumb to bad spending habits, you, on the other hand, will have laid a massive foundation that will allow you to build something great.

SECRET #76

Beating debt requires intellectual and emotional control.

Your friends probably will prefer to believe you have some trick. They will think that it is something you have invested in or your high annual income. When you tell them it is merely that you have learned to shift your financial thinking, they will be bored and go off to look for other people to ask instead of you. Let them go.

You will know that the journey to beating debt lies in your mind-set. Everyone knows that if you take in more money than you spend, you do not go into debt. Fewer people understand how it feels to live that way. Very few people manage to do it. There are many temptations. Temptations play with the ego and the emotions, and the topic of money is filled with emotion. Emotions introduce confusion; confusion destroys goals.

Everyone knows that if you save money you will have more money and less debt. But because you will be living that way, your values will have developed in a different way. You will actually understand what it means to avoid debt. It is a lot like fighting in a war. We have all seen movies and know what a war is, but until we have actually fought in one, we do not actually understand war. Your job is to use what you have learned from this book to go out and begin fighting the war for debt-free college.

COLLEGE IS NOT JUST MONEY

Though you seek a debt-free education, there are other parts to being successful and happy. When you compare family, friends, or health to finance, finance isn't important at all. Make no mistake; if you ignore health, friends, or spirituality for the sake of finance, you're on a dangerous road.

If you ask people about their memories of college, you will find that they never dwell upon the nice restaurants they went to, the fancy clubs they frequented, or the cars they drove. Instead, they refer to the friends they made, the student events they led, and sometimes a few favorite professors they had. They usually do not have many stories about the things that cost money. Instead, they have stories about the relationships they made and the causes they served. In the end, spending money is not what makes college memorable. It is actually the things that are free and that surround us all the time that make the difference. Those things are usually relationships and causes, which are things that are worth investing time in.

Of course, unless you have control of your money and savings, you will not be able to support your family or friends when they need help, nor will you be able to afford birthday gifts. That is exactly why it is important to think about money—so you can form your habits and then quit thinking about money.

Once you have the debt-free mind-set, you will have a wealth of time left over to meet people and join clubs. You will find satisfaction in knowing you are not sinking into a cycle of debt. You will have time for meeting people and pursuing hobbies. We have all heard that the best things in life are free, and if you ask people what they remember about college, you will see that it is true.

DEFINING SUCCESS

For one person, winning an Olympic gold medal might be the definition of success. For another person, getting their dog to stop peeing on their new leather sofa might be the definition of success. For one person, saving a million dollars might be success. For another person, reducing their credit card debt to $5,000 might be success. People's ideas about success are different and their standards are different as well.

There are many different roles we play as people, and each of those roles makes us pay a price in order to be successful. To be a good student, you must earn good grades. To be a good daughter, you must communicate with your parents. To be a religious person, you must develop religious understanding. There are so many different roles we are asked to hold that it is easy to forget about debt-free college. We are told that if we simply go to college and do well, we will get a "good job" and be "financially successful." This is a dangerous, untrue way to look at things.

SECRET #77

It is not going to college or getting a good job that makes us financially successful; it is being financially responsible that makes us financially successful.

If you are making $100,000 as a dentist, but you are spending $110,000, what is the point of your education and fancy job? You could be a bum and be $10,000 in debt. A dentist with no financial defense would *not* be financially successful, no matter how much he made.

RICH COUPLE, POOR COUPLE

My aunt told me about a couple she knows. They are in their sixties, and their net worth is in the millions. They have enough money to last them the rest of their lives, plus a lot more. But they have no stories. Their entire life, they have focused only on earning and saving money. They have never traveled or pursued hobbies with their money. They are boring people, content with one private excitement—saving more money.

On the other end of the spectrum, a different couple cannot even see retirement in sight because they have spent themselves into a deep hole. They have to hope they do not get sick, just so they can work for more years. They have a comfortable lifestyle—nice cars, a nice house, and a history of interesting vacations. But they might have to work until they are seventy-five in order to afford the kind of care they could require as they get older.

Most people would not want to be like either of these couples. To have money and no stories is a shame. To have stories and no money is a disgrace. To have some stories and some money is the best approach.

SECRET #78

A middle-of-the-road philosophy leads to balance and happiness.

How do you end up with some stories and some money? You manage your expenses so you do not sink into debt. You save some and then spend the rest on the things that make life interesting and fun. Neither the rich couple nor the poor couple could accomplish this balance. Hopefully, by the time you graduate from college, you will have perfected balance.

TRIVIA: The name for the clothing item "sweater" is believed to have originated by college athletes because their knitted jerseys were sweat-soaked after workouts—*www.uselessknowledge.com*

THE $100,000 JOB!

Doesn't a $100,000 job sound wonderful? *Not necessarily*—once you know what lies behind the impressive salary. Many people earning that much money are working eighty or a hundred hours a week. They are likely too busy to do anything besides work, breathe, eat, and sleep. If money has become that important to you, then something is wrong.

There is only one good reason to spend time learning to think financially. That reason is so you can stop having to worry about money and have more time to do the types of things that will eventually make you feel successful—spending time with family and friends, learning, worshiping, and playing.

Remember, it is not always how much money you make, but how much money you keep that is important. Even if you play great financial offense, you will go nowhere unless you play defense, too. Debt-free college, as well as other long-term financial goals, begins with playing defense. Offense just speeds up the process.

The Rat Race

The vicious cycle of earning and spending, earning and spending, earning and spending is called the rat race. After you graduate, you step right into the maze. You have to face the rat race. You have to go to work, you have to buy a new wardrobe, you have to find a place to live, and you might have a marriage to plan. Your salary will be higher, but so will your expenses.

THE RAT RACE WITH POOR FINANCIAL HABITS

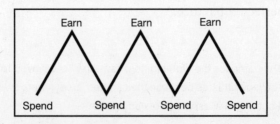

The problem with this pattern is that there is no way to exit—you end up working until you're too old to work. This is an undesirable spending pattern. It allows you to have lots of desirable toys, but it traps you in a very unpleasant rat race. The rat race after debt-free college looks different, however. With good financial habits, you still earn and spend, but your superior financial offense and defense begin to help you exit the rat race.

THE RAT RACE AFTER DEBT-FREE COLLEGE

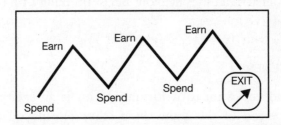

The "real world" is an entirely new set of financial challenges. The more nice things you accumulate, the longer you have to go on earning and spending to pay for them. But you will have quite a head start if you graduate debt-free because you will have grown financial roots during college. A more advanced system will seem easy.

INVEST

One way to escape the rat race is to invest. More than likely, this is an opportunity you will lack while you are in college because investing requires extra money.

Investing allows your money to work for you instead of you having to race around working for money. The fantastic thing about graduating from college debt-free is that you will be able to devote a portion of your income to investing as soon as you begin working and earning. This will give you a substantial lead over all those student debtors out there. Your money will have much more of a chance to work for you, thus allowing you to spend your time thinking about how to get out of the rat race.

SET NEW GOALS

Just because you graduate debt-free does not mean you are in the clear! After having achieved debt-free college, you should be able to capitalize on your good habits and continue avoiding debt.

There are many exciting things to work for—traveling to see the world, buying a nicer car, living in a good neighborhood. Perhaps your new goal will be to capitalize on your skills and knowledge to start your own business. Your personal financial management skills will truly come in handy once you begin thinking of having a business.

THINK RETIREMENT

What age do you want to work until? This is an exciting question if you are ahead of the game, or a scary one if you are behind. Knowing when you'll be able to retire depends on how quickly you outline your goals after you graduate debt-free. Then, it is simply a matter of learning the art of investing. You will already understand budgeting, saving, and thinking up money. Once you integrate investing into your arsenal, you will be moving on your way.

KEEP YOUR PIE IN MIND

Your good friend the PIE will follow you around even after college. It is your best friend or your worst enemy, depending on how you feed it. If you learn to use your PIE well, you will begin working toward your freedom quickly. The fact that you are a college graduate will help your earning capacity, which in turn can feed your PIE better.

In college, the tendency is to hover around this pattern and eat up your asset base:

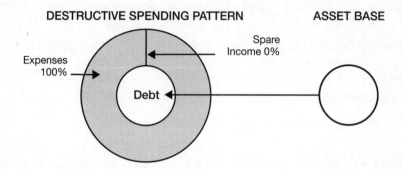

After college, you will more easily be able to have a healthy PIE. In fact, you should be able to go on building an asset base that is used entirely for investing, thus helping you escape the rat race. Because you graduated from college debt-free, you can move to a more desirable PIE as soon as you begin working.

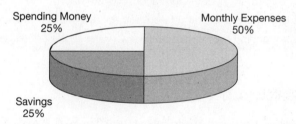

This PIE can be adjusted to fit your goals. Perhaps you only wish to save 10 percent and still be able to take a vacation every year. Perhaps you wish to save 40 percent and quit working by age forty. Either way, you will be able to focus on your freedom instead of spending all your time paying down debt.

WORDS OF ADVICE

The payoff of graduating debt-free is a sweet one. It feels a lot like getting a gigantic promotion. But before you go toasting yourself and changing the philosophy that got you there, think twice. As long as you have the energy and the humility to learn, you will never know limits in your personal life or with your bank account. But don't take the authors' word on it. Look through the pages of a few essential books that are sure to challenge your financial thinking.

SECRET #79

Don't toast yourself too early!

Rich Dad, Poor Dad by Robert Kiyosaki is an amazing book on asset-building.

The Millionaire Next Door by Thomas Stanley and William Danko is a fantastic book that gives you colorful statistics and case studies about millionaires.

The Richest Man in Babylon by George S. Clason is a classic that reveals age-old truths about saving and financial freedom.

TRIVIA: The football "huddle" formation was created by the students of Gallaudet University, a liberal arts college for the deaf, to prevent other schools from reading sign language—*www.uselessknowledge.com*

BECOME YOUR OWN MAN OR WOMAN

One aspect that you will discover as you learn the art of debt-free college is something that is hard to describe in a book. In a word, it can be described as pride.

To realize that you are supporting your way through college is great. Once you have developed the mindset of beating debt and developing good financial habits, you will be amazed at what you begin to accomplish. *You will put yourself through college.* Once you are finished with college, you will realize the power of what you have accomplished when you hear how much debt other people have.

"It's a good thing I got hired by Intel. I've got to pay off $20,000 of student loans."

"I hate credit cards. Eighteen percent interest! I can't believe I owe $8,000."

"Great. Now that I'm graduating, my $30,000 interest-free loan is going to start charging interest."

Surely you can imagine the painful struggle such debtors are going to have in paying back their loans. Even if such people do have high salaries, it will be difficult and slow to pay off such large amounts. There are two reasons for this:

- People with heavy debt tend to accumulate more debt.

- There is usually a high-cost period after college—getting a new apartment or house, purchasing a car, and buying a new wardrobe.

There will always be challenges in your future, but the financial game plan will always be similar. Take care of the financial details, then use the rest of your time and money for whatever else you wish—invest, take guilt-free vacations, or buy a Corvette. However, you can do fine things in life without big wads of money. This is because doing fine things does not take wads of money. It merely takes a lot of courage and effort and a little money management.

Crossing the Finish Line

You (hopefully) have a debt-free mindset. Now you must tailor the concepts to your life. Once you have learned the lessons, you can apply them in creative ways. There are a million different ways to follow the truth, and none of them is the right or wrong way. If you keep your debt-free mindset, then debt-free college is just around the corner. And when you find your balance and graduate debt-free, then,

Congratulations—you've crossed the finish line!

Glossary and Terms

academic credit—A form of academic measurement given at institutions to students when they complete a course or meet a degree or subject requirements as described by the institution.

academic year (AY)—A time period during which school is in session, usually from September through May, for a minimum of twenty-four semester hours or thirty weeks of instructional time. Academic years vary from school to school and from educational program to educational program and do not always match the financial aid award year.

accrued interest—Interest that is accumulated on loan that must be paid by the borrower to the lender, generally in installments, at a later time.

achievement tests—A group of tests designed to measure the student's proficiency and learned knowledge in specific subject areas (reading, math, writing). Achievement tests are used by most colleges as an evaluation standard to admit students into their colleges. The required tests vary from institution to institution.

adjusted gross income (AGI) / discretionary income—Taxable income after all allowable deductions are taken, including IRAs, pension plans, alimony, health care, and federal taxes.

Advanced Placement exam (AP)—A type of achievement test given to eligible high school students for college credit.

American College Test (ACT)—A type of achievement test used for college placement.

amortization—The gradual repayment of a loan through periodic installments of the loan principal and interest over an extended period of time.

appeal—A formal application or request to a recognized authority, such as a financial aid administrator, to review eligibility, aid award, or possibly use professional judgment to adjust the numbers to improve financial aid award.

asset—An item of value that has income-producing properties, sometimes resulting in passive income such as a home, a business, cash, certificates of deposits (CDs), bank accounts (checking, savings), trust funds, property, and investments (stocks, bonds, mutual funds).

assistantship—Type of student employment referring to research or teaching assistant positions.

associate degree—A degree granted by two-year colleges and institutions.

award letter—An official written notification to financial aid applicants describing the amount awarded for the academic year. The letter provides details on the aid analysis (EFC), type of aid awarded (grants, scholarships), and the terms and conditions of aid acceptance. The award letter is also known as the "financial aid notification" and/or the acceptance form.

award year—A defined period of time, established by the federal government, for which college federal aid may be awarded. The award year begins on July 1 and ends on June 30 of the following year.

bachelor's degree—An undergraduate degree granted by four-year institutions.

base year—The tax year preceding the academic year of expected attendance used to determine financial aid eligibility and amount. The base year starts on January 1 and ends on December 31.

borrower—A person who requests and receives a sum of money from a lender for a determined period of time.

budget—A formal plan outlining living expenses to coordinate financial resources (money) to manage expenses.

bursar's office—The university office responsible for billing and collection of university charges such as tuition, fees, and room and board.

campus-based aid programs—Programs that are administered by each college's financial aid office but funded by the federal government. These programs have a fixed amount of money and are distributed based on federal guidelines. The three campus-based aid programs are Federal Work-Study (FWS), Federal Perkins Loan (FPL), and the Federal Supplemental Educational Opportunity Grant (FSEOG).

cancellation—A loan provision that allows the borrower to reduce their loan balance based on special circumstances—death, permanent disability, military service, or teaching in national shortage areas. Cancellation policies vary for each loan.

capitalization—A practice of adding unpaid interest charges to the principal balance, thereby increasing the size of the repayment. Interest is first charged based on the beginning balance and then added to the balance, which becomes the outstanding loan balance. For the next period, the interest is then calculated on the new remaining balance (principal and previously charged interest).

Central Processing System (CPS)—The U.S. Department of Education's processing facility that reviews students' FAFSA applications. The CPS determines the official EFC and returns the information on the Student Aid Report (SAR) and the Institutional Student Aid Report (ISAR) for award distribution.

College Board (CB)—A nonprofit national membership organization of colleges, secondary schools, and other educational associations that monitors admissions policies, college examinations, and placement and provides general guidance on financial aid distribution and educational reform.

College Entrance Examination Board (CEEB)—An institutional membership organization that administers the taking of achievement tests.

College Level Examination Program (CLEP)—A college-level placement achievement exam offered to all college students. A satisfactory score on this exam can advance the student farther in a subject area and grant credit for the course.

College Scholarship Service (CSS)—An arm of the College Board that processes financial aid information and applications for institutional aid awards.

compound interest—Interest that is periodically added to both the principal balance and on any accrued (unpaid) interest. Capitalizing interest on an unsubsidized loan is a form of compounding.

consolidation—A repayment option where an eligible lender pays the existing loans for the borrower and creates one new loan. This usually lowers interest payments and increases the period of repayment.

cooperative education (co-op)—An educational program in which students attend alternate periods of schooling and employment, generally paid, which can lengthen the average baccalaureate program by one or two years.

co-signer—A second creditworthy party who co-signs a promissory note with the borrower guaranteeing that the loan will be repaid if the borrower defaults; generally student loans require a co-signer.

cost of attendance (COA) / cost of education (COE)—An estimated annual expense to attend one full academic year of college for a full-time college student. COA includes tuition and fees, room and board, books and supplies, transportation, and personal expenses. Some estimates also include dependent care, disability, moderate entertainment, as well as study-abroad program fees.

credit bureau—An agency that maintains records on credit and personal financial history. Information is available for a fee to creditors (banks, lenders) to assess your ability to pay.

credit rating—An evaluation of the borrower's likelihood to default on a loan; typically assessed by credit bureaus.

debt—An amount of money that is owed to an entity.

default—Failure to meet financial obligation(s) in accordance with the terms of the promissory note, or failure to submit requests for deferment or cancellation on time. Defaults appear on permanent credit records and may result in legal action and/or loss of future borrowing possibilities.

deferment—An approved postponement of loan payments for a specific period of time.

Department of Education (DOE, ED)—An arm of the U.S. government focused on educating and administering the college financial aid process.

dependent student—A student dependent on his/her parents for financial support and uses parental financial information for the calculation of EFC.

Direct Lending (also known as Federal Direct Student Loan [FDSL])—A federal student loan program that allows students to borrow directly from the institution with the federal government providing the funds. This allows for faster turnaround time and less bureaucracy than the "bank loan" program.

disbursement—The process by which funds are delivered to the borrower to meet educational and living expenses.

doctorate—See *Ph.D.*

educational benefits—Aid funds, generally federal, distributed to specific categories of students (veterans, children of deceased, physically disabled) to help finance education despite their inability to demonstrate need in the traditional sense.

electronic data exchange (EDE)—An electronic format by which financial aid forms and applications can be submitted to federal processors and received by participating schools.

eligibility—The process by which someone becomes qualified to participate in a program.

endowment—Institutional funds owned and invested by the institution to produce income to be used for educational programs.

enrollment—The process by which students register for academic courses at an institution to receive academic credit.

entitlement program—Financial aid programs such as the Pell Grant, FSEOG, or work-study that are not dependent upon institutional allocations but rather on student eligibility and enrollment and availability of funds.

equity—The monetary value of a property, investment, or other financial instrument. Owning assets leads to equity.

estimated financial assistance (EFA)—The amount of financial aid a student can expect from possible sources—federal, state, school, grants, scholarships, and work-study.

expected family contribution (EFC)—A determined amount of money a family/student is required to contribute toward the cost of education as calculated by the Federal Methodology and the FAFSA application.

Federal Direct Student Loan Program (FDSLP, FDSL, FDLP, FDL)—The collective name for federal loan programs (PLUS, Stafford) where the student borrows directly from the government. See also *Direct Lending*.

Federal Educational Loan Program (FELP), Federal Family Education Loan Program (FFELP)—The collective name for all federal loan programs where the student borrows from a commercial lender (bank, credit union, savings and loans, private organizations) but the loans are guaranteed against default by the federal government.

Federal Methodology (FM)—A standard method established by Congress to calculate expected family contribution (EFC) using the need analysis formula. The Methodology evaluates taxable and nontaxable income, assets, family size, number of family members in college, and benefits.

Federal Pell Grant—A federally sponsored need-based grant to help undergraduates pay for their education. The maximum grant award amount is set by Congress and varies annually.

Federal Perkins Loan—A federal low-interest need-based loan that lets students (undergraduate and graduate) borrow a predetermined amount based on class standing for a cumulative sum of $30,000 for graduate and undergraduate education.

Federal PLUS Loan (FPLUS)—A federal nonsubsidized loan program designed to assist parents of undergraduate students—under the DSL umbrella.

Federal Stafford Loan (FSL)—A type of DSL loan that comes in two forms—subsidized and unsubsidized.

Federal Supplemental Educational Opportunity Grant (FSEOG)—A campus-based federal grant available to undergraduate students who exhibit exceptional financial need as determined by the federal methodology.

Federal Work-Study (FWS)—A federal, need-based aid program through which eligible students (undergraduate and graduate) can earn a portion of their college expenses through part-time work during the school year.

fellowship—A form of financial aid (tuition waivers, living stipends, tuition payments) given to graduate students to continue postgraduate studies that may require teaching or research.

financial aid (FA)—A combination of self-help aid (loans, work-study) and gift aid (grants, scholarships) provided to a student to help pay for their education.

financial aid administrator (FAA)—An individual responsible for preparing and communicating the financial aid package and its contents, as well as advising, reporting, counseling, and supervising student financial aid functions.

financial aid notification (FAN)—See *award letter*.

financial aid package—A combination of federal, private, and institutional aid awarded to a student for the academic year.

financial aid profile—Formerly known as Financial Aid Form (FAF). A specific financial aid application developed by the College Scholarship Service (CSS) for colleges to help determine aid distribution from institutional funds.

financial aid transcript (FAT)—A formal written record of awarded financial aid from previously attended institutions required by colleges used to determine current financial aid award.

financial need—The amount by which a student's resources fall short of covering the cost of attending school—the difference between estimated cost of attendance (COA) and expected family contribution (EFC); the financial aid package is determined based on financial need.

fixed interest—A constant interest rate set at the time of loan negotiation for the life of the loan.

forbearance—A condition where student loan principal payments can be temporarily postponed, but the borrower is required to continue making interest payments. Forbearance is granted at the discretion of the lender in cases of financial hardship.

Free Application for Federal Student Aid (FAFSA)—A free financial aid application used to grant need-based aid that must be submitted by the student to the Central Processing System (CPS) in order to receive financial assistance for college costs.

gapping—The cost of education that is not met after calculating the difference between the student's total available aid resources and the total cost for the student's attendance at a specific institution.

gift aid—Financial aid such as grants and scholarships that does not have to be repaid.

grace period—A defined period of time, usually following graduation or a change in enrollment status, during which the borrower does not accrue interest and does not have to begin payments on a loan.

graduate student—A student pursuing studies above the baccalaureate level such as a master's or Ph.D. program.

grant—Gift aid awarded on a need-basis. Does not have to be repaid.

gross income—Individual income before taxes, deductions, and other allowances have been subtracted.

guarantee fee—A small percentage fee of the loan (not to exceed 3 percent) paid by the borrower to the guaranty agency to insure the loan against default.

Guaranteed Student Loan Program (GSL)—Formerly known as the FFELP. See *Federal Educational Loan Program*.

guaranty agency—A state or private nonprofit agency that administers FELPs in each state and insures lenders against borrower's default, death, disability, or bankruptcy.

income—The amount of money received from employment, profit from financial instruments, and other sources such as welfare, disability, child support, Social Security, and pensions.

indirect costs—All nontuition related college expenses such as room, board, transportation, medical, and personal expenses.

in-state student—A student who meets the state residency requirements and is eligible for reduced student tuition at public colleges and universities in the state.

Institutional Methodology (IM)—An alternative methodology used by individual colleges to determine eligibility in awarding institutional funds such as grants and scholarships.

Institutional Student Information Report (ISIR)—The electronic version of the Student Aid Report (SAR) for institutions.

interest—A fee, usually a percentage of the loan principal, that a lender charges the borrower for the privilege of using the lender's money.

internship—Part-time or full-time employment opportunities to gain professional experience in a specific field of interest during college.

lender—An entity from which students can borrow funds—a bank, savings and loan association, credit union, stock savings bank, trust company, or mutual savings bank.

liability—A financial obligation where you must pay money; many liabilities lead to debt.

loan—Money that is borrowed with a formal agreement for repayment with interest.

loan disclosure statement—Statement provided to borrowers by the lender disclosing information about the cost of the loan, interest rate, origination, insurance and loan fees, and other finance charges.

master's degree—A type of post-baccalaureate degree granted by graduate schools.

maturity date—The date when a financial obligation or a financial investment comes due.

merit-based aid—Financial aid that is awarded based on personal achievement such as student's academic, athletic, or artistic merit or other criteria or individual characteristic; does not depend on the existence of financial need.

need analysis—The process of analyzing household and financial information from a student's financial aid application to calculate expected family contribution (EFC).

need-based aid—Financial aid that is awarded based on a student's ability to demonstrate financial need.

non-need-based aid—See *merit-based aid*.

origination fee—A loan-processing fee charged to a borrower by a lender for the cost of administering the loan, typically runs to 3 percent of the amount disbursed.

out-of-state student—A student who does not meet the state residency requirements but attends that state's public college/university and is often charged a higher tuition rate.

outside resource—A form of aid or benefit that comes from sources other than the school and the federal or state government such as scholarships, prepaid tuition plans, and Veteran Administration (VA) educational benefits.

parent contribution (PC)—A quantitative estimate, determined by the need-analysis formula, of the parents' ability to contribute to postsecondary educational expenses from their income and assets.

Parent Loans for Undergraduate Students (PLUS)—See *Federal PLUS* Loan (FPLUS).

passive income—Income that is generated merely from holding on to assets or financial instruments—including real estate, farms, stocks, and other investments.

Pell Grant—See *Federal Pell Grant*.

Perkins Loan—See *Federal Perkins Loan.*

Ph.D.—A type of degree granted by graduate schools.

postsecondary school—Any educational institution that provides educational services beyond the level of high school. Sometimes used interchangeably with proprietary schools, trade and technical schools, and a range of nontraditional facilities as well as colleges and universities.

prepaid tuition plan—A type of college savings plan that locks in current tuition prices for future attendees.

principal—The total amount of money borrowed or remaining unpaid on a loan. Interest and other fees are charged based on the principal amount.

priority dates—Early deadlines set by colleges for students when filing the FAFSA and other applications to increase the chance of receiving the most possible financial aid from that school.

private loans—Loans established by private lenders to supplement the federal student and parent education loan programs.

professional degree—A degree in a field like law, education, medicine, pharmacy, or dentistry.

professional judgment (PJ)—The legal authority of a financial aid administrator to change expected family contribution (EFC) or any elements used in determining financial need based on additional information or individual circumstances to represent a more accurate financial situation. PJ can be used to change the dependency status of the student or adjust elements of EFC or cost of attendance (COA), disability, or parents' employment. This is done on a case-by-case basis and documented in the student's file.

promissory note—A binding legal document that the borrower signs promising to repay the loan, with interest, in specified installments before the lender disburses loan funds.

renewable scholarship—An awarded scholarship that will provide funds for more than one year, as long as the student maintains certain academic standards and formally reapplies for the scholarship.

repayment schedule—A formal plan that discloses the repayment terms—amount, time period, the frequency of payments, due date, and interest rate.

resident student—A student who lives on or around the college campus during the academic year.

Satisfactory Academic Progress (SAP)—A required minimum level of academic achievement expected of a student in order to continue receiving financial aid.

scholarship—A type of gift aid usually from private sources that does not have to be paid back. Some scholarships are awarded based on need, but most are based on personal achievements.

secured loan—A loan backed by collateral.

selective service—Required by law. All male citizens or eligible noncitizens eighteen years old or more must be registered with selective service in order to receive federal student aid.

self-help aid (assistance)—Aid provided through the work and effort of the student, including loans, student employment, savings from past earnings, income from present earnings, or a loan to be repaid from future earnings.

self-help expectation—The principle that a student has an obligation to help pay for a portion of their education, which is usually included in the analysis of a student's resources.

service academy—A four-year college focused in one of the five areas of the U.S. Defense that offers a bachelor's degree and commission in the military. Service academies include the U.S. Air Force Academy, U.S. Coast Guard Academy, U.S. Merchant Marine Academy, U.S. Military Academy, and U.S. Naval Academy.

simple interest—Interest that is calculated only on the original amount of a loan.

simplified needs test (SNT)—A need-analysis formula used for families whose total adjusted gross income (AGI) is less than $50,000 and who are eligible to file a 1040EZ or 1040A, or who do not file a tax return.

Stafford Loans—Federal direct loans that come in two forms: subsidized (based on need) and unsubsidized (not based on need). See also *direct lending*.

Statement of Educational Purpose—Formerly known as the "Affidavit of Educational Purpose," this document must be signed by the student acknowledging that any funds received will be used solely for educationally related purposes.

student accounts office—See *bursar's office*.

student aid report (SAR)—A report that summarizes the information included in the FASFA and contains the expected family contribution (EFC) that must be reviewed and submitted to the financial aid office prior to receiving any financial aid.

Student Financial Aid (SFA) Programs—Programs administered by the Office of Student Financial Assistance (OSFA) of the U.S. Department of Education—Federal Pell Grants, Federal Supplemental Educational Opportunity Grants, Federal Work-Study, Federal Perkins Loans, Federal Stafford Loans, Federal PLUS Loans, State Student Incentive Grants, Byrd Scholarships, and Federal Consolidation Loans.

subsidized loan—Formerly known as the guaranteed student loan (GSL). A need-based loan where the government pays interest for the borrower during college, during deferment periods, and/or during the grace period.

Supplemental Educational Opportunity Grant (SEOG)—See *Federal Supplemental Educational Opportunity Grant (FSEOG)*.

transcript—A document that shows all classes taken and all grades received by a student, usually sent by the school with an original signature of a school official.

truth-in-lending statement—See *loan disclosure statement*.

tuition—The amount of money colleges charge for instruction and use of facilities.

undergraduate student—A student who is in the process of earning a bachelor's or a first professional degree.

unsubsidized loan—A federal loan where the government does not pay interest for the borrower during college, during deferment periods, or during the grace period.

variable interest—A rate of interest that changes during the life of a loan on a regular basis because the interest rate is tied to an index.

verification—A random procedure in which a financial aid office substantiates the accuracy of the information provided on the student's financial aid application. Documentation of proof is usually required.

W2 form—A government form that lists an employee's earned wages and taxes withheld for the calendar year.

Resources

HIGH SCHOOL CALENDAR

MONTH	FRESHMAN/SOPHOMORE/JUNIOR	JUNIOR/SENIOR	SENIOR

January	• Evaluate college as a future
	• Develop an overall plan
	• Build résumé
	• Join high school organizations and groups
	• Gather information about possible colleges
	• Attempt summer internships in possible careers
	• Study for college examinations—PSAT, SAT, ACT
	• Work toward AP and honors classes
	• Create a database of potential colleges and
	  financial aid resources
	• Attend college fairs and workshops
	• Take PSAT
		• Take steps to maximize base year
		  financial situation–asset restructur-
		  ing
			• Apply for colleges and housing
			• Complete and file taxes

February		• Register for college exams	• Review and send SAR
March			• Continue to apply for scholarships • Mail FAFSA
April			• Continue to build asset base • Compare aid packages • Send in acceptance letters
May			• Evaluate asset base • Evaluate aid gap, if any
June		• Start an asset base • Plan on-campus visits • Request applications	• Build a budget

MONTH	FRESHMAN/SOPHOMORE/JUNIOR	JUNIOR/SENIOR	SENIOR
July		• Apply for scholarships • Study for college exams	
August		• Fine-tune college database	
September		• Collect college application require-ments • Gather recommendations • Compose essays	• Start college • Find part-time work • Select course work
October		• Take SAT • Get FAFSA	
November		• Create Expense PIEs • Evaluate financial situation	
December		• Narrow college choices • Apply for colleges	

COLLEGE CALENDAR

MONTH	FRESHMAN/SOPHOMORE/JUNIOR/SENIOR
January	• Renew FAFSA
February	• Complete and file taxes • Submit SAR
March	• Apply for scholarships
April	• Seek summer internships
May	• Rebuild asset base • Graduate without debt (senior)
June	• Rebuild asset base • Evaluate budget
July	• Forecast expenses and build budget
August	• Find part-time work, if needed • Apply for federal work-study positions
September	• Start academic year
November	• Update scholarship databases
December	• Interview on-campus for full-time positions post graduation (senior)

FINANCIAL AID CALENDAR

JANUARY	FEBRUARY	MARCH	APRIL	MAY	SEPTEMBER
• 1— First day for FAFSA application • 1–31— Renew FAFSA	• 1–28— Complete and submit taxes • 1–28— Submit SAR with corrections, if received	• 15— Last day for FAFSA application • 1–31— Submit SAR corrections • 1–31— Evaluate financial aid package, if received	• 1–31— Work toward meeting aid gap with other options	• 1–31— Absolute latest to accept financial aid package	• 1–15— Apply and find federal work-study positions

GENERAL INFORMATION

- *www.collegeboard.com* is an introductory website for high school students and parents. It discusses college planning, college selection, and college financing. It also guides the prospective student and parents through the college-going process with interactive tools to calculate cost and possible options.
- *www.collegesavings.org* is an informational website about college prepaid tuition and college savings plan options.
- *www.ed.gov* is supported by the U.S. Department of Education. It presents current information on deadlines, changing federal regulations and rules, programs, and the federal aid application process.
- *www.finaid.org* is a "how-to" website that offers valuable information on the financial aid process, grants, federal aid, scholarships, and guidelines to obtaining financial aid. It also has an extensive scholarship search engine.
- *www.financialaid.about.com* is an informational website about college tests, college rankings, study abroad, financial aid, and scholarships.
- *ifap.ed.gov* focuses on administration of financial aid guidelines. It acts as a frame of reference to students applying for federal aid.
- *www.nasfaa.org* is administered by the National Association of Student Financial Aid Administrators. It provides updates on the latest government regulations, legislation, and changes in the status quo.
- *www.oldschool.org* features additional resource websites and links to general financial aid information.
- *www.petersons.com* is managed by Peterson's Education and Career Center. It is a comprehensive website that discusses scholarships, financial aid, study abroad, distance learning, types of college programs, and test-taking.
- *www.wiredscholar.com* addresses all aspects of college attendance. It also provides checklists, interactive tools for managing cost, and financial aid processing.
- *www.xap.com* offers general information regarding higher education including federal aid, scholarships, and grants.

COLLEGE CULTURE

- *www.collegeclub.com* is the largest online college community website. It offers a venue for college students to communicate about college culture, student discounts, and college issues, nationwide.
- *www.collegenet.com* provides online applications for colleges in the

United States and overseas. It also provides a mini-scholarship search engine.

TAILORED WEBSITES

- *www.aacc.nche.edu* is supported by the American Association of Community Colleges. It is a comprehensive website about community colleges, including a strong database for research about nationwide colleges, scholarships, and other financial aid.
- *www.collegeparents.org* is supported by the College Parents of America. It helps parents understand the cost of attendance, how to save for college, how to avoid scholarship scams, and how to manage money with their kids.
- *www.edupass.org* is designed for international students planning to study in the United States or who are already studying in the United States. It focuses on college planning—culture, living, admissions, college prerequisites (language, tests, and passports), and college financing.
- *www.iefa.org* (International Education Financial Aid) offers insight to college planning and financing for all international students.
- *www.internationalstudent.com* contains general information about attending college in the United States.

SCHOLARSHIP SEARCH DATABASES

- *www.collegenet.com* is an online resource for applications to more than 1,500 colleges and universities.
- *www.collegequest.com* is supported by Peterson's Learning Center and offers online scholarship, fellowship, and financial aid tools.
- *www.college-scholarships.com* provides online scholarship applications to more than 1,000 colleges and universities. It also includes information on admissions, financial aid, and college tests.
- *www.collegeview.com* is a comprehensive scholarship database engine for all types of students and colleges.
- *www.absolutelyscholarships.com* is dedicated to finding national scholarships from a pool of more than 200,000 opportunities nationwide.
- *www.fastaid.com* is a scholarship engine designed by Dan Cassidy, author of *The Scholarship Book*.
- *www.fastweb.com* is a popular, customized financial aid search engine with more than 300 references and more than 150,000 scholarships, fellowships, loans, and grants available to students for free.

- *www.freescholarship.com* is a free scholarship search engine with links to other scholarship information.
- *www.srnexpress.com* (Scholarship Resource Network Express) is a free website with access to a database of numerous scholarships, fellowships, and grants.

LOAN AND MONEY MANAGEMENT

- *www.college-student-loans.com* provides a list of lenders and a directory for loan assistance.
- *www.ed.gov/DirectLoan* is a U.S. Department of Education website that details the direct loan borrowing process. It offers tips and advice on borrowing direct loans.
- *www.edfund.org* is a loan financial planner website directed toward parents.
- *www.educaid.com* is a student loan lender with an extensive loan information center. It has loan comparison tools and calculators, professional advice, and a monthly newsletter.
- *www.educationone.com* is supported by Bank One and has information about various college loan options with Bank One. It also has loan cost calculators.
- *www.estudentloan.com* is tailored to the specific needs of borrowers and guides prospective borrowers with loan comparison tools.
- *www.istudentloan.com* features online loan approval for Stafford, PLUS, and other private student loans.
- *www.kaploan.com* is supported by Kaplan. It provides information and advice on student loans and financial aid.
- *www.salliemae.com* (Sallie Mae) is a financial institution that offers interactive calculators to estimate the cost of college, forecast savings, and estimate loan payments. It also provides valuable information about the borrowing process.
- *sfahelp.ed.gov* is a government website that discusses the various federal loans and details about borrowing, including tips on borrowing cost-efficiently.

POPULAR ORGANIZATIONS

- *www.irs.ustreas.gov/prod/cover.html* is the place to find tax information and forms.
- *www.rotary.org* is a foundation that focuses on offering education scholarships on various criteria.

- *www.sss.gov/regist.htm* or *www.sss.gov* offers online registration for selective services for male students.
- *www.va.gov* (Department of Veterans Affairs) offers tailored financial aid and scholarships to veterans.

FORMS AND PUBLICATIONS

- *www.act.org* provides online registration for the American College Test.
- *www.ed.gov/prog_info/SFA/StudentGuide* is *The Student Guide,* a free booklet about financial aid from the U.S. Department of Education.
- *www.ed.gov/offices/OSFAP/Students/apply/fexpress.html* is an online request for *FAFSA Express* software.
- *www.ed.gov/offices/OSFAP/Students/apply.html* provides a list of federal school codes needed to complete FAFSA.
- *www.ets.org* is the Education Testing Service, which creates the college placement exams. The website has information about test dates, locations, mini-exams, test-taking tactics, and also offers online registration.
- *www.fafsa.ed.gov* provides information about FAFSA.
- *www.insideedgenewsletter.com* is a college newsletter for college students about reaching and achieving college education.
- *www.review.com* is administered by *The Princeton Review.* It discusses test-taking tactics and has exam preparation courses, test locations, and dates.

BOOKS

- *The Insider's Guide to Paying for College*
- *College Financial Aid for Dummies*
- *How to Go to College Almost for Free*
- *Debt-Free by 30*
- *Kaplan's Guide to Distance Learning*
- *Scholarships and Loans for Adult Students: The Only Guide to College Financing for Students 25 and Over*
- *Cyber Graduation: Earning a Degree Online*

TELEPHONE NUMBERS

General information about student financial assistance programs, completing the FAFSA, and requesting aid publications	1-800-4-FED-AID 1-800-433-3243 1-800-730-8913 (TDD/TTY) 1-319-337-5665 (foreign callers)
Technical assistance with *FAFSA on the Web* or to order *FAFSA Express* software	1-800-801-0576
To report fraud, waste, or abuse of federal aid	1-800-MIS-USED 1-800-647-8733
Information on the Direct Loan Consolidation	1-800-557-7392
Internal Revenue Service	1-800-829-1040
Veterans Affairs	1-843-953-6502
CSS Profile Application Form	1-800-778-6888

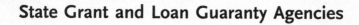

State Grant and Loan Guaranty Agencies

ALABAMA

Alabama Commission on Higher
Education
PO Box 302000
Montgomery, AL 36130-2000
334-242-1998
1-800-843-8534
Fax: 334-242-0268
hhector@ache.state.al.us
www.ache.state.al.us

ALASKA

Alaska Commission on
Postsecondary Education
3030 Vintage Boulevard
Juneau, AK 99801-7100
907-465-2962
1-800-441-2962
TTY: 907-465-3143
Fax: 907-465-5316
customer_service@acpe.state.ak.us
www.state.ak.us/acpe

ARIZONA

Arizona Commission for
Postsecondary Education;
Suite 275

2020 North Central Avenue
Phoenix, AZ 85004-4503
602-229-2591
Fax: 602-229-2599
toni@www.acpe.asu.edu
www.acpe.asu.edu

ARKANSAS

Arkansas Dept. of Higher
Education
114 East Capitol
Little Rock, AR 72201-3818
501-371-2000
Fax: 501-371-2003
ronh@adhe.arknet.edu
www.adhe.arknet.edu/

COLORADO

Colorado Commission on Higher
Education
1380 Lawrence Street, Suite 1200
Denver, CO 80204
303-866-2723
Fax: 303-866-4266
tim.foster@state.co.us
www.state.co.us/cche_dir/
hecche.html

CALIFORNIA
California Student Aid Commission
PO Box 419026
Rancho Cordova, CA 95741-9026
916-526-8047
Fax: 916-526-8002
jgarcia@csac.ca.gov
www.csac.ca.gov

CONNECTICUT
Connecticut Dept. of Higher
Education
61 Woodland Street
Hartford, CT 06105-2326
860-947-1833
1-800-842-0229
Fax: 860-947-1310
jlyddon@ctdhe.org
www.ctdhe.org

DELAWARE
Delaware Higher Education
Commission
Carvel State Office Building,
Fifth Floor
820 North French Street
Wilmington, DE 19801
302-577-3240
1-800-292-7935
Fax: 302-577-6765
dhec@state.de.us
www.doe.state.de.us/high-ed

DISTRICT OF COLUMBIA
District of Columbia Dept. of
Human Services; Office of
Postsecondary Education,
Research, and Assistance
2100 Martin Luther King, Jr.
Avenue, SE, Suite 401
Washington, DC 20020
202-698-2400

Fax: 202-727-2739
dhs.washington.dc.us/

GEORGIA
Georgia Student Finance Authority
State Loans and Grants Division
2082 East Exchange Place,
Suite 200
Tucker, GA 30084
770-724-9000
1-800-776-6878
Fax: 770-724-9225
info@mail.gsfc.state.ga.us
www.gsfc.org

HAWAII
Hawaii State Postsecondary
Education Commission
2444 Dole Street, Room 209
Honolulu, HI 96822-2302
808-956-8213
Fax: 808-956-5156
iha@hawaii.edu
www.hern.hawaii.edu/hern

IDAHO
Idaho State Board of Education
PO Box 83720
Boise, ID 83720-0027
208-334-2270
Fax: 208-334-2632
board@osbe.state.id.us
www.sde.state.id.us/osbe/board.htm

ILLINOIS
Illinois Student Assistance
Commission
1755 Lake Cook Road
Deerfield, IL 60015-5209
847-948-8500
1-800-899-4722
TTY: 847-831-8326
Fax: 847-831-8549

isac@wwa.com
www.isac-online.org

INDIANA
State Student Assistance
Commission of Indiana
150 West Market Street, Suite 500
Indianapolis, IN 46204-2811
317-232-2350
1-888-528-4719
Fax: 317-232-3260
grants@ssaci.state.in.us

IOWA
Iowa College Student Aid
Commission
200 10th Street, Fourth Floor
Des Moines, IA 50309
515-281-3501
1-800-383-4222
Fax: 515-242-3388
icsac@max.state.ia.us
www.state.ia.us/collegeaid

KANSAS
Kansas Board of Regents
700 SW Harrison, Suite 1410
Topeka, KS 66603-3760
785-296-3421
Fax: 785-296-0983
kim@kbor.state.ks.us or
jbirmingham@kbor.state.ks.us
www.kansasregents.org

KENTUCKY
Kentucky Higher Education
Assistance Authority
1050 U.S. Highway 127 South
Frankfort, KY 40601-4323
502-696-7200
1-800-928-8926
TTY: 1-800-855-2880
Fax: 502-696-7496

webmaster@kheaa.com
www.kheaa.com

LOUISIANA
Louisiana Office of Student
Financial Assistance
PO Box 91202
Baton Rouge, LA 70821-9202
225-922-1012
1-800-259-5626
Fax: 225-922-0790
custserv@osfa.state.la.us
www.osfa.state.la.us

MAINE
Maine Education Assistance
Division
Finance Authority of Maine
(FAME)
5 Community Drive
Augusta, ME 04332-0949
207-623-3263
1-800-228-3734
TTY: 207-626-2717
Fax: 207-632-0095
info@famemaine.com
www.famemaine.com

MARYLAND
Maryland Higher Education
Commission
Jeffrey Building
16 Francis Street
Annapolis, MD 21401-1781
410-260-4500
1-800-974-1024
TTY: 1-800-735-2258
Fax: 410-974-5994
ssamail@mhec.state.md.us
www.mhec.state.md.us

MASSACHUSETTS
Massachusetts Higher Education
Information Center

Boston Public Library
700 Boylston Street
Boston, MA 02116
617-536-0200
1-800-442-1171
Fax: 617-536-4737
iriarte@teri.org
www.adinfo.org/

MASSACHUSETTS
Massachusetts Board of Higher
Education
One Ashburton Place, Room 1401
Boston, MA 02108
617-994-6950
Fax: 617-727-6397
bhe@bhe.mass.edu
www.mass.edu

MICHIGAN
Michigan Higher Education
Assistance Authority
Office of Scholarships and Grants
PO Box 30462
Lansing, MI 48909-7962
517-373-3394
1-888-447-2687
Fax: 517-335-5984
oir@state.mi.us
www.MI-StudentAid.org

MINNESOTA
Minnesota Higher Education
Services Office
1450 Energy Park Drive, Suite 350
Saint Paul, MN 55108-5227
651-642-0533
1-800-657-0866
TTY: 1-800-627-3529
Fax: 651-642-0675
info@heso.state.mn.us
www.mheso.state.mn.us

MISSISSIPPI
Mississippi Postsecondary
Education
Financial Assistance Board
3825 Ridgewood Road
Jackson, MS 39211-6453
601-432-6997
1-800-327-2980
Fax: 601-432-6527
sfa@ihl.state.ms.us
www.ihl.state.ms.us

MISSOURI
Missouri Dept. of Higher
Education
3515 Amazonas Drive
Jefferson City, MO 65109-5717
573-751-2361
1-800-473-6757
Fax: 573-751-6635
cheryl.kesel@mocbhe.gov
www.gov.state.mo.us/boards/cgi/
boards.cgi

MONTANA
Montana University System
2500 Broadway
PO Box 203101
Helena, MT 59620-3103
406-444-6570
Fax: 406-444-1469
sherry.rosette@state.mt.us
www.montana.edu/wwwoche

NEBRASKA
Nebraska Coordinating
Commission for Postsecondary
Education
PO Box 95005
Lincoln, NE 68509-5005
402-471-2847
Fax: 402-471-2886
staff@ccpe.state.ne.us

www.ccpe.state.ne.us/
PublicDoc/CCPE/Default.asp

NEW HAMPSHIRE
New Hampshire Postsecondary
Education Commission
2 Industrial Park Drive
Concord, NH 03301-8512
603-271-2555
TTY: 1-800-735-2964
Fax: 603-271-2696
kdodge@nhsa.state.nh.us
www.state.nh.us/postsecondary

NEW JERSEY
Higher Education Student
Assistance Authority (New Jersey)
PO Box 540
Building 4
Quakerbridge Plaza
Trenton, NJ 08625-0540
609-588-3226
1-800-792-8670
TTY: 609-588-2526
Fax: 609-588-7389
www.hesaa.org

NEW MEXICO
New Mexico Commission on
Higher Education
1068 Cerrillos Road
Santa Fe, NM 87501
505-827-7383
1-800-279-9777
TTY: 1-800-659-8331
Fax: 505-827-7392
highered@che.state.nm.us
www.nmche.org

NEW YORK
New York State Higher Education
Services Corporation
99 Washington Avenue
Albany, NY 12255

518-473-7087
1-888-697-4372
Fax: 518-474-2839
www.hesc.com

NORTH CAROLINA
North Carolina State Education
Assistance Authority
PO Box 13663
Research Triangle Park, NC 27709-
3663
919-549-8614
1-800-700-1775
Fax: 919-549-8481
emcduffie@ga.unc.edu
www.ncseaa.edu

NORTH DAKOTA
North Dakota University System
North Dakota Student Financial
Assistance Program
Dept. 215
600 East Boulevard Avenue
Bismarck, ND 58505-0230
701-328-4114
Fax: 701-328-2961
ndus_office@ndus.nodak.edu
www.nodak.edu

OHIO
Ohio Board of Regents
State Grants and Scholarships
Dept.
PO Box 182452
Columbus, OH 43218-2452
614-466-7420
1-888-833-1133
Fax: 614-752-5903
www.regents.state.oh.us/sgs

OKLAHOMA
Oklahoma State Regents for
Higher Education

Oklahoma Guaranteed Student
Loan Program
State Capitol Complex
500 Education Building
Oklahoma City, OK 73105-4500
405-524-9120
Fax: 405-524-9235
tsimonton@osrhe.edu
www.okhighered.org

OREGON
Oregon Student Assistance
Commission
1500 Valley River Drive, Suite 100
Eugene, OR 97401
541-687-7400
1-800-452-8807
Fax: 541-687-7419
thomas.f.turner@state.or.us
www.osac.state.or.us

OREGON
Oregon University System
PO Box 3175
Eugene, OR 97401
541-346-5700
TTY: 541-346-5741
Fax: 541-346-5764
bob_bruce@ous.edu
www.ous.edu

PENNSYLVANIA
Pennsylvania Higher Education
Assistance Agency
1200 North Seventh Street
Harrisburg, PA 17102-1444
717-720-2800
TTY: 1-800-654-5988
info@pheaa.org or
kwoollam@pheaa.org
www.pheaa.org

RHODE ISLAND
Rhode Island Higher Education
Assistance Authority
560 Jefferson Boulevard
Warwick, RI 02886
401-736-1100
1-800-922-9855
TTY: 401-734-9481
Fax: 401-732-3541
www.riheaa.org

RHODE ISLAND
Rhode Island Office of Higher
Education
301 Promenade Street
Providence, RI 02908-5748
401-222-6560
TTY: 401-222-1350
Fax: 401-222-6111
ribghe@etal.uri.edu
www.ribghe.org/riohe.htm

SOUTH CAROLINA
South Carolina Commission on
Higher Education; Suite 200
1333 Main Street
Columbia, SC 29201
803-737-2260
1-877-349-7183
Fax: 803-737-2297
shubbard@che400.state.sc.us
www.che400.state.sc.us

SOUTH DAKOTA
South Dakota Board of Regents
306 East Capitol Avenue,
Suite 200
Pierre, SD 57501
605-773-3455
Fax: 605-773-5320
info@ris.sdbor.edu
www.ris.sdbor.edu

TENNESSEE
Tennessee Higher Education
Commission
Parkway Towers, Suite 1900
404 James Robertson Parkway
Nashville, TN 37243-0830
615-741-3605
Fax: 615-741-6230
www.state.tn.us/thec

TEXAS
Texas Higher Education
Coordinating Board
PO Box 12788
Austin, TX 78711
512-427-6101
1-800-242-3062
Fax: 512-427-6420
www.thecb.state.tx.us

UTAH
Utah State Board of Regents
Three Triad Center; Suite 550
355 West North Temple
Salt Lake City, UT 84180-1205
801-321-7100
Fax: 801-321-7199
heyring@utahsbr.edu
www.utahsbr.edu/

VERMONT
Vermont Student Assistance
Corporation
Champlain Mill
1 Main Street, Fourth Floor
PO Box 2000
Winooski, VT 05404-2601
802-655-9602
1-800-642-3177
TTY: 1-800-281-3341
Fax: 802-654-3765
info@vsac.org
www.vsac.org/

VIRGINIA
State Council of Higher Education
for Virginia
James Monroe Building, 9th Floor
101 North 14th Street
Richmond, VA 23219
804-225-2600
TTY: 804-371-8017
Fax: 804-225-2604
bradford@schev.edu
www.schev.edu/

WASHINGTON
Washington State Higher
Education Coordinating Board
PO Box 43430
917 Lakeridge Way
Olympia, WA 98504-3430
360-753-7800
TTY: 360-753-7809
Fax: 360-753-7808
info@hecb.wa.gov
www.hecb.wa.gov

WEST VIRGINIA
West Virginia Higher Education
Policy Commission
1018 Kanawha Boulevard, East
Charleston, WV 25301
304-558-2101
Fax: 304-558-0259
healey@hepc.wvnet.edu
www.hepc.wvnet.edu

WISCONSIN
Wisconsin Higher Educational Aids
Board
131 West Wilson Street,
Room 902
Madison, WI 53707-7885
608-267-2206
Fax: 608-267-2808
heabmail@heab.state.wi.us
heab.state.wi.us/

WYOMING
Wyoming Community College
Commission
2020 Carey Avenue, Eighth Floor
Cheyenne, WY 82002
307-777-7763
Fax: 307-777-6567
sbutler@commission.wcc.edu
commission.wcc.edu

AMERICAN SAMOA
American Samoa Community
College Board of Higher Education
PO Box 2609
Pago Pago, AS 96799-2609
684-699-1141

NORTHERN MARIANA ISLANDS
Northern Marianas College
Olympio T. Borja Memorial
Library
As-Terlaje Campus
PO Box 1250 CK
Saipan, MP 96950-1250
670-234-3690
Fax: 670-234-0759
www.nmcnet.edu

PUERTO RICO
Puerto Rico Council on Higher
Education
PO Box 19900
San Juan, PR 00910
787-724-7100
Fax: 787-725-1275
sa_espada@ces.prstar.net

REPUBLIC OF THE MARSHALL ISLANDS
Republic of the Marshall Islands
RMI Scholarship Grant and Loan
Board
PO Box 1436
3 Lagoon Road
Majuro, MH 96960
692-625-3108

VIRGIN ISLANDS
Virgin Islands Joint Boards of
Education
Charlotte Amalie
PO Box 11900
St. Thomas, VI 00801
340-774-4546
Fax: 340-774-3384

Bibliography

BOOKS

Betterton, Don (2000). *The Insider's Guide to Paying for College: Find Out How to Get More Money for College!* Washington, D.C.: Peterson's Thomson Learning.

Davis, Herm, and Joyce Lain Kennedy (1999). *College Financial Aid for Dummies* (2d. ed.). California: IDG Books Worldwide.

Dr. Seuss (1990). *Oh, the Places You'll Go!* New York: Random House.

Johnson, Ronald W. and Marc Robinson (2000). *Financial Aid for College: Understand and Plan Your Funding Options.* New York: Dorling Kindersley Publishing, Inc.

Kaplan (2000). *Parent's Guide to College Admissions: What Every Parent Should Know* (2d. ed.). New York: Simon & Schuster.

Peterson's Thomson Learning (2000). *Scholarships and Loans for Adult Students: The Only Guide to College Financing for Students 25 and Over.* New Jersey: Peterson's Thomson Learning.

ONLINE ARTICLES

ACCRA Cost of Living Index. Chart. St. Louis: America's Center for Business. Summer 2001. <www.econdev.stlrcga.org/profile13.html/>.

Associated Press: Permission from Norm Goldstein. "Who Tops the List of Party Colleges?" *CNN.* 21 Aug. 2001. Aug. 2001. <fyi.cnn.com/2001/fyi/teachers.ednews/08/21/party.schools.ap/>.

Distance Learning and the Internet. 2001. Harvard, MIT. Summer 2001.

<www.caso.com/home/articles.phtml?id=4&p=7&sID=522ad0f520
ddf4f22aa51dddfd556117>.

Ezell, Hank. "Too Many College Students are Singing the Debt Blues."
Atlanta Journal and Constitution. 2000. Summer 2001. <www.azfcu.
org/smartmoney/azsmarticle2.htm>.

The Rising Cost of a College Education. Chart. Kansas City: Masters Financial Group. Summer 2001. <mastersfinancialgroup.com/>.

Sanchez, Rene. "Report Documents Rising Debt of College Students."
Washington Post. 22 Sept. 1995: 115(43). Summer 2001. <www.nagps.
org/Student_Aid/debt/ed-debt-post.html>.

Slobogin, Kathy. "Cyber-Graduation: Earning a Degree Online." *CNN*. 24
May 2001. Summer 2001. <fyi.cnn.com/2001/fyi/teachers.ednews/05/
24/cyber.education/>.

Wirt, John. *NCES Fast Facts*. The Department of Education: National Center for Educational Statistics. Summer 2001. <www.nces.ed.gov>.

ONLINE RESOURCES

Bureau of Labor Statistics. 2001. National Bureau of Labor Statistics. Summer 2001. <www.bls.gov/home.htm>.

College Board. 2001. The College Board Association. Summer 2001.
<www.collegeboard.com/>.

College Business Officers Page. 2001. National Association of College and
University Business Officers. Summer 2001. <www.nacubo.org/account-
ing_finance/endowment_study/>.

College Preparation Website. 2001. Sallie Mae, Inc. Summer 2001.
<www.wiredscholar.com>.

Community College Association Page. 2001. American Association of
Community Colleges. Summer 2001. <www.aacc.nche.edu>.

Dear Susan & Co. 2001. CCCS of the Gulf Coast Area, Inc. Summer 2001.
<www.cccsintl.org/susan/cd.htm>.

Dept. of Education Student Guide 2000/2001. 2001. U.S. Department of
Education. Summer 2001. <www.ed.gov/prog_info/SFA/StudentGuide/
2000-1/>.

Embark: College Research Page. 2001. *The Princeton Review*. Summer
2001. <www.embark.com/>.

FinAid! The Smart Guide to Financial Aid. 2001. FinAid Page, LLC. Summer 2001. <www.finaid.org/>.

IRS Website. 2001. Internal Revenue Service. Summer 2001. <www.
irs.gov>.

Military Website. 2001. MyFuture.com. Summer 2001. <www.myfuture.com>.

NASSGAP. 2001. National Association of State Student Grant and Aid Programs. Summer 2001. <www.nassgap.org/>.

ROTC Website. 2001. U.S. Army. Summer 2001. <www.armyrotc.com>.

SallieMae. 2001. USA Education, Inc. Summer 2001. <www.salliemae.com/>.

Student Financial Aid Services Page. 2001. Student Financial Aid Services. Summer 2001. <www.fafsa.com>.

Trends in College Pricing Page. 2001. The College Board. Summer 2001. <www.collegeboard.com/press/cost01/html/TrendsCP01.pdf>.

Trivia Website. 2002. Cool Quiz Network, Inc. March 2002. <www.useless knowledge.com>.

Trivia Website. 2002. Funtrivia.com. March 2002. <www.funtrivia.com>.

U.S. Department of Education Page. 2001. U.S. Department of Education. Summer 2001. <www.ed.gov>.

U.S. Military Website. 2001. U.S. Military. Summer 2001. <www.todays-military.com>.

Index

Page numbers in **bold** indicate charts or tables; those in *italic* indicate figures.

About the Authors

Robert A. Sparks graduated debt-free with a degree in business. During college, he mentored over one hundred students as a resident assistant. He currently works as a network administrator and information technology consultant in Austin, Texas.

Mamatha Vaddi works as a consultant in Dallas, Texas. During college, she organized and led various campus-wide events in addition to serving as residence hall president. She completed a finance degree in Thailand using financial aid and also graduated with a bachelor's degree in MIS.